LV

DEC 12, 2013

POPE FRANCIS
UNTYING THE KNOTS

D0395861

About the Author

Paul Vallely has an international reputation as a commentator on religion, society and ethical issues. As a journalist he has produced award-winning reporting from 30 countries over three decades. As an activist on international development he has worked with Bob Geldof and Bono and was co-author of *Our Common Interest*, the report of the Commission for Africa. As a writer his books include *The New Politics: Catholic Social Teaching for the 21st century* and *Bad Samaritans: First World Ethics and Third World Debt*. He co-wrote Geldof's best-selling autobiography *Is That It?*

He writes on political, cultural and ethical matters in *The Independent on Sunday, the Church Times, Third Way and The Tablet*. A former associate editor of *The Independent* and editor of *The Sunday Times* News Review section, he is now Visiting Professor in Public Ethics and Media at the University of Chester. He was Chair of the development agencies Traidcraft and the Catholic Institute for International Relations and has been an adviser to the Catholic Bishops of England and Wales. He was made a CMG 'for services to journalism and to the developing world' in the 2006 Birthday Honours. He lives in Manchester with his wife and son.

www.paulvallely.com

Pope Francis

Untying the Knots

Paul Vallely

3 1336 09525 8381

BLOOMSBURY
LONDON • NEW DELHI • NEW YORK • SYDNEY

First published in Great Britain 2013

Copyright © Paul Vallely, 2013

The moral right of the author has been asserted

No part of this book may be used or reproduced in any manner
whatsoever without written permission from the Publisher except in the
case of brief quotations embodied in critical articles or reviews. Every
reasonable effort has been made to trace copyright holders of material
reproduced in this book, but if any have been inadvertently overlooked
the Publishers would be glad to hear from them.

A Continuum book

Bloomsbury Publishing Plc
50 Bedford Square
London WC1B 3DP

www.bloomsbury.com

Bloomsbury is a registered trade mark of Bloomsbury Publishing Plc

Bloomsbury Publishing, London, New Delhi, New York and Sydney
A CIP record for this book is available from the British Library.

ISBN 978 1 4729 037 09

10 9 8 7 6 5 4 3 2 1

Typeset by Fakenham Prepress Solutions, Fakenham, Norfolk
NR21 8NN

Printed and bound in Great Britain by CPI Group (UK) Ltd, Croydon
CR0 4YY

Picture section images © Caleb Bassett http://www.flickr.com/photos/
maven/, Getty, Rex Features, and Thomson Reuters

For Christine
*without whom
nothing would be possible*

Contents

Foreword

You could be forgiven for thinking that there is nothing unusual about the suburban church of San José del Telar in Buenos Aires. Yet the steady trickle of women who enter it, on an ordinary weekday, make only the most cursory genuflection towards the rococo gold of the central altar and its sultry crucifix. Then they immediately turn their backs on it. They move, instead, to the side aisle on the left, at the rear of the church, where the painting hangs.

It is a copy, and not a terribly good one, of the eighteenth-century original in a church in Augsburg where in 1986 it was discovered by a visitor from Argentina, Fr Jorge Mario Bergoglio SJ. He could not have known then that some twenty-seven years later he would surprise the world by appearing on the balcony of St Peter's in Rome. This virtually unknown priest would be elected the 266th Pope of the Catholic Church. More than that, he would break a number of precedents: as the first pope from the Americas, the first from the Southern hemisphere, the first Jesuit, and the first to take the name of Francis – in a signal of his intent that hence-forth things would be very different for the Church and its billion or more members.

He appeared a man of great confidence, in himself and in God. But he had been a man in turmoil on the day that he first came across the Baroque artwork in that German church. Painted in oils on wood panelling by one Johann George Schmidtner, it bore the enigmatic title of *Mary Untier of Knots*. Behind it lay an intriguing story.

In 1610, as the tale was told, a Bavarian nobleman, Wolfgang Langenmantel, had travelled to the city to seek the sage counsel of a Jesuit priest named Fr Jakob Rem. The aristocrat's marriage was in difficulties. He and his wife Sophia were on the brink of separating – which would have been a scandal of enormous proportion in Catholic Bavaria in those times. Rem had asked the nobleman to bring with him the long white ribbon used in the celebration of the couple's wedding. The Jesuit had in mind something which had been written by one of the first great Christian theologians and apologists, the second-century church father St Irenaeus, who had written of how 'the knot of Eve's disobedience was loosed by the obedience of Mary'. Rem invoked the Virgin to intercede over the difficulties of Wolfgang and Sophia. 'In this act of piety,' he prayed over the wedding ribbon, 'I raise up the bond of marriage that all knots be loosed and resolved.' The couple subsequently overcame their problems and remained together. Around 1700 their nephew commissioned the painting, which hangs in the church of St Peter am Perlach in Augsburg. It shows Mary unravelling the entanglements in the ribbon, assisted by two angels and surrounded by cherubs, while her foot casually crushes the head of a serpent representing the Devil.

It is not difficult to understand why the Marian painting spoke so potently to the 50-year-old priest from Argentina. He had been sent to Germany purportedly to do research for a PhD on Romano Guardini, the Catholic philosopher who wrote in the 1930s about the moral hazards of power. But his superiors wanted him out of Argentina, where his leadership of the Jesuit province over the previous fifteen years – as Novice Master, then Provincial and finally as Rector of its seminary – had divided his religious order so deeply, and so bitterly, that the leader of the Society in Rome eventually decreed that a Jesuit from outside Argentina must be sent in to heal the wounds. There were knots aplenty for the Virgin Mary to untie for Bergoglio.

Yet untied they were. Within a few months he was back in Argentina. But after an unhappy period in Buenos Aires, the scene of his long years of controversy, he was exiled to the Jesuit community in that country's second city Córdoba, some 400 miles from the capital. There he languished in penitential obscurity for years before then being plucked by the Cardinal Archbishop of Buenos Aires to be made – highly unusually for a Jesuit, for Jesuits take a vow to avoid ecclesiastical preferment – an assistant bishop, back in the city of his birth.

An extraordinary journey had begun. It was to transform Jorge Mario Bergoglio into the Bishop of the Slums, a passionate defender of the disenfranchised, an unwavering enthusiast for dialogue as a way to build bridges between people of all backgrounds and beliefs – and eventually a Pope who announced his intention to transform the cultured silk-brocaded propriety of the Rome of Pope Benedict XVI into 'a poor Church, for the poor'.

There are still knots to be disentangled, not least for a Church and a world only just getting to know this Pope of paradox. Jorge Mario Bergoglio is a doctrinal traditionalist but an ecclesiastical reformer. He is a radical but not a liberal. He seeks to empower others and yet retains a streak of authoritarianism. He is a conservative yet was on the far left of his nation's reactionary Bishops' Conference. He combines religious simplicity with political guile. He is progressive and open, yet austere and severe. The first Pope to have been ordained a priest after the Second Vatican Council, he nonetheless imposed a pre-conciliar training on his novices. He has opposed same-sex marriage and gay adoption but he has kissed the feet of homosexuals with Aids. He is of the South, yet has deep roots in the North: a Latin American whose parentage is Italian and who has studied in Spain, Ireland and Germany. He is a diocesan priest and yet also a member of a religious order. He is a teacher of theology but a pastor with the common touch. In him humility and power come together.

When he returned to Argentina from Germany he brought with him a postcard of the Augsburg painting. The people of his native land took the image to their hearts. A decade later the parishioners in one church took it upon themselves to raise the money to have a full-size copy of the painting made by an Argentinean painter. It is to that, in the otherwise nondescript church of San José del Telar in Agronomeia, a middle-class suburb of Buenos Aires, that pilgrims now flock. Later, in his time as Archbishop of Buenos Aires, the man who liked to be known only as Padre Bergoglio would slip in among them, dressed in the anonymity of plain clerical black, to sit in the pews before the painting to unravel the knots of his higher office.

'The copy has become more famous now than the original', said Fr Ricardo Aloe, as he sat in the right aisle, in a clear glass-sided confessional, on hand in case any of that steady trickle of pilgrims wanted to be shriven. 'People come from all over Argentina, indeed all over the world to see it. On the eighth of every month we have 10,000 people here. On the eighth day of December, the Feast of Mary's Immaculate Conception, more than 30,000 come. They all feel they are listened to and understood by the Virgin. As Mother she is very attentive to our problems. The knots are metaphors of the difficulties we have. She appeals to God to help us with them.'

A metaphor. Jorge Mario Bergoglio knew that only too well. And it seems he obtained the forgiveness he was seeking. Though it has never been enough.

Dirty Tricks in the Vatican

No one admitted to sending the email. The ambassador said he did not do it. So did the lawyer. So did the journalist. So did several high-ranking officials the Society of Jesus, the world's biggest and most powerful religious order. But the dossier that dropped anonymously into the inbox of senior cardinals as they gathered in Rome was damning. Or so it was clearly intended to be. Someone did not want Jorge Mario Bergoglio to be Pope.

When a pope dies, cardinals from all over the world collect in the Vatican and begin to meet in what they call General Congregations. In April 2005 the first few days of these meetings were spent in absorbing the implications of the death of the man the Vatican swiftly dubbed John Paul the Great. *Santo Subito*, the crowds in St Peter's Square had cried: Make him a Saint Now! The old Pope had died a long lingering public death, making himself an icon of suffering, as if to chastise a world which has become so fixated with the busyness of doing that it had forgotten about the business of simply being. But while in those Congregations the cardinals of the Roman Catholic Church were publicly deliberating on the details of what was to be the biggest funeral in human history, in private they were talking about something else: who should be the next Pope?

It was in the midst of this that the dossier arrived. Just three days before the 2005 conclave, a human rights lawyer, Marcelo Parrilli, in Argentina, filed a complaint charging Bergoglio with complicity in the kidnapping of two Jesuit priests whose work with the poor in a Buenos Aires shanty town was considered by Argentina's military death squads in 1976 to be subversive. The priests – whom he had dismissed from the Society of Jesus a week before they disappeared, for disobeying his order to end their work with the poor in the slums – were tortured and held in hoods and shackles for five months before being released.

The allegations, which the cardinal's spokesman in Buenos Aires in 2005 dismissed as 'old slander' – and which we will examine in detail in a later chapter – were based on the investigations of a campaigning journalist, Horacio Verbitsky, who had interviewed the kidnapped Jesuits after their eventual release. He had also compiled accounts from priests and lay workers which he claimed corroborated the accusations. And he had found documents in old government files implicating Bergoglio from his time as leader of the Jesuit province in Argentina. The lawsuit filed against Bergoglio was eventually dismissed, but the debate had raged on unabated.

Defenders of Bergoglio claimed that Verbitsky had an ulterior motive. He was a political ally of the previous and current presidents, Néstor and Cristina Kirchner. Verbisky's most detailed allegations against Bergoglio had been published in a book, *El Silencio*, earlier that year which was written after Cardinal Bergoglio publicly criticised President Néstor Kirchner for his record on corruption and failure to help the poor. The main Argentine newspaper *Clarín* claimed that the Kirchner government distributed the dossier to cardinals via its ambassador to the Holy See. But both government and ambassador issued denials. Verbitsky countered by pointing out that he had begun investigating the allegations in 1999, four years before the Kirchners came to power.

There were other potential culprits in the frame. Alicia Oliveira, a former Argentinean human rights lawyer and judge who had been persecuted by the military junta – and who is still a close friend of Bergoglio – blamed conservative elements in the country's hierarchy linked to Opus Dei for the attempt to block his election to the papacy in 2005. Yet others laid the blame for the email at the door of fellow Jesuits who had fallen out with Bergoglio when he was the Provincial of the order in Argentina, and it is certainly true that there were heavy reservations among Jesuits about Bergoglio;

they had complained about his behaviour many years before to the Jesuit Curia in Rome. And there were emails in circulation from Jesuits complaining that Bergoglio was a man 'who never smiled'. Whoever sent the dossier to a large number of cardinals, there was clearly a Stop Bergoglio campaign in place. Catholics like to say that, in the selection of a pope, the Holy Spirit guides the Church. Yet here there were clearly other forces seeking to steer the outcome. But did they succeed?

***

The cardinals met for the first of their General Congregations in the Synod Hall in the shadow of the great dome of St Peter's basilica. An undistinguished post-war building, with a boring beige interior like a university lecture theatre, it feels somehow suited to the dreary formality of ecclesiastical policy. But the real politics went on elsewhere, during the lunch breaks and at dinners hosted by those key cardinals who became conclave power brokers. 'Ever since the Last Supper, the Church has decided its most important affairs at the dinner table,' one cardinal-elector quipped. Some cardinals knew each other well beforehand. But they were in a minority. Pope John Paul II had over the years internationalised the College of Cardinals and new electors were arriving from all over the world. One cardinal's aide recounted seeing 'clutches of developing-world cardinals wandering around Rome as dazed as first-time tourists'. One even asked: 'Where are these dinners they are all talking about?'

Cardinal Cormac Murphy-O'Connor, then Archbishop of Westminster, hosted a gathering of the English-speaking cardinals in the Irish College. But he did his real business in a smaller group of European liberals, which included Cardinals Carlo Mario Martini of Milan, Walter Kasper of Stuttgart and Godfried Daneels of Brussels. The group had met at least once a year for many years and Martini, who was also a Jesuit, had long been their candidate for the papacy. But by 2005 Martini was, at 78, felt to be getting too old and his health was so poor he had retired as a serving archbishop three years before. Bergoglio of Buenos Aires was another option for them. He and Murphy-O'Connor had been made cardinals in the same consistory in 2001. That meant, according to official Vatican seating plans, they always sat near one another at official Vatican events. The two men had become friends.

For many, though, Cardinal Joseph Ratzinger was the obvious candidate. He had been John Paul II's right-hand man for twenty-four years and had been watchdog of the Vatican's doctrinal orthodoxy as the Prefect of the Congregation for the Doctrine of the Faith. That post meant he was one of the few senior officials whom every cardinal saw on routine visits to Rome. He was also Dean of the College of Cardinals and therefore took the chair at the General Congregations, as well as presiding at John Paul II's funeral Mass and at the *Pro Eligendo Papa* (For the Election of the Pope) Mass on the morning the conclave began. At the General Congregations Ratzinger, a man with a phenomenal memory, called each cardinal by name and spoke to each in a language he knew they understood. For new cardinal-electors – who hardly knew one another, had poor Italian and had little sense of whom to vote for – he seemed the obvious choice. He had, after all, been the closest aide to the late John Paul II of whom the conclave was in such awe. And he conducted himself with grace and purpose in the Congregations, and spoke with warmth in his homily at the funeral Mass and with analytical lucidity on the shortcomings of contemporary society at the pre-conclave Mass. Many of the cardinals who had arrived with the question 'if not Ratzinger, who?' began to ask 'why not Ratzinger?'. After 26 years of Pope John Paul II no one wanted another long papacy, so it did not seem to matter that Josef Ratzinger was 78. Somehow it seemed apt that on his birthday, shortly before the conclave, someone had presented the German cardinal with an arrangement of white and yellow tulips, the papal colours.

Had the Stop Bergoglio dossier not been circulated, would it have made any difference to the election, given the momentum which was building in Ratzinger's favour? On the first day of the conclave the cardinals began their solemn procession into the Sistine Chapel at 4.30 p.m. It took almost an hour for the 115 cardinal-electors to take their solemn oaths of seriousness and secrecy. Then all outsiders left to the formal cry of *Exeunt Omnes* (Everybody Out) and the doors were locked – *con clave* means 'with a key' – so the voting could begin.

The outcome of all the formal Congregations, and informal meetings, was that attention was focused on four cardinals: Joseph Ratzinger, Carlo Mario Martini, Camillo Ruini (the papal vicar of Rome) and Jorge Mario Bergoglio. Other names were in the air too: Dionigi Tettamanzi of Milan, Angelo Scola of Venice, and the African cardinal Francis Arinze of Nigeria. The Dean asked the assembly if they preferred to vote immediately or retire for the evening. They chose to vote.

On that first ballot, Ratzinger received 47 votes, 30 short of the 77 required to obtain the necessary two-thirds majority. But the real surprise of the first round was that the Argentine, Bergoglio, received 10 votes – one more than the liberals' candidate Martini of Milan. Ruini got six and the man who had been Pope John Paul II's chief minister, the Vatican secretary of state, Cardinal Angelo Sodano got four. The Honduran cardinal Oscar Rodriguez Maradiaga of Tegucigalpa had three and Tettamanzi of Milan just two. A few others received a single vote.

The cardinals closed the voting for the day and went to dinner. Across the tables in the dining hall, and in small knots in the corridor or in their private rooms, then meeting in groups of two or three in their rooms, or smoking outside on the patio, the talk was of Bergoglio and how he had beaten his fellow Jesuit Martini. Those who knew little about him began to exchange information. Some remembered him from the 2001 Synod of Bishops four years earlier. The Archbishop of New York, Cardinal Edward Egan had been given the job of *relator*, or summariser of the discussion and conclusions, but the 9/11 terrorist attacks had forced him to return to New York. Pope John Paul II had asked Bergoglio to take over, and some of his peers recalled warmly the collegial nature of his chairmanship. He had topped the poll at the Synod on the Americas which followed.

More intriguingly, the dining room analysis noted something else. Bergoglio had over the years developed a relationship with one of new movements of lay people within the Church, *Comunione e Liberazione*, on which Pope John Paul II had been so keen. Bergoglio had written a chapter in a tribute-book to the Italian founder of the movement, Fr Luigi Giussani; he had spoken several times at its annual mass gathering in Rimini. This had an additional significance, since the movement had previously been seen as the main opposition in Milan to Bergoglio's Jesuit rival, Cardinal Martini.

Bergoglio was tight-lipped over whether or not he wanted to be Pope. Those who are still close friends in Argentina found him hard to read too. Some believed he wanted it, others not. 'Sometimes it's hard to know what a Jesuit is thinking,' one said. But certainly Bergoglio did not campaign behind the scenes. But Cardinal Karl Lehmann, president of the German bishops, began lobbying on his behalf. Cardinal Danneels, Archbishop of Brussels persuaded a significant group of cardinal-electors from both the North and South Americas to back him. Two senior Vatican bureaucrats among the cardinals swung behind him. They argued that he was an effective unifying alternative to Ratzinger: conservatives could admire him as a man who had held the line against liberalising currents among the Jesuits and opposed Marxist trends in Liberation Theology; on the other hand, moderates could view him as a symbol of the Church's commitment to the poor and the developing world. And conservatives and moderates alike could respect his keen pastoral sense and his personal frugality – a Prince of the Church who had given up a grand archbishop's palace for a simple apartment in his episcopal office-block, who cooked his own meals and eschewed a chauffeur-driven limousine in favour of taking the subway and the bus. He was also a man of deep prayer.

Next morning the voting recommenced at 9.30 a.m. Beneath the Latin legend *Eligo in summum pontificem* (I elect as supreme pontiff), each cardinal wrote his selection for Pope on a rectangular ballot paper, disguising his handwriting in accordance with the rules, and folded it lengthwise before posting it in a specially designed voting urn. The second round of voting showed that Ratzinger's votes had risen to 65 but Bergoglio's had more than trebled – to 35, a quarter of the votes. Martini and Ruini received none. The smaller votes of Sodano and Tettamanzi were unaltered.

At 11 a.m. the third round began. This time Ratzinger received 72 votes, six short of the 77 needed for the required majority. But Bergoglio got 40 – enough to constitute a blocking minority and prevent Ratzinger from attaining the two-thirds he needed to be declared Pope.

But there was another factor. In 1996 Pope John Paul II had issued a new Apostolic Constitution *Universi Dominici gregis*. It changed the voting system so that, in the event of deadlock, after 34 ballots a simple majority would be all that was required to win. Some of Ratzinger's supporters let it be known that all they had to do was persist in 13 days of inconclusive voting and their candidate would win anyway, for he had already passed the 58 votes needed for a simple majority.

At this decisive point the cardinals broke for lunch. What they shared in their whispered discussions was this question: would the next vote see Ratzinger become Pope? Or had his support peaked, in which case his votes might shift towards another candidate, perhaps Jorge Mario Bergoglio?

Away from the Sistine Chapel the Argentine cardinal knew that in every round he had received the second-highest number of votes. On every round his vote had increased. And the 40 votes he had won in the third ballot were the highest number ever obtained by a Latin American. But he also knew that if enough of Ratzinger's supporters took a hard line they could hold out until the simple majority kicked in. A conclave that long would be bad for the Church's image in the outside world. It would be read as a sign of discord.

Bergoglio let it be known – more in gestures than in words – that his supporters should switch their votes to Ratzinger. On the fourth ballot Bergoglio polled just 26 votes; Ratzinger received 84. Joseph Ratzinger was declared Pope and was taken off to the robing room for the new pontiff, which is known as the Room of Tears, though it is never specified whether they be of anguish or of joy.

Bergoglio tried to follow to talk to the new Pope, who had declared, as he accepted, that he would take the name Benedict. The guards would not let him in. The mechanism of the papal court had swung immediately into place to elevate and separate the new shepherd from his sheep. The bells pealed. Out on the balcony, before the waiting multitudes in St Peter's Square, Pope Benedict XVI beamed and raised his arms in clasped exultation like a triumphant prize-fighter.

The next morning in the *Sala Clementina* on the third floor of the papal apartments Cardinal Jorge Mario Bergoglio paused longer than almost any other cardinal to talk to the new pontiff as he made his obeisance and pledged his loyalty as cardinals have done since the Middle Ages. In his heart he must have pondered that this was not the way things should be done. Without the dossier might it have been a different story?

***

A pope is sometimes not like the cardinal he was before. As Prefect of the Congregation for the Doctrine of the Faith – the Vatican department previously known as the Supreme Sacred Congregation of the Roman and Universal Inquisition – Joseph Ratzinger had been upholder of orthodoxy and the scourge of debate and dissent within the Church. But when he became Pope Benedict XVI the man who had infamously been called 'God's rotweiller' turned into a gentler German shepherd. His views were as clear as before but he expressed them in a different tone. He displayed an unexpectedly gentle smile and, on his international travels, came across as a pope who was open to dialogue with the wider secular world. 'He made us sit up and think,' said Britain's prime minister David Cameron after Benedict's series of sensitively-judged speeches in the UK. But if he was a wise teacher and a gentle pastor, Benedict XVI was a weak governor and a poor politician.

His eight years in office were marked by a series of ill-fated judgements and public relations disasters. These began with his 2006 lecture at Regensburg which offended Muslims around the world and went on to include the readmission to the Church of a Holocaust-denying bishop, the imposition across the globe of deeply conservative bishops more interested in culture wars than pastoral ministry and the creation of an Ordinariate to woo traditionalist Anglicans to Rome without consulting the leaders of the Anglican Communion. There were new allegations of money-laundering at the scandal-mired Vatican Bank, the imposition of controversial new translations of the Mass, and the disciplining of US nuns considered too liberal on issues such as homosexuality which, in the words of one commentator, had reduced relations between the Vatican and Catholic theologians to their lowest point since the Reformation. Hanging over it all was the continuing scandal of the cover-up of priestly sex abuse and a Vatican bureaucracy which was careerist and out of control.

The response of Jorge Mario Bergoglio in Argentina to all this was illuminating. His reaction to the Regensburg row brought him into direct conflict with the Vatican. The incident began with a thoughtful lecture on faith and reason given by Benedict XVI at his old university of Regensburg. In it the new Pope quoted a highly inflammatory remark by a Byzantine emperor linking Islam and violence which he appeared to endorse. Riots followed around the world and Christians died. The Pope apologised but seemed bemused that remarks which would have gone unnoticed when he was an academic now carried such power.

But Jorge Mario Bergoglio, over in Latin America, understood the implications well enough. Through a spokesman he told *Newsweek Argentina* of his 'unhappiness' with Benedict's words. 'Pope Benedict's statement doesn't reflect my own opinions,' the Archbishop of Buenos Aires declared. 'These statements will serve to destroy in 20 seconds the careful construction of a relationship with Islam that Pope John Paul II built over the last twenty years.' The Vatican was outraged; it demanded he sack his press aide, Fr Guillermo Marcó, who had been Bergoglio's public spokesman for eight years and who had been the one to speak to *Newsweek*; Marcó took the blame and stood down, saying he had made the comments not as Bergoglio's spokesman but as President of the Institute of Inter-religious Dialogue. But few believed he had not reflected Bergoglio's thinking. Bergoglio responded by immediately organising an interfaith meeting, though he demonstrated his political finesse by getting someone else to chair it.

He was similarly unimpressed with Benedict's 2009 decision to lift the excommunication of four schismatic Lefebvrists bishops of the Society of Pius X – one of whom, Bishop Richard Williamson, turned out persistently to insist that millions of Jews were not gassed in Nazi concentration camps. Benedict later admitted a simple internet check might have detected that fact – but so might a call to Bergoglio. Williamson lived in Argentina, where he was considered so extreme that even the Lefebvrists expelled him as the head of one of their seminaries there. Bergoglio's friends in Buenos Aires reported that over the year he had had numerous problems with the Lefebvrists, both ecclesiologically and politically. 'He saw them as supporters of the military dictatorship,' said Alicia Oliviera. 'He had a lot of problems with them.' It had emerged, during the trials of the military junta when democracy was restored to Argentina, that the founder of the breakaway group, Archbishop Marcel Lefebvre, had travelled to Buenos Aires. There he had congratulated the military on the repression of left-wing dissenters, tens of thousands of whom were tortured and killed by military death squads. Bergoglio saw the Lefebvrists as supporters of the junta.

Nor was Bergoglio enthusiastic about Pope Benedict's attempt the same year to persuade discontented traditionalists inside the Anglican church to swim the Tiber. Not long after it was instituted, the Cardinal Archbishop of Buenos Aires telephoned his Anglican counterpart, Gregory Venables, Bishop of Argentina and sometime primate of the *Iglesia Anglicana del Cono Sur*, and invited him to breakfast. Venables later said Bergoglio had 'told me very clearly that the Ordinariate was quite unnecessary and that the Church needs us as Anglicans'.

The Pope and Bergoglio were moving in opposing directions, too, on the legacy of the Second Vatican Council. For all his lip service to Vatican II, Benedict XVI, like his predecessor John Paul II, clearly felt that many of its reforms had gone too far. Both did their best to dampen the energy and expectation the spirit of the Council had generated within the Church. Benedict, as he grew older, retreated yet further into a sacristy bounded by traditional styles of liturgy, Gregorian chant, Latin and the monarchical robes of the pre-Vatican II Church. His decision to put Pope John Paul II on a super-fast track to sainthood was, in part, an attempt to consolidate the legacy of the past. Meanwhile, in Buenos Aires, the city's cardinal continued to celebrate the liturgy in a free and open style in contemporary vestments, interacting with the congregation in ways designed to connect with the ordinary people. Extreme traditionalists in Buenos Aires complained that Bergoglio had set such prescriptions around the saying of the Latin Mass that it was almost impossible to hear one. Priests who disobeyed the limitations were personally ordered to stop by the man who would later describe Vatican II as 'a great work of the Holy Spirit' and insist there could be no 'turning back the clock'.

On priestly sex abuse and paedophilia the two men took a closer line. But even here there was a significant difference. Throughout Benedict's time as Pope, fresh allegations of sexual abuse committed by priests, and inadequate responses by the institutional Church, continued to emerge. The constant news dealt continuing blows to the moral authority of the Catholic Church in the wider world. Benedict took a much stricter line than his predecessor Pope John Paul II, under whom the Curia had protected serial abusers like the Mexican founder of the Legionaries of Christ, Marcial Maciel. One of Benedict's first moves on taking office was to remove Maciel from active ministry and order him to spend the rest of his days in prayer and penance. In his later years as Cardinal Ratzinger he had insisted that every allegation of priestly sex abuse was passed to him personally. He dealt with the cases personally every week, on what he called his 'penitential Fridays'. He was much firmer in dealing with paedophile priests and other clerical abusers than was widely supposed. But he had the Church's old instincts for private action and public reticence. Though he made public apology in country after country on his international travels, and in each place made efforts to meet the victims of such crimes, he acted largely behind closed doors, thereby reinforcing the impression that the Church continued to care more about institutional self-preservation than it did about promulgating the values of the gospel.

The Cardinal Archbishop of Buenos Aires was altogether more robust. He went out of his way to preface his position by insisting that there is no connection between celibacy and paedophilia. 'There are psychological perversions that existed prior to choosing a life of celibacy,' he said. 'If a priest is a paedophile, he is so before he becomes a priest.' And he also introduced his remarks with a statistic that 'seventy percent of the cases of paedophilia occur in the family and in the neighbourhood: grandparents, uncles, stepparents, neighbours'. But having done that, he insisted on a policy of zero tolerance. When a priest abuses, he said, 'you must never look away. You cannot be in a position of power and use it to destroy the life of another person.'

Church attempts to cover up the problem were both wrong and counter-productive, he believes. 'I do not believe in the positions that some hold about sustaining a certain corporate spirit so as to avoid damaging the image of the institution,' he said. 'The solution … of switching them to other parishes is stupid, because the priest continues to carry the problem in his baggage.' Argentina has not been hit by a sex abuse scandal of anything like the proportions elsewhere. Only 23 priests have been investigated for sexual abuse there since 1987. Bergoglio had none in his archdiocese. Even so, the advice he gave to other bishops was clear: 'A bishop called me once by phone to ask me what to do in a situation like this and I told him to take away the priest's faculties, not to permit him to exercise his priestly ministry again, and to initiate a canonical trial.' Many survivors' support groups feel that this is still not enough; the priest should be reported to the police, not merely subjected to a church trial, but Bergoglio's approach made a significant step towards greater openness as well as zero tolerance. He was also outspoken on the broader issue of the sexual exploitation of children in society, describing Buenos Aires as a 'meat grinder' because of prostitution and trafficking in sex-slaves.

In 2005, when Ratzinger was elected Pope, there were many who hoped that he was the man to bring the necessary reforms to the Curia which had grown unchecked in the twenty-six-year pontif-icate of John Paul II. Pope Paul VI was the last pontiff properly to govern the Curia with its Secretariat of State, nine congregations, three tribunals, twelve pontifical councils and various other offices intended to provide support to the Pope. He placed significant power in the hands of the office of his chief minister, the Secretariat of State, and various other Vatican departments, but he required regular meetings of the heads of the different curial offices in the manner of the cabinet style of administration found in many secular governments. But the practice had lapsed under John Paul II, who allowed the heads of the different departments to govern themselves like independent fiefdoms. Bergoglio was irritated to find his recommendations were routinely being disregarded by the Vatican's Congregation for Bishops.

At the conclave after the death of Pope John Paul II, who had been globe-trotting parish priest to the world but had let Vatican governance atrophy, cardinals hoped that a time-serving insider would know how to fix the problem. It did not happen. Instead the system collapsed further under Benedict XVI, who put his supporters in positions of administrative power because he knew and trusted them, rather than because they had the qualities required to do the job. His Secretary of State, Cardinal Tarcisio Bertone was to come in for particular public criticism from cardinals during the General Congregations in 2013. He was seen as a Yes man, with no diplomatic experience or linguistic skills, who saw his main job as protecting Benedict from bad news. While Benedict got on with writing his books and private prayer, the different departments of the Roman Curia formed policy and administered the various parts of the Church without consultation or coordination. Some department heads began to behave like medieval barons, jealous of their autonomy and resentful of what they perceived as interference. Rather than reform the Curia, Benedict just ignored it.

Eventually it all got too much for the German Pope. His health was deteriorating. His hearing had worsened. He could not see with his left eye. His body had become so thin that the tailors had difficulty keeping up with newly fitted clothes. By the end of 2012, his biographer, the German journalist Peter Seewald, said: 'I'd never seen him so exhausted-looking, so worn down.' In March 2012 on a trip to Mexico and Cuba he lost his balance in his room and fell, hitting his head on a bathroom sink. The accident was kept secret by the Vatican, but for the failing Pope it was a decisive moment. When he returned from the gruelling trip he spent many hours praying before the large bronze figure of Christ which looked down from the wall of his small private chapel in his apartments in the Apostolic Palace. Before him, also, was the memory of how John Paul II had chosen to die in public; there was an almost carnivalesque atmosphere to those final dying days of which the austere reserved Bavarian disapproved. After long prayer he decided to do something which no pope had done for 598 years, since Pope Gregory XII in 1415 stepped down to end the Western Schism between rival popes and anti-popes, each recognised by different factions and kingdoms within in the Catholic Church. He would resign.

For a long time he kept the decision to himself. He wanted to time the announcement to cause minimum disruption to the liturgical life of the Church. After Pentecost or before Lent were the obvious times. But before he could make an announcement, a new drama hit the Church, which had been reeling for years as it staggered from one crisis to another. It shook Benedict's already shaky confidence to the core.

On 23 May 2012 the Pope's personal butler, Paolo Gabriele was arrested and charged with stealing sensitive documents from the pontiff's desk – and leaking them to the media. Gabriele was one of a handful of people who had a key to an elevator that led to the Pope's private apartments. He had been Benedict's butler for six years. The Pope, insiders said, regarded him like a son. The betrayal was devastating.

Much of the media reported the affair as if it were a comic caper. 'What the Butler Leaked' was just too good a headline. Yet when Gabriele was prosecuted, anyone who followed the court case more closely realised the affair was devastating in a different way. Gabriele had passed to a journalist papers that the Pope had marked 'to be destroyed' and he had done it not for venal motives, but out of a sense of violated loyalty because he was worried at the extent to which underlings were pulling the wool over the pontiff's eyes.

The leaked documents revealed scandalous intrigue and in-fighting, ambition and arrogance, greed and glory-seeking, clerical careerism and corruption, secrecy and sexual lapses in the Vatican civil service. And they showed the Pope to be an intellectual who, ill at ease with the day-to-day running of the Church, let himself become isolated in the Vatican. The butler was not so much a traitor as a whistle-blower.

The story that emerged was of a pope who had begun to be out-manoeuvred by those who were supposed to serve him. It had begun at least five years earlier when Benedict was persuaded by Rome's vested interests to move a Curia reformer, Archbishop Carlo Maria Viganò, formerly the Vatican City's second-highest ranking administrator, and pack him off to be papal ambassador in the United States. Viganò had been clamping down on internal waste and corrupt practices that cost the Holy See millions in higher contract prices. Projects were routinely being assigned to the same companies at twice the normal commercial cost. One of the leaked letters was a plea to the Pope from Viganò not to be moved before the job was done. But Viganò was smeared by his opponents, who got Benedict to move him out of their way to Washington. Other documents in the affair the media dubbed Vatileaks revealed the attempts of vested interests to resist efforts to reform the Vatican Bank by introducing greater financial transparency and complying with international norms to fight money-laundering. There were also tales of wealthy individuals and bodies paying large sums to secure an audience with the pontiff.

The impact of all this on Pope Benedict was shattering. 'He was never the same after that,' one intimate of the pontiff said. The Pope appointed a commission of three cardinals to investigate the leaks. They handed their dossier to the Pope on 17 December 2012. He locked it in a safe in the papal apartments for his successor to handle. Then Benedict visited his butler in jail, where he had languished since being convicted in October, and pardoned him. Gabriele was released three days before Christmas.

But if the Vatican's self-serving bureaucracy thought their entrenched resistance had defeated Benedict XVI they were wrong. Just after 11.30 a.m. on the morning of 11 February a group of cardinals gathered in the *Sala del Concistoro* in the Apostolic Palace to hear the Pope announce a new collection of saints. He spoke in Latin and many of the cardinals allowed their minds to wander to such an extent that they did not notice Benedict had appended an addendum. He had written the 350-word statement himself and sent it to a Latin expert in the Secretariat of State to make sure the grammar was correct. The translator had been sworn to secrecy. Benedict now read the words from the dead language in a weak but steady voice. To run the Church, it said, 'Both strength of mind and body are necessary, strength which in the last few months, has deteriorated in me to the extent that I have had to recognise my incapacity to adequately fulfil the ministry entrusted to me'. The cardinals exchanged silent glances, unsure of what they had heard, as the pontiff left the room.

News of Benedict's resignation was so surprising that when an official from Rome called Cardinal Scola, who by now had been promoted to Milan, he refused to believe the news. Benedict had decided that heads in the Vatican should roll, but he knew that he did not have the operational grip to know how to get rid of the Machiavellian characters who had been deceiving him for years. So he came up with a response none of them could have anticipated: that his own head should be the one to roll. By this device he check-mated his opponents entirely.

History may well determine Benedict XVI's resignation to be the defining act of his papacy – and his greatest service to the Church. Becoming the first pope in modern times to stand down he redefined the papacy as a job, rather than a vocation, with particular tasks and targets, which may with propriety be set aside when the time is ripe. He has set a benchmark and future popes who find they are not up to the job will feel liberated, or indeed may come under pressure, to retire. His final act may turn out to be his most modernising.

Had the Stop Bergoglio dossier not been sent might things have been different? Perhaps a pope who was a true outsider to the Curia would have been better placed to resist its machinations. A man who had governed his own archdiocese as a distinctive leader for more than a decade might well have achieved what proved impossible to a man who had spent decades working as a faithful lieutenant to a charismatic master like John Paul II. In the meantime Jorge Mario Bergoglio has gone from strength to strength. Within six months of coming runner-up in the 2005 conclave Bergoglio was elected head of Argentina's Conference of Bishops. Two years later he was elected president of the commission of his entire continent's gathering of bishops at Aparecida and given responsibility for writing that meeting's final summarising document. It lamented the fact that a process of secularisation in Latin America is arresting the faith which has animated the life of the continent for five centuries. And it endorsed firmly the 'preferential option for the poor' which those same bishops and their predecessors had set out at the seminal meetings of the Latin American bishops' conference CELAM at Medellín, in 1968 and Puebla in 1976. 'We live in the most unequal part of the world, which has grown the most yet reduced misery by the least,' Bergoglio said. 'The unjust distribution of goods persists, creating a situation of social sin that cries out to Heaven and limits the possibilities of a fuller life for so many of our brothers.'

The way forward, it set out, was to put 'poor people's culture' at the centre and get rid of all the 'transient structures that no longer encourage the transmission of the faith'. The people of South America would not receive the Good News 'from evangelisers who are dejected, discouraged, impatient and anxious' but from 'ministers who have primarily received the joy of Christ in themselves'. That meant bishops who walk every day alongside their people. It meant priests who do not live secluded in their parishes but who were to be found in the streets, in soup kitchens, in schools, in all the endless social and charitable works where they truly came across people's struggle to continue. 'Only within the concrete circumstances of daily life,' it concluded, 'can one share in the faith and joy for the living presence of Christ.'

The conference lasted three weeks. In all that time only one homily provoked applause. It came on the day that Jorge Mario Bergoglio had been chosen to say Mass. During the conference breaks the other participants sought out the cardinal to talk and have their photograph taken alongside him as they would with a celebrity. But this was no rock star or sporting legend; it was a man who had crystallised a new vision for the Church, combining social justice, poor people's culture and spreading the good news of the gospel to those outside the Church. Even as Pope Benedict was weakening, Bergoglio was going from strength to strength.

Perhaps in his heart he pondered with gratitude how fortunate he had been not to have been handed Benedict XVI's poisoned chalice. Or perhaps he thought how different things might have been had the outcome of the 2005 conclave been different. His friends are not so sure. 'Pope John Paul II was a hard act to follow,' one cardinal told me. 'Perhaps the Holy Spirit held off until the house was collapsing around our ears. God is good at writing straight with crooked lines.'

On his continuing visits to Rome Bergoglio stayed, as he always had, in the Domus Internationalis Paulus VI clergy house in Via della Scrofa in the heart of Rome. The floors are made of marble but the rooms are spartan. It is some considerable distance from the Vatican but it allowed Bergoglio the chance to walk through the cobblestone byways, past the shops and bars, homes and banks, monuments and churches in which the people of the city and its visitors live out the routine of daily existence with its chores, trials and small acts of kindness and love. His dark overcoat covered his pectoral cross and he did not wear his cardinal's red skullcap. But he was among them. When he returned from his Vatican meetings he would eat at the common table with their other visiting clergy. Most did not give him more than a glance. They knew he was the Nearly Man, who back in 2005, at the age of 68, had missed his chance. You didn't get a second chance, did you?

'Back then, in 2005, wasn't his moment,' said one close friend in Buenos Aires, who now gets weekly phone calls from Bergoglio in Rome on a Sunday afternoon. 'Things needed to get a lot worse for the Church before they would be brave enough to choose Bergoglio. God knows what he's doing.'

2

The Common Touch

The crowd to see the new Pope was enormous. St Peter's Square was filled with an excited mass of people, shouting and laughing and pushing forward as the long white popemobile containing Francis swung through the roped-off pathways between the tens of thousands of visitors. Flags of many nations waved. Pilgrims and tourists shouted, giddy in the windy day. Parents held up their bewildered toddlers to be blessed as he passed. Some thrust their babies to security men to be raised up, so the Pope could ruffle their hair or kiss the top of the head. The joy was infectious.

How Pope Francis could have spotted a single individual amid the tumult is a mystery. But, all at once, he instructed his driver to stop. He climbed down to the line of people, waving and shaking the hands extended towards him. Then he stopped before a tiny woman in black with a walnut-wizened face. Grabbing his arms she spoke volubly, a torrent of words gushing over him. She was too far away for me to hear what language she was speaking. But whether he knew her or not, whether her words made sense, he took her ancient face in his two great hands and cradled it with huge tenderness. His grandmother, Rosa Margherita Vassallo Bergoglio, had lived to see him ordained a priest. But how proud she would have been to see her eldest grandson as Pope. This, he must have known, is how she would have reacted.

It was Grandma Rosa who had taught him to pray and educated him in the faith. She had arrived in Argentina from Italy in 1929, just six years before her grandson was born. Family legend has it she came down the gangplank of the steamship *Guilo Cesare* on a sweltering morning wearing a full-length fox fur, not because she had failed to appreciate that she would be arriving in the southern hemisphere where January would be high summer, but because sewn into its lining was the entire proceeds of the sale of the family's home and café back in Piedmont. With her in the third-class quarters of the ship had been her husband Giovanni and her son Mario José Bergoglio. They were late. The sale of their assets had been delayed and they had had to change their tickets in Genoa from those they originally had. Providentially, it transpired, for their original ship – the ocean liner *Principessa Malfalda* – had fractured a propeller shaft which pierced the hull. The ship sank in the Atlantic with the loss of 314 lives, most of them in the steerage class in which the Bergoglio family would have travelled.

Five years later Mario met a young woman, Regina María Sívori, an Argentinean whose family were originally from Genoa, at Mass in the San Antonio Chapel in the Almagro neighbourhood of Buenos Aires where they lived. Within twelve months they were married. The future Pope Francis was born Jorge Mario Bergoglio a year later on 17 December 1936 and was baptised eight days afterwards on Christmas Day.

Though he was born an Argentine, Jorge Mario Bergoglio was raised on pasta and in a culture and a faith tradition which were distinctively Italian. Since he was the first of five children Jorge was, in his early years, collected from his home by his grandmother every morning. He then spent the day at her home around the corner, returning only in the evening. As a result, of all his brothers and sisters, Bergoglio was the one who 'took the family's traditions most to heart', he later said. His grandparents spoke Piedmontese to one another and he learned it from them. 'They loved all of my siblings, but I had the privilege of understanding the language of their memories.' That is why today Pope Francis is completely fluent in Italian as well as Spanish, and can get by in German, French, Portuguese and English as well as Latin. He can also sing a few risqué songs in the Genoese dialect, thanks to a reprobate great uncle.

His father's brothers were confectioners and when they visited the family home his father would switch to Italian too, though he discouraged his children from speaking it; he wanted them to be fully Argentinean. Mario and his brothers were veterans of the First World War and would talk about their experiences and discuss the rise of Mussolini in their homeland, of which Mario disapproved.

Mario José Bergoglio was an accountant by trade, but, because his Italian qualifications were not recognised in Argentina, he took a lower status job as a book-keeper in a hosiery factory. He earned less than he should have, but he was a cheerful man who did not show any resentment. The family was comfortably off, though they had no luxuries. 'We had nothing to spare, no car, and didn't go away on holiday over the summer, but we still never wanted for anything,' Bergoglio has said.

Jorge and his sister María Elena, who is his junior by over a decade, are the only two of the siblings still alive. They recall a happy childhood despite the fact that their mother was paralysed for some years after the birth of her fifth child. Jorge and his siblings would help with the cooking. He recalled getting home from school to find her sitting peeling potatoes with all the other ingredients laid out on the kitchen table. She would then instruct them how to do the cooking. 'We all know how to do it, at the very least *cotolette alla milanese*,' Bergoglio said. The skill has come in useful throughout his career – he cooked for the other students at seminary on Sundays when the chef was off, he fixed his own meals as an archbishop in Buenos Aires, and he has even now had modest cooking facilities installed in his papal rooms in the Casa Santa Marta.

When he was 13 he was shocked to hear his father announce it was time for him to start work. He had just begun a six-year vocational course at the Escuela Nacional de Educación Técnica leading to a diploma as a chemical technician. The school hours were from 8 a.m. to 1 p.m. so his father arranged for him to work from 2 p.m. to 8 p.m. in the hosiery factory. After two years as a cleaner, and then a third doing clerical work, he got a job in a food laboratory. 'I had an extraordinary boss there, Esther de Balestrino de Careaga, a Paraguayan woman and communist sympathiser,' Bergoglio later told the interviewers Francesca Ambrogetti and Sergio Rubin, who published *El Jesuita*, a book of autobiographical interviews with Bergoglio, in 2010. Esther taught him a key lesson about work: that a job needs to be done properly. 'I remember that when I handed her an analysis she'd say "Wow, you did that so fast" and then she asked "Did you do the test or not?". I would answer "What for, if I've done all the previous tests it would surely be more or less the same". And she would chide me "No, you have to do things properly". She taught me the seriousness of hard work. I owe a huge amount to that great woman.' Looking back he feels very grateful to his father for making him take those part-time jobs. 'The work I did was one of the best things I've done in my life. In particular in the laboratory I got to see the good and bad of human endeavour.'

It also taught him something about how work confers dignity upon an individual, a theme to which he regularly returned as an archbishop and as Pope. 'Unemployed people are made to feel like they don't really exist,' he has said. 'Dignity is not conferred by one's ancestry, family life or education. Dignity comes solely from work … It's very important that governments cultivate a culture of work.' That is, he says, a key part of Catholic Social Teaching. But so is the principle of work-life balance. 'One of the questions I would ask young parents during confession is whether or not they spend time playing with their children. Many go to work before the children wake up and come home after they've gone to sleep. And on weekends, overwhelmed by tiredness, they don't pay attention to them like they should. Too much work dehumanises people. Man is not for work; rather, work is for man.'

Family leisure was a key part of his childhood. He treasures the memory of Saturday afternoons when his mother would make all the children listen with her to the 2 p.m. broadcasts of complete operas. 'She'd sit us around the radio and before the opera got underway, she'd explain what it was about. Saturday afternoons with my mother and siblings, enjoying music, was a wonderful time.' Today he still listens to classical music to relax before bed. Beethoven is a favourite. He reads fiction too, with Borges and Dostoevsky among the authors he most frequently revisits.

But his family was, above all, where his deep faith was nurtured. When he was baptized it was his grandmother Rosa who came forward to be his godmother. It was she who taught the young Jorge how to pray. 'She had a big influence on my faith,' he recalled in a radio interview in 2012. His grandfather would tell him stories about World War I but 'she'd tell me stories about the saints. She left a deep spiritual imprint in me.' His sister María Elena remembers she did not just go to church on Sundays: 'Grandma Rosa very devoted; very, very devoted to the Santisimo (Jesus). We all used to pray the rosary with her. Jorge was particularly devoted to the Virgin.' María Elena is in no doubt that his grandmother was responsible at least in part for her brother's vocation to the priesthood. Bergoglio himself has quoted lines the nineteenth-century German poet Friedrich Hölderlin dedicated to his own grandmother; they end 'may the man not betray what he promised as a child'. For Bergoglio the poem reminds him that 'I feel a special devotion to my grandmother for all that she gave me in the first years of my life'. Bergoglio has regularly lamented the fact that grandparents' role has 'gradually fallen by the wayside' in a society where we shove 'our elders into nursing homes with a couple of mothballs in their pockets as if they were an old overcoat'. Being with our grandparents brings us, he said, face-to-face with our past.

Grandma Rosa transmitted a similar strength of faith to her son, Mario, who in his own turn passed his on to Bergoglio. Mario would gather his family to pray the rosary before dinner. He encouraged his son, while still in primary school at Wilfrid Barón de los Santos Ángeles, to rise hours before his classmates so that he could serve Mass for one of the school's Salesian priests, a Ukrainian named Fr Stefan Czmil. There was, Bergoglio later recalled, a puritanical streak to the religion he inherited; divorced or separated people were not allowed to enter the family home and the Bergoglios were suspicious of Protestants, though he recalls when he was about six years old being told by Grandma Rosa that two women from the Salvation Army were 'Protestants, but they are good'. But the boy Jorge was sufficiently zealous that when he arrived in high school he sought permission to ask classmates if they had made their first Holy Communion. When it transpired that four had not, 13-year-old Bergoglio gave them catechesis in the sacrament. He was shocked, about the same time, when someone died from a heart attack at a family wedding, to hear a relative doubt the existence of God.

The religious worldview in which Bergoglio was enfolded as a boy was one of security and certainty. It took God for granted. Faith was as much about what you did as what you thought. His boyhood church, San José in the middle-class Flores district of Buenos Aires, still shows that today. I visited it one Saturday afternoon recently and found a busy bustling place, high-vaulted and imposing, ornate and gilded in the Rococo style, but bursting with colour and activity. At the front, a couple of hundred people were gathered for a Christening. The priest was engaging them with an interactive style of sermon in which he asked questions and the congregation shouted replies. I have seen Bergoglio do the same with a great crowd of children at his annual Mass for the young people of the archdiocese. It is the style of the *porteños*, the slang term which residents of Buenos Aires use of themselves; it has its roots in the fact that the city was first a busy port and conveys something of the swagger and self-assurance found in dockers all over the world. 'We're the New Yorkers of Latin America,' one told me, laughing. In the side aisles of the church individuals of all ages were engaged in private prayer, moving in and out of the dark confessionals, progressing down the side aisles in contemplation of the cornucopia of religious murals, brooding paintings, passionate crucifixes, golden effigies and brightly painted statues. The church was alive with colour and sound, as busy as the notice board with the paraphernalia of rosaries, novenas, pilgrimages and processions.

In pride of place, near the door at the back of the church, was a statue of *Nuestra Señora de Luján*, the patron saint of Argentina, whose story summarises the popular piety of the place. Copies of the celebrated icon of the Virgin, depicted with a long trailing gown of lace like the vapour trail of a rising rocket, have replicated everywhere in Argentina since the day the original arrived in 1630. The image of Mary Immaculate had been made in Brazil and had disembarked in the port of Buenos Aires to be transported to a settler in Santiago. But the oxen pulling the cart stopped unaccountably in Luján and refused to move, despite all manner of cajoling. Only when the cart containing the statue was unloaded would the beasts continue their journey with the rest of their cargo. A local peasant was so amazed at the miraculous determination of the Virgin to remain there that he set up a small shrine in her honour. Last year 1.5 million people went there in pilgrimage. Many intellectuals discount such legends as the residue of a superstitious peasant religion. Bergoglio never has, and that faultline was one of the subjects of the entrenched disputes he was to have in later years within the Jesuit order (see Chapter 3).

But as a young man there was more to life for Bergoglio than religion. As a boy he was a keen footballer – 'never seen without a ball at his feet,' according to one of the nuns who were his first teachers. His father would take him to see San Lorenzo, the soccer team local to the Almagro neighbourhood in which Bergoglio senior had first settled on arrival in Buenos Aires. The team had originally been started by a priest to keep the local lads off the streets and out of trouble. Bergoglio has remained a lifelong supporter, attending matches for many years, though as he became busier with his pastoral work he tended to listen on the radio while doing routine administrative tasks. In 2011 he celebrated mass for the club before posing with the players and holding up a team jersey for photographers. The Saturday after Bergoglio was made Pope the team trotted out for their next match with a photo of the new pontiff on the centre of their kit.

As a teenager he loved to dance. He was good at the tango, Argentina's celebrated national dance, but he preferred the *milonga*, its faster forerunner. He enjoyed the company of young women.

Indeed, according to his sister María Elena, he was planning to propose to one of the girls at his school's annual Student Day picnic one spring morning in September – but something happened on the way. On impulse, passing the family church of San José de Flores he popped in to say a prayer. There he encountered a new priest whom he had never met before. Bergoglio was struck by a sense of deep spirituality about the man and asked to go to confession with him. 'A strange thing happened to me in that confession,' he later told Rubin and Ambrogetti. 'I don't know what it was, but it changed my life … It was a surprise, the astonishment of a chance encounter … the astonishment of encountering someone who was waiting for you all along … God is the one who seeks us first.' The priest to whom he made his confession, a Fr Duarte, died within 12 months.

In later years he reflected on that moment as one in which he had been chosen. When he became a bishop he adopted as his episcopal motto *miserando atque eligendo*. It comes from a comment by the Venerable Bede on the gospel passage in which Jesus met the despised tax collector Mark. Translated it means *unworthy but chosen*, though Bergoglio likes to translate it rather more cumbersomely as '*by having compassion and by choosing*'. He now sees in that motto the moment he uncovered his vocation. 'That was how I felt that God saw me during that conversation. And that is the way he wants me always to look upon others: with much compassion and as if I were choosing them for him; not excluding anyone, because everyone is chosen by the love of God … It is one of the centrepieces of my religious experience.' Religion must contain such a measure of astonishment.

'I don't know what happened,' he later told an Argentine radio station. 'But I knew I had to become a priest.' He could not face the school picnic outing, and the girl to whom he had intended to propose, and he went home instead.

But the 17-year-old did not act upon his decision for four years. 'My thoughts were not focused only on religious matters. I also had political concerns,' he has said. The young Bergoglio had become aware of politics early on. When he was at primary school something else happened which was to shape the churchman that Jorge Mario Bergoglio was to become. His mother's father was a carpenter. Once a week a man with a beard, named Don Elpidio, would come and sell him aniline dyes. His grandmother would serve the two men a cup of tea with wine as they chatted on the patio. One day, after the man had gone, his grandmother asked the young Bergoglio if he knew who the visitor was. It turned out that he was Elpidio González who was once the vice-president of Argentina. Bergoglio was struck by the honesty and integrity of a man who had not corruptly profited from high office but had been content to return to the modest income of a dye salesman. Something has happened to our politics,' he later mused. 'It is out of ideas ...'

As he became a teenager Bergoglio became fascinated by politics. Elpidio González had been a member of Argentina's Radical Party. But the young Bergoglio was also intrigued by the ideas of communism. 'I had a political restlessness,' he later said, which was part of his growing intellectual exploration of the world. He devoured a Communist Party periodical *Nuestra Palabra y Proposito* and was particularly influenced by the articles of their celebrated cultural commentator Leonidas Barletta. 'It helped me in my political education, though I was never a communist.' Yet he cherished too a communist teacher at his high school. 'We had a wonderful relationship with him, he questioned us about everything and it was good for us, but he never lied to us. He always told us where he was coming from, what his hermeneutic and his worldview were.' As the years went by, however, the politics of Argentina polarised and as the Left became more atheistic and anti-clerical, Bergoglio more fully embraced Peronism (see Chapter 3), that peculiarly Argentinean political amalgam which sought to bring together the army, the unions and the Church in a vision of national unity with a distinctly authoritarian streak. He had long been drawn to Peronism; he was once punished at school for wearing a Peronist badge on his uniform.

But throughout all this Bergoglio's sense of vocation consolidated. When he graduated from technical school with a diploma in technical chemistry he told his mother that he intended to study medicine. Delighted, she cleared the attic overlooking the terrace of the family home 'so that he could study in peace, away from the rest of us', his sister María Elena recalled. Every day, after his morning job in the lab, he would arrive home and disappear into the room and work diligently. But one day, when he was out at work, his mother decided to clean his study. To her surprise she did not find textbooks on anatomy or pharmacology but only tomes on theology, many of them in Latin. When Jorge came home she confronted him.

'You said you were studying medicine,' she said, perturbed.

'I didn't lie to you,' Bergoglio responded coolly. 'I'm studying medicine – but medicine of the soul.'

His mother was angry and extremely upset. She told him to wait until he had finished university before making such a momentous decision. When, aged 21, he decided to enter the seminary he told his father first and let him break the news to his mother. Mario could be stern but Bergoglio knew he would be pleased by his decision. But his mother was so upset she refused to go with her son when he entered the seminary. Bergoglio later put his parents' differing reactions down to the fact that his father was an immigrant, which had helped him understand that strength as well as pain can come from being uprooted. His mother, he said, by contrast, 'experienced it as a plundering'. It was four years before she was reconciled to his decision and he only knew she had fully accepted it when she knelt before him after he had been ordained a priest, eleven years later, and asked for his blessing.

Having come to the priesthood relatively late, at the age of 21, he decided, not long after enrolling in San Miguel seminary in Buenos Aires, to join the Jesuits who ran the philosophy and theology courses there. As a teenager his spiritual director had been a Salesian, Fr Enrique Pozzoli, but Bergoglio was now drawn to the military symbolism which has imbued the Jesuit order since it began in the sixteenth century. It was founded by the soldier-turned-mystic Ignatius Loyala as he was recovering from wounds received on the battlefield. Loyola conceived the order's charism as one of being 'contemplatives in action'. 'I was attracted to its position on, to put it in military terms, the front lines of the Church', he said. He also liked the Ignatian tradition of intellectual and spiritual rigour and its emphasis on missionary work and had a hankering after becoming a Jesuit missionary in Japan.

It was not to be. Not longer after entering the seminary the 21-year-old came down with a mysterious fever. For three days and nights he was on the brink of death. Eventually the worried doctors diagnosed that he had pneumonia caused by three cysts in his right lung. His life was saved only by the removal of the upper part of the lung. He recovered, but his impaired breathing capacity put paid to the idea of working overseas. The pain, he later said, was tremendous. The drainage tubes in his lung were also extremely uncomfortable. Visitors tried to cheer him up with the usual comforting banalities but he was not placated, until he was visited by the nun who had prepared him for his first Communion, Sister Dolores. 'She said something that truly stuck with me,' he later recalled, 'and make me feel at peace: "you are imitating Christ"', he was told. Coming face to face with death strengthened his sense of what is important, and what is ultimately peripheral, in life. It strengthened his faith. It is, he later decided, a gift to understand and fully live through pain. 'Pain is not a virtue in itself,' he concluded, 'but you can be virtuous in the way you bear it.' Despite the severity of the experience it has not much impaired his physical ability, though breathing restrictions have produced some pain in the lower back, which is why today he needs special shoes and at times walks with a stick.

It was not an unswerving vocation. At one point in his seminary career he became besotted by a young woman he met at a family wedding. 'I was surprised by her beauty, the clarity of her intellect … and, well, I kicked the idea around for a while. When I returned to the seminary after the wedding, I could not pray during the entire week because when I prepared to pray, the girl appeared in my mind. I had to think about my choice again.' Eventually he reaffirmed his commitment to become a priest, though he added, 'it would be abnormal for these types of things not to happen'.

Through all this Grandma Rosa, both before and after her death in the mid–1970s, was to Bergoglio a supportive and sustaining presence. His breviary is the first thing he opens in the morning and last thing he closes at night. Inside it he carries two pieces of paper. One is a letter she wrote in 1967, half in Italian and half in Spanish, two years before his ordination. It was written because she feared she might die before the great day arrived when he would become a priest and, in that event, left it to be handed to him on the day. Fortunately she was there to give it to him in person. It read:

> On this beautiful day on which you hold Christ our saviour in your conse-crated hands, and on which a broad path to a deeper apostolate is opening up before you, I bequeath to you this humble gift, of very little material but very great spiritual value.

With it came a personal creed she had written for herself in the form of a spiritual last will and testament. In one paragraph she wrote:

> May these, my grandchildren, to whom I gave the best my heart has to offer, have long and happy lives, but if someday sorrow, sickness, or the loss of a beloved person should fill them with distress, let them remember that a sigh directed toward the tabernacle, home to the greatest and noblest martyr, and a look to Mary at the foot of the Cross, can drop a soothing balm onto the deepest and most painful of wounds.

Jorge Mario Bergoglio has remained faithful to that, and to the style of spirituality with which she imbued him. In an order as intel-lectual as the Jesuits he has had to find ways of reconciling with criticisms that he is pandering to the superstitions of folk religion. Another Argentinean Jesuit, Fr Humberto Miguel Yáñez, who is now the head of the moral theology department at the Gregorian University in Rome, thinks Bergoglio has done that. 'He has always had a favourable attitude to popular religiosity,' said Yáñez. 'Some see it as including an element of superstition which is not part of the faith and some bishops were against that. But Bergoglio saw it as an important way that people linked to the spiritual. His influence gradually shaped a different culture among the bishops of Argentina, among other things pushing them to be much closer to their own priests.'

Any movement in that direction in the wider Church will be a significant departure. Benedict XVI was far more cautious about popular piety. 'Through it, faith has entered into men's heart, forming part of their sentiments, customs, feeling and common living', he acknowledged to the Latin America bishops gathered at Aparecida in 2007. 'Faith has become flesh and blood. That is why, popular piety is a great patrimony of the Church.' But he warned: 'It cannot be denied, however, that certain deviated forms exist of popular religiosity that, far from fomenting an active participation in the Church, create instead confusion and can foster a merely exterior religious practice detached from a well-rooted and interior living faith. Popular piety can incline toward the irrational and perhaps also remain on the outside. Popular piety must certainly always be purified and point to the centre.' Bergoglio has always been a good deal less suspicious.

The popular devotion to a woman named the Difunta Correa is a good example of the way popular piety is being accepted into the mainstream, Yáñez said. She died around 1840 in the province of San Juan in Argentina. 'She was a woman so consumed with grief when her husband was forced to go to war that she walked into the desert carrying her infant child. She died of thirst but her breasts continue to produce milk to nourish her child.' Her body was found days later by *gauchos* driving cattle nearby. To their astonishment they found the baby still alive, feeding from the dead woman's 'miraculously' ever-full breast. Her devotees, who now number in their hundreds of thousands, believe her still to intercede for the living to perform more miracles. 'Her cult was for years not recognised by the Church', said Yáñez. 'But nowadays the bishops do not discourage it.' That change in attitude has been in part due to the influence of Bergoglio. He believes that it is through devotions like these that the ordinary people express their spirituality and the Church should be part of that. Bergoglio, he recalls, once organised an international conference on the relationship between faith and culture. 'Bergoglio understands that the attitudes of people like those who follow the Difunta Correa creates a place where faith and culture meet.'

Bergoglio's frequent references to the Devil offer another example of his ease with combing the two approaches. After Vatican II many Catholic priests and theologians dispensed with the Devil, preferring to see evil in more abstract terms. But Bergoglio does not. He is what another Jesuit called 'a more concrete person with a more folksy religiosity', and yet the founder of the Jesuits, St Ignatius Loyola, very much saw the Devil as a person, a fallen angel. That idea still remains in parts of Catholic spirituality though some Jesuits tend to emphasise it more than others. 'Bergoglio's attitude to popular religiosity is that you don't judge it, you work alongside it', said Fr Augusto Zampini, a diocesan priest who taught at the *Colegio Máximo* where Bergoglio was once Rector. 'To disregard popular faith is in a way to disregard the option for the poor. Bergoglio would say: "This has to do with the spirit, let's work with it, rather than against it".'

Argentinean Catholicism is replete with examples of this folk religion, which the nation's theologians prefer to call the Theology of the People. Cars carry bumper stickers invoking Gauchito Gil, a legendary Robin Hood character from the eighteenth century, whom devotees insist protects drivers. St Cayetano is upheld as the patron saint of bread and work. St Expedito is the saint of urgent cases. St Pantaleon, doctor and martyr, protects from the gripe, the flu and other illnesses of the winter season. 'There is a calendar of saints days, a saint for health, a saint for work and so on, Fr Bergoglio loves all that', says Fr Guillermo Marcó, who was for eight years Bergoglio's public spokesman in the archdiocese of Buenos Aires. The foreign incomers into the slums of the city also bring with them their own Virgins: *Nuestra Señora de Caacupé* from Paraguay, *Nuestra Señora de Copacabana* from Bolivia and *Nuestra Señora de Cuzco* from Peru. Saints and manifestations of the Madonna appear through popular acclamation by simple folk who make bargains with them, like the woman in one shanty town in Bergoglio's former diocese who has converted her home into a chapel and provides lunches for forty hungry children a day because she promised St Cayetano she would do that if the saint found her husband a job.

In all this Bergoglio is 'a man very close to popular devotion', said Fr Francisco de Roux, the provincial of the Jesuits in Colombia. 'He is a man of popular piety. He captures the experience of God in the simplicity of popular practices, processions, shrines, the Christmas novena, the family saying the rosary. To him the strength of Catholicism is in the way simple people live their faith.' The approach is summed up in the chalice being designed in Argentinean silver for Pope Francis by a local goldsmith, Juan Carlos Pallarols. It will feature images of Our Lady of Luján, Mary Untier of Knots, Jesuit symbols and an Argentine icon.

All this is not some strategy of Bergoglio's to keep close to the people; it goes to the core of his being. A small order named the Franciscan Friars of the Immaculate posted an item on their webpage after Pope Francis was elected, about how they noticed ten years ago that at 9 a.m. every morning a middle-aged man would come into their little church dedicated to the Virgin of the Annunciation in Lungotevere, not far from St Peter's basilica in Rome. They were intrigued, not just by his clockwork timekeeping – Bergoglio is an extremely punctual man – but by the fact that he always went straight to a statue of St Theresa of the Child Jesus and prayed before it with great devotion. 'At the end of the prayer,' they wrote, 'he used to do as many old ladies – who are sometimes looked down upon in this country – do, he touched the statue and kissed it.' Then one day they noticed the man, who clearly visited on his way to meetings at the Vatican, had red buttons on his cassock. Alone and unobserved Cardinal Jorge Mario Bergoglio, Archbishop of Buenos Aires, was at prayer in the way that Grandma Rosa would have been.

'I remember two rhymes from my grandmother', Bergoglio said in *On Heaven and Earth*, his book of conversations with the Argentinean rabbi Abraham Skorka.

> See that God watches you,
> See that He is watching you
> See that you will have to die
> And you do not know when.

'She had that saying under the glass top of her little nightstand, and each time that she went to bed she would read it. After seventy years I still have not forgotten it. There is another rhyme that she told me that she had read at an Italian cemetery:

> Man who walks,
> stop and think
> about your pace,
> your steps,
> the final step.

'She impressed on me the awareness that everything must end, that everything has to be left behind in good order. With respect to the Christian life, death has to accompany you on the way. In my case, for example, I think every day that I am going to die. This does not distress me, because the Lord and life have given me the proper preparation. I saw my ancestors die and now it is my turn. When? I do not know.'

His thoughts turned to a previous pope. 'John XXIII, until the moment of his death, continued being a rural peasant. On his death bed, his sister placed on his head cold cloths with vinegar, just like they did in the country.' It is hard to believe that Jorge Mario Bergoglio, likewise, will ever leave behind the popular spirituality of his devotional roots.

3

Jesuit Secrets

It was not exactly an endorsement. As soon as the name of the new Pope had been announced the internet buzzed with emails. Who was Jorge Mario Bergoglio? What was he like? Members of the Jesuit order were particular targets for these inquiries. What many replied was far from flattering. One of the most senior figures in the Society of Jesus, a serving Provincial in another Latin American country, wrote this, in a private email (seen by the author):

> Yes I know Bergoglio. He's a person who's caused a lot of problems in the Society and is highly controversial in his own country. In addition to being accused of having allowed the arrest of two Jesuits during the time of the Argentinean dictatorship, as Provincial he generated divided loyalties: some groups almost worshiped him, while others would have nothing to do with him, and he would hardly speak to them. It was an absurd situation. He is well-trained and very capable, but is surrounded by this personality cult which is extremely divisive. He has an aura of spirituality which he uses to obtain power. It will be a catastrophe for the Church to have someone like him in the Apostolic See. He left the Society of Jesus in Argentina destroyed with Jesuits divided and institutions destroyed and financially broken. We have spent two decades trying to fix the chaos that the man left us.

Given the otherwise universal acclaim that greeted the election of Pope Francis – the simple and humble Pope for the poor who would restore integrity to a compromised Church – this consti-tuted an extraordinary counterblast. And it was far from a lone voice inside the religious order in which Jorge Mario Bergoglio was formed and was a leading figure until the age of 50. Within hours an instruction had gone out from head office, the Jesuit Curia in Rome, ordering Jesuits around the world to be prudent in their recollections and keep to themselves any unhappy memories they had of the new Pope. Even so, such was the feeling within the order that some leading Jesuits put their names to critical comments. The senior English Jesuit, Fr Michael Campbell-Johnston, a veteran of the persecution of the Church by the Western-supported military dictatorship in El Salvador where Oscar Romero was martyred, wrote in the Catholic journal *The Tablet* about how Bergoglio was out of step with other Jesuit provinces on issues of social justice. And the distinguished Spanish theologian Fr José Ignacio González Faus wrote in *El Pais* that Bergoglio's time as an archbishop offered great grounds for hope but that his time as a Jesuit – as 'a man with an amazing ability to charm, but with a passion for power' – raised real fears. What could create such strength of feeling among the ranks of those who might have been expected to applaud the first Jesuit Pope as one of their own?

***

It takes fifteen years' study and preparation to become a Jesuit. Given that, the progress of Jorge Mario Bergoglio through the ranks of the Society of Jesus was remarkably speedy. After entering the Society as a novice on 11 March 1958 he undertook a year of study in the humanities in Chile and then did two years of philosophy at the *Colegio Máximo de San José* in the San Miguel district of Buenos Aires. Three years of teaching literature and psychology followed, in a Jesuit *Colegio de la Inmaculada Concepción* in Santa Fé which was much sought-after by wealthy families seeking a traditional education for their sons, and then at the prestigious *Colegio del Salvador* in Buenos Aires. He was, said his pupils, a firm but enthusiastic teacher, with a great memory for his charges' names, home towns, acquaintances and interests. He brought all manner of outsiders into the classroom to enliven proceedings. The most famous of these was the great Argentinean novelist Jorge Luis Borges, whom the charismatic Bergoglio persuaded to write a foreword to a collection of the students' short stories.

For the next three years, from 1967–70, he studied theology at *Colegio Máximo*. In that time he was ordained a priest, on 13 December 1969, just a few days before his 33rd birthday, by Archbishop Ramón José Castellano. There others began already to remark upon the austerity of his lifestyle. He also earned a reputation for inscrutability, so much so that his fellow scholastics – as Jesuits in their second stage of formation training are known – teased him with the nickname La Gioconda, after the Mona Lisa, because it was impossible to know what he was thinking. His tertianship, the third stage of formation, was spent at the university of *Alcalá de Henares* in Spain from 1971 to 1972. He was so highly regarded, by his fellows and his superiors alike, that on his return to Argentina he was made Master of Novices, and also served for a short time as Rector of *Colegio Máximo*, even before he came to take his final vows as a Jesuit. Indeed within just three months of taking those perpetual vows, in April 1973, at the age of just 36, he was made Provincial Superior, the head of all the Jesuits in Argentina.

The tension which was to grow between what developed into *Bergogliano* and *anti-Bergogliano* factions divided the province in two. There were two main areas of conflict. One was religious, the other political. The religious division was over the Second Vatican Council. Though Bergoglio went on to become the first Pope who had been ordained as priest after the Second Vatican Council, his formation was essentially pre-Vatican II in its style and content. As different sections of the Church began to explore how to put the insights of the Council into practice, a polarisation occurred, and then deepened, between progressive and conservative factions within the Argentinean Jesuits. But there was another polarisation growing in Argentina, in politics.

To understand Jorge Mario Bergoglio it is essential to under-stand something of the politics of Argentina, for Bergoglio is not comprehensible outside his own national context. Conventional paradigms of Left and Right do not greatly help here. Politics in Argentina is dominated by Peronism, a curious amalgam of forces not normally associated with one another: the military, the trade unions and the Church. General Juan Domingo Perón was President of Argentina for a decade from 1945 onwards. An immensely skilled populist politician, he and the legend of his second wife Evita shaped the nation's politics for many decades more; in many ways his is still the defining model through which Argentineans do their politics.

Peronism had its roots in one of the major documents in the history of Catholic Social Teaching – an encyclical called *Quadragesimo Anno*. It was issued in 1931 by Pope Pius XI to mark the fortieth anniversary of the first Catholic social encyclical, *Rerurm Novarum*, which in 1891 had set out to discover a third way between capitalism and communism. The idea was to increase social justice while dissuading Catholic workers from allying themselves with socialist movements. By 1931 Pope Pius XI had come to the conclusion that there was no alternative to capitalism; Pius gave it, implicitly, his blessing and exhorted it to behave more responsibly. But *Quadragesimo Anno* was published two years after the 1929 Wall Street crash and the worldwide collapse of money markets. Something clearly was needed to address the fact of economic depression and the consequence of mass unemployment. The mechanism to control this which Pius XI proposed was a grand corporate plan for the reconstruction of the social order which would do away with class struggle between bosses and workers, and promote harmonious co-operation within industries and professions in its place. The problem was that the obvious vehicles for that in the 1930s were the fascist movements of Italy, Germany and Spain.

Though World War II had discredited fascism, its underlying principles lingered on in Perón's holy alliance of Church, workers and the military, which he announced was based on *Quadragessimo Anno*. His approach involved a new industrialisation to boost the economy, nationalisation and a substantial redistribution of wealth to ensure the new working class benefitted from it. The physical might of the military and the moral authority of the Church were to enforce it, though in practice it also involved the authoritarian suppression of the opposition and the freedom of the press. Unfortunately Perón's approach led to a combination of economic stagnation, bloated state bureaucracy, inflation, falling living standards and rising unemployment. In 1955 the military overthrew Péron, who went into exile until 1973 when he returned to become President again, though only for a year until his death in 1974.

There is one final key factor to be grasped to understand the political worldview of the man who went on to be the first Pope from the Americas. Peronists thought of themselves as socialists but many of their policies were closer to the fascism of Mussolini's Italy or Franco's Spain. The lack of ideological consistency led the movement to split into dissenting factions. Some extreme leftists known as the Monteneros took inspiration from Mao, Castro and Che Guevara and developed anti-clerical, anti-Catholic positions. Right-wing Peronists saw themselves as the defenders of the nation, private property and of Catholicism against the atheist communist hordes; the most extreme groups on the Right included the *Alianza Anticomunista Argentina* (also known as the Triple A) and *Guardia de Hierro* (the Iron Guard), a name taken from an ultra-nationalist, fascist, anti-communist, anti-semitic movement in Romania which claimed to be acting in defence of Orthodox Christianity. These Peronist factions did not just disagree; eventually they set up death squads which roamed the streets in killing sprees targeted upon opponents at the other end of the Peronist spectrum. At one point, as we shall see, Bergoglio became a spiritual adviser to the Iron Guard. What pushed him in that direction was the other great polarisation in his life – the religious split which developed between Catholics all across Latin America, and particularly in Argentina and inside the Society of Jesus there. It was over Liberation Theology.

Between 1962 and 1965 the Catholic Church had been shaken to its foundations by the Second Vatican Council. Before it, the Church had been a body turned quietly inward on its own inner sacramental life; Vatican II famously threw open the windows of the Church, seeking greater interaction with, and influence on, secular society. In Latin America a number of theologians began to work out how the teachings of Vatican II should be applied on the ground.

A few individual priests took it upon themselves to move into the *villas miserias*, or 'misery villages', which Argentineans most commonly translate as 'slums'. Calling themselves the *Movimiento de Sacerdotes para el Tercer Mundo* (Movement of Priests for the Third World) they insisted the gospel was about bringing good news to the poor and fought for the rights of their parishioners. Jesuits were in the vanguard of this; one of the pioneers was a former Jesuit Provincial, Juan Marcós Moglia, who served in the slums for 20 years until his death. But the movement began to take greater shape in 1968 when the Brazilian theologian Rubem Alves wrote a book called *Towards a Theology of Liberation* which set a template for the movement which was developed by thinkers like Gustavo Gutiérrez in Peru, Juan Luis Segundo in Uruguay, Jon Sobrino in El Salvador and Leonardo Boff of Brazil. The common ground was to seek a liberation from unjust economic, political or social conditions in the under-developed region where an elite class exploited resources and labour largely for their own benefit – and that of the rich world with which they traded. It was to be expressed in what Gutiérrez, in the movement's seminal work *A Theology of Liberation* (1971), called the 'preferential option for the poor' – the radical idea that in the Bible God takes sides and gives preference to the impoverished, the marginalised and the oppressed. The notion was endorsed at gatherings of all the continent's bishops at Medellín in Colombia in 1968 and again at Puebla in Mexico in 1976. The Medellín documents spoke of the 'institutionalised violence' of poverty; Argentina's bishops, however, who were overwhelmingly traditionalist and reactionary, were notably unenthusiastic.

What the conservatives particularly disliked was that Liberation Theology allowed a critique of society, and of the Church, through the eyes of the poor. And it introduced a bottom-up model of Christian base communities where biblical interpretation and liturgy were designed by ordinary people – a notion which went down very badly in a top-down organisation like the Catholic Church. The hierarchy in the Vatican objected to that and also to the use by some liberation theologians of Marxist sociological analysis. The Church could not endorse notions of class struggle, Rome said. Most of all it utterly rejected the idea adopted by a handful of Liberation Theology's most extreme enthusiasts that the gospel offered a justification for the poor to engage in armed struggle against the rich.

There were a good number of liberation theologians who took such a view. Just before Medellín 1,500 priests from the Movement of Priests for the Third World signed a letter to Paul VI condemning 'the violence of the upper class' and 'the violence of the state' as the first violence. In the face of this, they argued, the violence of the poor was an understandable response.

But there was an element of deliberate and wilful misunderstanding of the basis of Liberation Theology by some in Rome. Most liberation theologians, when they talked about the need for revolution, were advocating a complete turnaround of existing exploitative economic and social structures. Opponents caricatured this as an endorsement of armed violence, but most liberation theologians were not advocating that the poor should take up guns. What they wanted was that the Church should stand alongside the poor and help as they learned to organise themselves in unions and co-operatives to gain bargaining power. Liberation Theology proper was about giving the poor priority in their fight to overturn unjust relationships, bring about structural change, and the Church standing in solidarity with that.

But this was the time of the Cold War when the Soviet Union – and, more nearby, Fidel Castro in Cuba – were intent on exporting revolutionary communism to what was then called the Third World.

Elites in Latin America saw Liberation Theology as the first sign of the continent's slide toward Marxism. The United States took a similar view and deployed its Central Intelligence Agency (CIA) to galvanise the split of the Church into conservative and progressive elements – and back the conservatives. It even set up a special unit dedicated to working on the issue with the Vatican. Rome was happy to co-operate. It saw Liberation Theology as a threat to Catholic orthodoxy and the power of the Vatican hierarchy. Pope Paul VI was persuaded that Liberation Theology needed curbing. He appointed the Colombian bishop Alfonso López Trujillo, an Opus Dei member, to become its principal scourge. Cardinal Antonio Samorè, President of the Pontifical Commission for Latin America, was given the job of liaising between the Roman Curia and the Latin America bishops to stem the influence of this new theology of the poor.

What sharpened the significance of these religious and political distinctions was violence. In 1966 a military coup in Argentina had placed in power the authoritarian General Juan Carlos Onganía who banned Peronism – along with mini-skirts and long hair on men – and presided over what its citizens later called a 'soft dictatorship' (in contrast to the horrors that were to follow). The Movement of Priests for the Third World issued a declaration supporting revolutionary socialist movements. In response Juan Carlos Aramburu, the acting Archbishop of Buenos Aires, forbade priests from making political declarations. Onganía's administration ended in a chaos of instability, discontent and demonstrations, ushering in the first elections for a decade.

The return of the exiled Juan Perón which followed in 1973 was supposed to calm society's troubled nerves. It did exactly the opposite. The barely suppressed antagonisms between the Left and Right of Peronism erupted into open warfare with murders, kidnappings and bombings. Left-wing guerrillas battled the government, while right-wing death squads cruised the streets, murdering with impunity. Among those who died was the first of the 'slum priests' to be martyred, the charismatic Fr Carlos Mugica, who was shot dead by the *Alianza Anticomunista Argentina* outside the church of *San Francisco Solano* where he had just finished celebrating Mass. He was talking to a couple of young people about their forthcoming wedding when the bullets struck. Between 1973 and 1976 a virtual civil war reigned on the streets of Buenos Aires. Some historians have suggested that as many people died in those three years as were killed by the military dictatorship in the so-called Dirty War in the years that followed the military coup that took place in 1976. Things were so bad that many ordinary citizens sighed with relief when the army stepped in.

It was against this background of a titanic struggle for the soul of Catholicism in Latin America that Jorge Mario Bergoglio became Provincial Superior of the Society of Jesus in Argentina. His predecessor was Fr Ricardo 'Dick' O'Farrell, whose name discloses that the Irish were, along with Bergoglio's Italians, a major component in the melting pot of Argentinean immigration. O'Farrell was a sociologist who had embraced the changes of Vatican II. He was open to new ideas, including Liberation Theology. He supported base communities. He encouraged Jesuits like Fr Orlando Yorio and Fr Franz Jalics to work with the poor in the slums – from which they would be kidnapped by the military in an incident which has cast a shadow over Jorge Mario Bergoglio's ministry ever since (see Chapter 4).

But O'Farrell presided over a dramatic decline in vocations. In 1961 there were twenty-five novices; by 1973 that had dropped to just two. The reason for this is disputed. The Jesuit historian Jeffrey Klaiber has suggested it was merely a reflection of a general post-Vatican II crisis in vocations. Professor Fortunato Mallimacci, who runs the *Society and Religion* course at the University of Buenos Aires, suggests many Jesuits left at this time 'as an act of rebellion against the intellectual support the order had given to the regime of the dictator Onganía who was one of a thousand members of the elite recruited to be a member of Opus Dei'. But Marina Rubino, a theology student at the *Colegio Máximo* at the time, recalled that it was because O'Farrell and his teaching staff, which included Jalics and Yorio, were taking seriously the changes set out by the Second Vatican Council and Medellín – and this was driving old-style conservative seminarians away.

Whatever the explanation, the order was in turmoil, according to Fr Michael Campbell-Johnston, who was later sent on a visitation to Argentina on behalf of the Jesuit Superior General, Fr Pedro Arrupe in Rome. 'The Argentinean Jesuits had been going through a lot of trouble', he recalled. 'A lot of people had been leaving the order and even the priesthood. Some ten to 15 were leaving every year. That was quite exceptional.'

What was clear was that there were many Jesuits who were unhappy with the rapid pace at which things were changing in the order after the Second Vatican Council. They did not like the shifts of emphasis within Ignatian spirituality. Jesuits were supposed to be 'contemplatives in action'. The old guard prefer the contemplation to the action but the new progressives inverted the priority. Progressive Jesuits wanted to downplay, or even abandon, the order's traditional role of educating the next generation of the nation's elite. Instead they wanted to move to working with the uneducated poor in the shanty towns. The conservatives did not approve and, more than that, they were afraid that the progressives who were working politically in the slums would make all Jesuits targets for the right-wing anti-communist murder squads.

Something extraordinary then happened. The conservatives staged an unprecedented rebellion in which a number of them complained to the Superior General in Rome about their Provincial, Dick O'Farrell. They petitioned that he should be removed from office. The Jesuit Curia in Rome, fearful of the division that was being caused in the Argentinean province, acceded to their request. O'Farrell, who might have expected to serve for six years, as is the norm, found himself removed after less than four. On 31 July 1973 Bergoglio was made Provincial and O'Farrell, humiliatingly, was told to swap jobs with the younger man and become Novice Master, a post he only then held for eighteen months.

As Provincial in charge of fifteen Jesuit houses, 166 priests, thirty-two brothers and twenty students in their care, Bergoglio immediately set about reversing many of O'Farrell's changes and moving back to the pre-Vatican II values and lifestyles in which his own formation as a Jesuit had been shaped. O'Farrell had had the chapel at *Colegio Máximo* remodelled and replastered so that the traditional church now looked like an awesome giant white cave – the Vatican II enthusiast intended it to feel like the inside of Moses' tent in the desert – totally unadorned save for a great dark crucifix. It was a breathtaking transformation, as visitors to the *Colegio Máximo* can still see today. Entering the chapel is like emerging into an astonishing whitewashed catacomb. Bergoglio hated it, but knew he could not justify the cost of reordering the chapel again so he swiftly installed a statue of the Virgin and what he felt was a more reverential tabernacle. But that was only the start.

The job of a Jesuit novice master is to test whether novices have a genuine vocation; some do that through gentle discernment, others as a strict disciplinarian. Bergoglio had been the latter. Now he used the same approach as Provincial. He made changes in the liturgy, setting aside modern Vatican II songs and replacing them with pre-conciliar songs, psalms and Gregorian plainchant. He introduced the service of Lauds, which is not part of the Jesuit tradition, and which many in the Society did not like. 'He tried to make us more like a religious order, wearing surplices and singing the office', recalled one of his students, Miguel Mom Debussy, who joined the order in 1973 and was ordained a priest by Bergoglio in 1984. As Rector he introduced a fixed schedule for the students and insisted on integrating manual labour into their formation, remembered another student, Fr Humberto Miguel Yáñez, who is now the head of moral theology at the Gregorian University in Rome. O'Farrell had been a modernising influence on everyday clothing, allowing students and priests to wear non-clerical clothing; Bergoglio put an end to that, insisting on clerical collars instead. He himself routinely wore a cassock, something only older members of the community routinely had done.

There were changes too in the curriculum. Bergoglio instructed the teachers of moral theology appointed by O'Farrell to work from an ancient textbook in Latin. 'That caused a problem because many of the novices had stopped learning Latin – or saying prayers in it – years before', said Mom Debussy, of Bergoglio's first few years as Provincial. 'We had to go to the older Jesuits, aged 45 or over, to get things translated. The teacher was a progressive type who obeyed the instructions given by the new Provincial but who would bite her lip with obvious disgust.' Bergoglio was unimpressed. He brought in conservative lay professors to replace teachers he considered too progressive. Among those sacked was the theology lecturer Fr Orlando Yorio, one of the two Jesuits later kidnapped and tortured by the military in 1976. Yorio had been one of Bergoglio's teachers. Books by the other Jesuit later kidnapped alongside Yorio, Franz Jalics, who had taught Bergoglio philosophy, were withdrawn from the college library and a teacher using them on a student course was asked to remove them from its reading list. 'Before long', said Mom Debussy, 'Bergoglio brought in an arch-conservative, the military chaplain from Moreno Air Base, to teach. He seemed unaware of any of the teachings of Vatican II. It was all St Thomas Aquinas and the old Church Fathers. We didn't study a single book by Gutiérrez, Boff, or Paulo Freire.'

'Liberation theology was actually forbidden', said another of Bergoglio's students, Fr Rafael Velasco, who is now the rector of the Catholic University of Córdoba. 'It was seen by him as very suspicious if you were interested in that. I had to wait to read it later in life.' Philosophy was similarly constrained. The course of study began with Pre-Socratic philosophers and then went through Descartes, Kant and Hegel to the modern period. 'But it stopped with Nietzsche, of whom there was just a little with critical analysis from a Catholic perspective, and very little Kierkegaard or Heidegger', said Mom Debussy. 'There was no Marx, Engels, Sartre, Foucault, structuralists, post-structuralists or postmodernists. Nobody who opposed one iota of traditional Catholic doctrine and dogma. All under the strict orders of Jorge Bergoglio.'

The resistance movement to the reforms of Vatican II was being led among the foremost intellectual religious order in Argentina by Jorge Mario Bergoglio.

O'Farrell had encouraged seminarians to study a wide range of subjects outside their mandated philosophy and theology: sociology, politics, anthropology, engineering – even, in one case, solar engineering. Bergoglio steered novices and scholastics away from such an approach. 'There is a tradition in the Jesuits that you're encouraged to do political science as a sociology', said Velasco. 'This was absolutely discouraged by Bergoglio.'

But if Bergoglio wanted to erase any trace of Liberation Theology inside the Argentinean Jesuits, he was keen for them to maintain their contact with the poor. 'From Monday to Friday we were at the college but at the weekends students had to go out to parishes including poor areas,' said Velasco, 'but our only duties there were religious. We had nothing to do with unions or cooperatives or even Catholic NGOs.' When students discovered a need in a parish Bergoglio was swift to act. Yáñez, who was received into the order in 1975, recalled how Bergoglio dispatched him to a poor area to visit families and discover what they needed. In response the Provincial immediately set up a soup kitchen for 200 children in the district. Even so, according to Velasco, 'his relationship with the poor was pastoral but a little bit patronising. It was to soften the consequences of injustice rather than to tackle the causes of injustice or poverty or to empower the poor.' The Bergoglio of those days might well have agreed. Presiding at his first provincial assembly in April 1974, he told the gathered Jesuits that they should avoid what he called 'abstract ideologies mismatched with reality'.

Many in the province agreed with him and found his changes helpful. 'He wanted to bring back certain elements of our formation that had been left aside after the Second Vatican Council, not for the sake of being pre-conciliar, but because he thought they reflected our reality', said Yáñez. 'At the time, things like a fixed schedule seemed like going back to the past. But he wanted to create a certain discipline. Integrating manual labour into our formation struck

me as a realistic way of living poverty.' Students had freedom but
he demanded there was a certain coherence in their lives. Another
student from that time, who asked not to be named, commented:
'The clerical dress was no big deal. In the 1970s in Argentina
everybody – lawyers, doctors, priests – wore clothes appropriate to
their job. It was not old-fashioned. It was just proper at the time.
The people expected the clerical collar from a student priest in
those days. I never found Bergoglio a control freak. As Provincial it
was just about authority not control.'

Then, as later when Bergoglio was an archbishop and Pope, many
were impressed by his personal lifestyle. 'He was very austere', said
Velasco. 'He always wore the same clothes and he rejected luxurious
food or drink.' He thought a priest should suit the action to the
Word too, as his old friend the human rights lawyer Alicia Oliveira
recalled. 'In those days the Jesuits ran a school for the wealthy, the
Colegio del Salvador in Buenos Aires. My sons went there. It was
actually two schools in one building with two separate entrances,
for those who paid and those who didn't. When Bergoglio was
Provincial he closed down the free school and moved all the poor
children into the rich one. He did not tell the parents. No-one knew.
He was always concerned about the poor.'

Already in his late thirties Bergoglio was a charismatic figure.
'His leadership was based on his personality', said Velasco. 'He loved
teaching the novices. He was not hierarchical in his style. He came
across more as a brother than a father. You wanted to be very close
to him.' The new Provincial was a dynamic force-of-nature figure
who swiftly set about building a big new library for the *Colegio
Máximo*. 'He was a marvellous leader', recalled an Irish Jesuit,
Fr James Kelly, who was living in the house in those years while
teaching scripture in Buenos Aires. 'In fact his leadership qualities
were quite remarkable … A very spiritual man, humble but with
strong convictions, he was responsible for attracting a large number
of young men to join the Jesuits at a time when numbers had fallen.'
But his charismatic style of leadership brought many problems. 'If
you liked him and he liked you, you'd be in a good position', recalled

Rafael Velasco. 'But if he didn't like you, you were in for some kind of trouble. And if you didn't agree with him you'd be relegated outside the circle of power.'

That is what happened to Miguel Dom Debussy. 'For the first four years, from 1973 onwards, I had a really good relationship with Bergoglio. He often chose me as his driver', he recalled, with a tart aside that the man who, in later years as Archbishop of Buenos Aires was celebrated for taking underground trains and buses, was earlier happy to be chauffeured around. 'Even when he went to celebrate Mass in a parish church just ten blocks away he'd ask me to drive him. And nor was he simple in his approach to the liturgy in those days; he wore pre-Vatican II vestments of velvet embroidered in gold, saying that "ordinary people like a touch of Evita". But we got on very well in the early years and he shared a lot of confidences in the car, such as the fact that he didn't like the fact that his brother was in Opus Dei. We were quite close though we later fell out as Bergoglio became increasingly more conservative.'

Fr Humberto Miguel Yáñez is still in touch with Bergoglio. He had received a phone call from Pope Francis not long before I met him to talk. He recalled Bergoglio as struggling to hold a divided religious order together in those days. 'These were years of a strong conflict between left and right,' he said, 'and I'd say that for the most part Bergoglio was in the middle.' But others tell a different story and see the young Provincial's injunctions about avoiding politics as distinctly one-sided.

By his own admission to his interviewers Francesca Ambrogettti and Sergio Rubin, Bergoglio was a political animal. As a teenager he had been interested in the relationship between faith and communism. But as Argentinean society polarised between an atheist anti-Church Left and a Right which claimed to be acting in defence of the Church and its values, Bergoglio was drawn inexorably to the worldview of the Right, if not with its tactics.

As he drove the Provincial's car through the streets of Buenos Aires, Miguel Mom Debussy gained insights into Bergoglio's political shift. 'I was a left-wing Peronist', said Mom Debussy.

'Bergoglio was on the right of Peronism, he was linked with the Iron Guard who were a traditional, right-wing, dogmatic group with an entryist strategy to various sources of power.'

Despite their name, the Iron Guard did not have much in common with their violent fascist Romanian namesakes. Argentina's Iron Guard were an odd bunch who liked to think of themselves as a secret order characterised by obedience, intellectual rigor and ascetic discipline – the Jesuit virtues – but whose intellectual influences were a mish-mash of Lenin, the mystic Romanian philosopher Mircea Eliade and the sixteenth-century Jesuit missionary to China, Matteo Ricci. But with their doctrine of preaching class harmony they had the appeal of constituting a third way between the violent activists of the extremes of Left and Right. That was something which drew Bergoglio; he had concluded that something in Peronism constituted Argentina's best hope for a solution to the nation's endemic problems of economic instability and political chaos. Various former members of the Iron Guard have confirmed that Bergoglio was from 1972 a spiritual adviser to the movement whose founder, Alejandro Álvarez later linked up with the Italian Catholic lay movement *Comunione e Liberazione* with which Bergoglio later developed links. The lawyer Alicia Oliveira acknowledges Bergoglio's links to the Iron Guard: 'He was involved. He gave them spiritual help. But I never heard him say any of the stupid things that a lot of people in the Iron Guard said.'

The Iron Guard would have remained a mere eccentric footnote in the Bergoglio biography had it not been for an initiative from the Jesuit's Superior General, Fr Pedro Arrupe. Just twenty days before Bergoglio was appointed Provincial an order had come from Rome. The 31st General Congregation of the Jesuit order, which had met while Vatican II was still in session, had decreed that the Society should reappraise its relationship with the lay men and women of the Church. In pursuit of that, Arrupe had decided that in Argentina the order should pass one of the two universities in its control over to the hands of the laity. On taking over, Bergoglio put the matter in train.

The *Universidad del Salvador* in Buenos Aires, he decided, would be given to the Iron Guard 'to facilitate the growth of the Kingdom of God'. It would represent a 'continuity of the Jesuit spirit' but in lay hands. In August 1974 he appointed a leading member of the Iron Guard, Francisco Jose Pinon, as the university's rector. The Iron Guard's chief of staff, Walter Romero and other leading figures in the Guard were also given senior university positions. Many in the Jesuits were furious at this decision, which was compounded three years later when the university awarded an honorary degree to Admiral Emilio Massera, the chief torturer in the military dictatorship's Dirty War (see Chapter 4). Bergoglio avoided the ceremony but sent along his deputy, Victor Zorzín to the ceremony. 'Handing the university to the Iron Guard,' said Fr Guillermo Marcó, who was for eight years Bergoglio's public spokesman in the archdiocese of Buenos Aires, 'is something for which many Jesuits have never forgiven him.'

But the divisions within the province were set to worsen – and again Bergoglio was the focus. The following year Superior General Arrupe convened the 32nd General Congregation in the history of the Society of Jesus. The Superior General wanted the order's highest body to address the question of how the Jesuits were putting into practice the vision of the Second Vatican Council. It was to prove a watershed in the four centuries of the existence of the Society.

On the agenda was the mission of the Jesuits 'to engage, under the standard of the cross, in the crucial struggle of our time: the struggle for faith, and that struggle for justice which it includes'. The Society of Jesus had been founded 'principally for the defence and propagation of the faith', but now, the agenda said, there could be no genuine conversion to the love of God without conversion to the love of neighbour and, therefore, to the demands of justice. The promotion of justice was indispensable to the promotion of the gospel. The Jesuit community was a community of discernment but final decisions would 'belong to those who have the burden of authority'. In other words the Congregation would decide on a possible change of direction and everyone else would have to do as they were told.

Arrupe knew that the decisions to be made would be controversial. He was keenly aware that a commitment to work for social justice would bring his priests and brothers into conflict, particularly in Latin America, where he knew right-wing dictatorships, with the backing of the United States, saw social justice as a back door to Cold War communism. Earlier that year he had travelled to Argentina, at the behest of the Holy See, to investigate the case of Bishop Enrique Angelelli in the diocese of La Rioja in the north-west of the country. Arrupe and the Archbishop of Santa Fe, Vincente Zazpe had been asked by Pope Paul VI to adjudicate on a dispute between Angelelli, who had supported the formation of trade unions locally, and local landowners and merchants who had rioted in church when Angelelli arrived to say Mass. Arrupe and Zazpe had backed the bishop, but it was clear to Arrupe what ire would be aroused by the Church siding with the poor. Revealingly, Bergoglio, who accompanied the official delegation, drew a different emphasis from the encounter; he later noted that 'many sectors of La Rioja society publicly expressed to us their discomfort with Jesuits working among the poorest'.

Many Jesuits, Bergoglio included, felt the changes Arrupe wanted to institute at the 32nd General Congregation would overly politicise the order. One group of conservatives in Spain objected so strongly to the plan that they decided to propose they should be allowed to form a new congregation, a society within a society, to preserve the older traditions. They set out for Rome by train from Spain. Arrupe feared that the Spaniards' plea to the Congregation could prove destructively divisive. Someone, he decided, had to go to meet them off the train – and persuade them to turn round and head home without disrupting the General Congregation.

Just before the group from Spain arrived, Bergoglio landed in Rome at the head of the Argentinean delegation. Arrupe knew that the Spaniards would listen to Bergoglio since he largely shared their fears. So he asked the Argentinean Provincial to go to Termini

Station to persuade the group from Spain to turn around and go home. Bergoglio, despite his own reservations, loyally obeyed and successfully persuaded the dissenters to get back on the next train. The Argentinean was uneasy, but obedience is a prime Jesuit virtue.

The debate at the 32nd Congregation on Decree Four, the measure containing the decisive shift which would move the Jesuits from a focus on educating the elite to one of serving the poor, was intensely debated – so much so that a vote was not taken until the last day of the Congregation, 7 March 1975. When it came, the change was passed with an overwhelming majority among the delegates. Bergoglio was not happy with the general direction of the 32nd General Congregation. He was against a number of the crucial decrees and in particular Decree Four on social justice, which he saw as flirting with Marxism. But he and Arrupe had a good relationship. 'He always took care to praise the Superior General in public', one Jesuit contemporary said. 'There was much they agreed upon. They both shared a strategy to make the Society get involved in issues of the outside world. And the option for the poor was essential for both of them. But they disagreed on what exactly that meant.' Bergoglio wanted to alleviate the symptoms of poverty; Arrupe wanted to challenge them. Bergoglio obediently returned to Argentina charged with the task of encouraging the priests to seek justice and defend and care for the poor. But he warned senior members of the Argentine province that 'the price of violence is always paid by the weakest'. Seminarians found that Decree Four was not to feature in their studies. 'We never heard anything about it at all', recalled Mom Debussy. Priests and students alike, as they left the *Colegio Máximo* to do pastoral work at the weekend, were told they were to work in conventional parishes rather than the new base communities.

For many in the Jesuits, Bergoglio's cautious and conservative approach was vindicated a year later. Fears that working in the slums would provoke a backlash were proved correct. In 1976 a junta comprising the heads of the army, navy and air force seized power and immediately instituted a terrifying crackdown on anyone it perceived to be a political opponent. Tens of thousands of people disappeared in a campaign of kidnappings, torture and murders. Among the victims were 150 Catholic priests as well as hundreds of nuns and lay catechists. Jorge Mario Bergoglio's controversial personal behaviour during this so-called Dirty War is examined in detail in the next chapter. But here it is worth noting the impact all this had on the Jesuits of Argentina. The division in the province hardened. The violence underscored to traditionalists that for priests to become involved in politics was both wrong and dangerous. To the progressives, however, the sudden spasm of violence by the state reinforced the responsibility of the Church to speak out in prophetic witness as priests were doing under military dictatorships in Chile, Brazil, El Salvador and elsewhere. The upshot was that, in the words of the Jesuit historian Jeffrey Klaiber, 'during those years, the Argentinean province did not march in unison with the rest of the Society of Jesus in Latin America.'

The disparity was noticed in Rome. The Superior General, Pedro Arrupe sent one of his assistants out from Rome to Buenos Aires in 1977 to talk to Bergoglio. Fr Michael Campbell-Johnston's job was to monitor the work around the world of the Jesuits' social institutes which were known as Centres for Investigation and Social Action (CIAS). 'I was Aruppe's representative for the social apostolate', Campbell-Johnston said. 'My job was keeping in touch with the social institutes. They needed a lot of support because in those days countries like Chile, Brazil and Argentina were ruled by harsh right-wing military regimes known as National Security States.' The governments in such countries, on the pretext of combating international communism, assumed total control over all dimensions of public life including education, the media, the unions and the judiciary. 'Anyone questioning the status quo was automatically considered subversive and such measures as arbitrary arrest and even torture were justified. In many of the countries our Jesuit institutes were facing opposition and even persecution.'

The social institutes were run by teams of Jesuits with expertise in the social sciences: economists, sociologists and political scientists. Typically there would be three to five Jesuits plus some lay academics, tackling issues like land reform and getting involved in the poorer parts of the communities. 'Throughout Latin America Jesuits in the social institutes were very critical of government,' the British Jesuit said, 'so much so that many had to go into hiding and continue their work under-ground. But this was not the situation for our institute in Buenos Aires which was able to function freely because it never criticised or opposed the government. As a result there were justice issues it could not address or even mention.

'At the time there were an estimated 6,000 political prisoners in Argentina and another 20,000 *disaparecidos* – people who had been "disappeared",' Campbell-Johnston said, 'and there was widespread evidence of torture and assassination. Yet in Argentina the institute was silent on all that. I discussed this at length with Fr Bergoglio. He defended his position, trapped between the Catholic military and the very secularist anti-Church Left. I tried to show him how it was out of step with our other social institutes on the continent. Our discussion was lengthy but in the end we could not agree.'

Bergoglio was unrepentant. He cut back funding for the social institute and, when he ceased to be Provincial, attempted to persuade his successor Andrés Swinnen to do the same. At one point he tried to close the Centre for Investigation and Social Action entirely but Rome intervened and refused permission. Members of staff were sacked. Mom Debussy claims that one professor was dismissed in his absence. 'I helped Bergoglio clear the man's room and found in a drawer a file of denunciations of Bergoglio which the professor had been planning to send to Rome', he claimed. Complaints from other Jesuits about him did arrive in the Superior General's office in the Jesuit Curia.

In the years that followed, Bergoglio's stances became increasingly dogmatic, the more so after John Paul II became Pope, according to his aide Miguel Mom Debussy. Certainly opposition to him within the province began to grow as post-Vatican II attitudes consolidated within the order and as, in 1983, the military junta was replaced by a civilian government and investigations into the human rights abuses of the Dirty War began. 'Other members of the teaching staff were more open to new methods in philosophical and social matters', said Rafael Velasco. 'Those opposed to him were in the majority by the 1980s. He was Rector but he was quite isolated.'

As his term of office as Rector ended in 1986, the polarisation within the Jesuits of Argentina has crystallised into *Bergoglianos* and *anti-Bergoglianos*, with his opponents referring to his supporters as 'the dinosaurs'. By this time there had been a change at the top in Rome; Superior General Pedro Arrupe had been replaced by Peter-Hans Kolvenbach, who was alarmed at Bergoglio's divisive legacy. 'There's no doubt that in the years after he left, the style of formation was different than what it had been under Bergoglio', said Fr Humberto Miguel Yáñez, with diplomatic understatement, having watched Bergoglio's career unfold over the previous decade. 'The new superiors felt it had been a little too conservative, and it needed to be renewed.' Professor Fortunato Mallimacci of the University of Buenos Aires said, more forthrightly: 'When Bergoglio left there was a huge crisis in the order in Argentina.' Some suggest that, twenty years on, the scars have not fully healed. When Pope Francis was elected, the eminent Jesuit theologian Fr José Ignacio González Faus wrote to the Spanish newspaper *El Pais* and said: 'He divided the Argentine province into two sides, sides that have not yet reconciled.'

Certainly when Bergoglio finished his term as Rector his superiors in Rome did not know what to do with him. It was decided that it would be best if he was removed from Argentina for a period. Bergoglio was dispatched to Germany, where he spent several months at the Sankt Georgen Graduate School of Philosophy and Theology in Frankfurt consulting the resident professors about possible topics for his PhD thesis. He returned to Buenos Aires several months later, far more swiftly than Jesuit colleagues back in Argentina were expecting, with piles of photo-copies and books. Among the subjects he explored was the work of Romano Guardini, the German Catholic philosopher whose work in the 1930s criticised Nazi views of Jesus, emphasising his

Jewishness, and critiquing the relationship between religion and violence in ways which must have resonated with Bergoglio's recent experience with the terror in Argentina. Guardini also laid the groundwork for many of the liturgical reforms of the Second Vatican Council. But Bergoglio could not settle on a topic and returned to Argentina undecided.

It was while in Germany, in the church of St Peter am Perlach in Augsburg, that Bergoglio came across the eighteenth-century painting *Mary Untier of Knots*, which so moved him that he bought a postcard of the image and took it back to Argentina (see *Foreword*). He was not happy in Bavaria, and not just because, as he later said, he always got homesick when away from the city of his birth, Buenos Aires. Someone who came across him taking an evening walk in a cemetery near the airport while he was researching possible thesis subjects, asked him what he was doing there. He replied: 'Waving to the planes. I'm waving to the planes bound for Argentina.'

On his return, the Jesuit's new Provincial in Argentina, Fr Victor Zorzín installed him in a Jesuit community in Buenos Aires. Bergoglio took up a part-time teaching job at *Colegio del Salvador*, returning to *Colegio Máximo* one day a week to lecture. But it was not long before tensions began to arise. Bergoglio seemed to have forgotten he was no longer Provincial or Rector. He started to voice his disapproval of the way his peers ran the school. The issues involved were petty details about courses and administration, but his fellow Jesuits made it clear that Bergoglio's interference was unwelcome. Eventually Zorzín, having decided that Bergoglio 'was getting into situations that weren't favourable or desirable for him', removed the meddlesome priest from the school and packed him off to 'a more tranquil place' – Argentina's second city Córdoba, some 400 miles away.

Bergoglio's duties there were simply to say Mass, hear confessions, act as a spiritual director to individuals who requested him, and continue work on his doctorate. He complied but, colleagues recalled, he also brooded. The man who had been for almost fifteen years the kingpin of the Jesuit province felt he had been sidelined and belittled. It was even suggested that the Jesuit Superior, General Peter-Hans Kolvenbach had forbidden him from visiting other Jesuit communities. 'Córdoba was, for Bergoglio, a place of humility and humiliation', said Fr Guillermo Marcó, who was for eight years Bergoglio's right-hand man on public affairs in the archdiocese of Buenos Aires.

Yet even in the several years he was in limbo the Bergoglio personality cult continued to divide the province. So much so that Kolvenbach, eventually, had to send in outsiders as both Provincial and Novice Master to sort out the deeply entrenched difficulties. When Fr Alvaro Restrepo, a Colombian who had formerly been an assistant to Superior General Arrupe, arrived he expected to find the Argentinean province divided between conservatives and progressives, he said. Instead he found a province bitterly divided over the personality cult that existed around Bergoglio. 'Some followed the formation of Jorge Mario,' Restrepo said, 'and others were a different generation.' Restrepo had to work hard to heal the wounds, which he did by fostering dialogue, being impartial, and making people with different opinions work together. But it was clear that the cause of the deep rift within the Jesuits of Argentina had become Bergoglio himself.

Bergoglio's exile ended abruptly in 1992 when the Archbishop of Buenos Aires, Cardinal Antonio Quarracino decided to rescue him and recommended to Rome that Bergoglio be made one of his auxiliary bishops. Earlier in their careers, when Bergoglio was Provincial and Quarracino was Bishop of Avellaneda, the Jesuit had directed retreats for Avellaneda's priests. 'Quarracino had been impressed by the depth of Bergoglio's spirituality and his cleverness', said Marcó. 'When he heard about Bergoglio's penance in Córdoba he decided to rescue him.' In his interviews with Francesca Ambrogettti and Sergio Rubin for El Jesuita, Bergoglio told the story of how he had met the papal nuncio to Argentina, Archbishop Ubaldo Calabresi, thinking he was advising on the names of suitable candidates for the episcopacy, only to be told that it was he who was to become the new Auxiliary Bishop of Buenos Aires.

That too divided the Jesuits. 'His being a bishop was totally unexpected', said Yáñez. 'We Jesuits must do what we can to avoid being bishops and only do so if the Pope expressly demands it.' One of the Jesuit callings is to radical sacrifice of personal ambitions; one of the undertakings which Jesuits make is to avoid high ecclesiastical office. But many saw Bergoglio's change of direction as a solution. 'It was a relief when he left the order and became a bishop,' said Velasco, 'a relief for him and for the order.'

Yet even as a new direction opened up in the ministry of Jorge Mario Bergoglio, the story of his problematic relationship with the Society of Jesus was not over. When he moved back to Buenos Aires as a bishop, instead of moving into a house at the archdiocese, he went back into a Jesuit residence. There, colleagues from that period say, he began to meddle again. Again it was over small things. One Jesuit who shared the residence with him, who spoke on condition that he should remain anonymous, gave the example of a parcel of pastries which was sent to the house as a present by a friend of the order. 'Bergoglio grabbed it and carried it to the kitchen, so the maids and cooks could share the goodies,' he recalled, 'but we didn't need a bishop to teach us how to share.' After a few months, some Jesuits began to ask when Bergoglio would leave. Eventually the order formally asked him to move. All of which may explain the Jesuit emails complaining about Bergoglio as 'a man who never smiles'. And it perhaps tells us why, over the two decades that followed in which Jorge Mario Bergoglio made countless visits to Rome, he never once stayed at a Jesuit house in the city.

4

What Really Happened in the Dirty War

For six years the very name ESMA sent a shiver of fear through the hearts of the people of Buenos Aires. The initials stood for nothing more than a training place for navy mechanics, the Escuela de Mecánica de la Armada. But after the military coup toppled the democratic government in Argentina in 1976 it became something more sinister. The ESMA training centre was one of 340 clandestine concentration camps into which tens of thousands of individuals 'disappeared' and were never seen again.

It was here that two Jesuit priests, Fr Francisco Jalics and Fr Orlando Yorio, were brought one Sunday morning in May, hooded and shackled, and very frightened, after being arrested in the poor neighbourhood where they had worked for the previous six years. They were taken down to the basement, stripped naked apart from their hoods, and tortured for five days in a fruitless attempt to get them to confess that they were in league with the left-wing guerrillas which the military junta had seized power determined to extirpate. What made matters worse was that they were convinced they had been kidnapped after being betrayed by their Superior, the Provincial of the Jesuit order, Jorge Mario Bergoglio.

Today tours can be taken around the white-stucco red-tiled colonnaded building, rather grand in its colonial style, with neatly trimmed gardens, painted curbstones, clipped conifers and beautiful deep pink *rosa china* hibiscus flowers by the door through which those about to die would enter. In May, which is autumn in the southern hemisphere, the trees turn rich shades of russet and chestnut.

The case for the prosecution was made, the day I visited, by a quietly spoken philosophy student who in his spare time guides visitors around ESMA. 'This is where they were brought in', he said, indicating an elegantly proportioned entrance hall with stout wooden pillars, hooped top and bottom with bands of black iron. 'No photographs please; this is still a crime scene.'

Thirty years have passed since the first crime occurred in this building, and yet the investigations are not considered complete. Prosecutions are still taking place now that the military's immunity from prosecution has been lifted. The wounds in Argentine society are not yet healed, which is why the controversy surrounding Jorge Mario Bergoglio is still alive and angry. There are many who do not like ESMA being a museum with tours for members of the public and foreign tourists; they want to knock it down and create a park with a golf course 'so that society can forget'. As the debate around Bergoglio illustrates, there are still many alive in Argentina who are unreconciled with their past.

Four marble steps took the blindfolded prisoners up to El Dorado, the golden room, with its herringbone parquet floor; this main building was called the *Casino de Oficiales*, and was once the recreation centre of the naval officers training here. When ESMA was a detention and torture centre, a phone booth was installed in this room from which the *desaparecidos* – the disappeared – were forced to ring their relatives back home to say they were being treated well. To the left was the staircase, and to the right the elevator shaft, down to the basement, where the torture was done. Today neither can be seen; the building was altered by the military to mask the evidence when the Inter-American Commission on Human Rights visited to check out reports of abuse. Before the foreign commissioners visited, the prisoners were rounded up and taken off to El Silencio, an island in the Rio de la Plata which had been the weekend home of the Archbishop of Buenos Aires.

The offence of the 5,000 prisoners who were held in ESMA – of whom a mere 150 survived – was that they were branded 'subversives' by the military junta headed by the army's General Jorge Videla, the navy's Admiral Emilio Massera and the air force's Brigadier-General Orlando Agosti. The *Proceso de Reorganización* was the military dictatorship's name for what the rest of the world came to call Argentina's Dirty War. At that time relations between the United States and the USSR had warmed a little but the two superpowers had transferred their Cold War hostilities to proxy arenas. The dictatorships of Argentina, Chile, Brazil, Bolivia, Paraguay and Uruguay came together – with the backing of the United States – in a plan called Operation Condor. Its aim was to stamp out communism across Latin America through a continent-wide campaign of murder and incarceration of anyone suspected to be involved in terrorism. The Argentinean junta believed themselves to be engaged in one of the first battles of the Third World War. They reckoned that the Argentinean public, which had been terrified by the campaigns of violence of the extremists of Left and Right in the previous three years, would accept the extermination of the leftist troublemakers. People were dragged from their houses in the middle of the night or snatched brazenly from the streets in broad daylight and bundled into unmarked Ford Falcons, the vehicles of choice of the Argentinean security services. A climate of fear spread swiftly throughout the nation.

'As many people as is necessary will die in Argentina to protect the hemisphere from the international communist conspiracy', Videla told army commanders the year before the coup. Videla saw the *Proceso de Reorganización* as a cleansing process, after which politics could be handed back to a chastened civilian population. But others in the junta saw it as a permanent change which would keep the military firmly in charge. They began by picking up left-wing militants and activists but soon moved onto trade unionists, academics, students, artists, writers, journalists and psychoanalysts until, two years on, they were picking up hapless individuals who happened to be in the wrong place at the wrong time – and priests like Jalics and Yorio who had done nothing more subversive than work among the poor.

At the bottom of the marble staircase which led off the entrance hall was a massive iron door. There the prisoners waited as they heard a command passed via the crackle of a radio to the guard who controlled the door from the other side. They stumbled through it and then, blindfolded still, cracked their heads on the great concrete beam which spanned the entrance to the place where they would be tortured. The guards laughed mirthlessly as each skull took the self-inflicted blow. The massive basement had been partitioned off into individual cells. To the right was one in which a few prisoners with the necessary skills forged the fake ID documents the death squad members used to infiltrate the leftist groups where they would find their next victims. 'This was where the false ID was prepared for agents like Alfredo Astiz, the naval intelligence officer who infiltrated the Mothers of the Plaza de Mayo', the guide explained. The Mothers and Grandmothers of the Plaza de Mayo were two groups of women who, for thirty years, gathered in the city's main square every Thursday afternoon to demand news of the whereabouts of their disappeared children and grandchildren. The handsome Captain Astiz, who became known as the Blond Angel of Death (and was later briefly arrested by the British during the Falklands War), had infiltrated the group with a bogus identity card, pretending that his brother was one of the 'disappeared'. When he had worked out who the key figures were he marked them – in grotesque imitation of the Judas of the gospels – with a kiss, watched from a distance by one of his death squads, who then pounced and bundled the women into cars and took them away.

'One of his victims', the guide explained, 'was Esther de Caragea, the woman who had been the first boss of the young Jorge Mario Bergoglio in his job in a chemistry lab.' She was kidnapped from Santa Cruz church in 1977 where she was working with other mothers to publish a list of disappeared family members. She had, very unusually, been successful in securing the release of her own daughter Ana Maria, who then fled to Brazil. But Esther insisted on staying in Argentina, despite her daughter's pleas. Other mothers have daughters who are not yet freed, she told Ana Maria. 'She was brought to ESMA and tortured for 10 days.' Secret United States government documents, declassified in 2002, showed that along with two French nuns and four other mothers she had been drugged, stripped naked, flown out to sea in a helicopter and thrown into the Atlantic Ocean. Her body was unrecognisable when it was washed ashore. When it was finally identified Bergoglio had her reburied in the garden of the church from which she had been kidnapped.

'For years the Mothers asked Bergoglio for a private meeting but he always refused. Within a month of his election as Pope he met Estela de Carlotto, the leader of the Grandmothers', my guide told me. With her was a young politician, Juan Cabandié, who was born in ESMA after his pregnant mother was kidnapped and imprisoned here. 'Pregnant women weren't exempt from torture,' the guide explained, 'but many were kept in isolation and then moved to small rooms to give birth. The babies were taken from their mothers almost immediately and priests and nuns found adopting families sympathetic to the military regime. Many of them were given to the torturers and other staff here.' When Cabandié found out that his father was one of the perpetrators of the horror he cut off all contact with him. 'They asked Pope Francis to open the archives of the Church so they could try to track their disappeared relative. We will see if he does.'

In the middle of the basement was a row of cells in which prisoners were tortured. A sign on the wall leading to cells 11 to 15 read, with cruel irony, Happiness Avenue. The two Jesuits, Yorio and Jalics, were heavily tortured here for five days, naked apart from the hoods which blinded and disorientated them, fastened with shackles hand and foot. The methods of torture involved semi-drowning and shocks from electric cattle prods. Torture throws up its own moral dilemmas. The guide pointed to a room where the electric goads were repaired when excessive use wore them out. 'They brought in an electrician to fix them', the guide explained. 'When he found out what they were used for he, very bravely, refused to do it. So the torturers used bare wires, which was far more dangerous.' The electrician was horrified by the quandary in which he had been placed. Should he collude with torture by fixing the goads? Or leave the victims to be subjected to even worse treatment? After an agony of indecisions he fixed the goads.

'The torture was extraordinarily effective', the guide continued, matter-of-factly. 'Everybody talked. Although not everything they said was true. Prisoners will say anything to get the torture to stop. Some of the Montenero leftist guerrillas carried cyanide pills in their pockets to avoid torture and avoid betraying their comrades. They knew they would talk if they were tortured enough. People sometimes even named the innocent in an attempt to get the torture to stop.' There was a sadistic creativity to the forms of violence the perpetrators invented, torturing wives in front of husbands or children in front of their parents. They even lined one cell with egg cartons to muffle the victims' screams.

But Jalics and Yorio had nothing to confess. At one point Yorio was injected with some kind of truth drug which made him babble deliriously, but all he talked about was God and Jesus. After five days one of the torturers said to Yorio: 'We know you're not violent. You're not guerrillas. But you've gone to live with the poor. Living with the poor unites them. Uniting the poor is subversion.'

Death, when it came, was called a 'transfer'. In the roof space the prisoners lay in coffin-sized wooden cells when they were not in the torture basement. At 5 p.m. the guards would read out a list of those who were to be 'transferred' to another detention centre. Those chosen were taken down to the basement where they were given an injection which rendered them woozy but still able to walk. Then over their heads were placed black fabric hoods stuffed with cotton which pressed painfully tight on the eyes, thanks to the elastic at the sides. They were never washed so an unbearable stench came off them. Then the drugged prisoners were made to climb the eleven stairs, along a wall where the paint today is peeling, grey, cream, light blue as the layers of history are revealed. The steps led to the courtyard to be taken to their final destination. Only a few, like Jalics and Yorio, were transferred to another jail – in their case to a country house in Don Torcuato, thirty miles from Buenos Aires. There for five months they were held – hooded, handcuffed and with their feet tied – but they were not tortured. Eventually they were taken by helicopter and dumped, drugged and naked, in a field. Most of the prisoners staggered up the stairs to lorries, drugged sufficiently to prevent protest but not enough to prevent faltering movement. At the airport they were loaded into planes or helicopters from which, dazed but conscious, they were pushed out into the Atlantic or the estuary of the River Plate. This was done in such numbers that eventually the friendly military dictatorship in neighbouring Uruguay complained about the number of bodies being washed up on its shores.

***

So was Jorge Mario Bergoglio complicit in all this, as Yorio and Jalics claimed on their release? To understand it is necessary to grasp something about the role of the Church and the shocking extent to which it endorsed and colluded in the systems set up by the military junta. The repression, which began immediately the military seized power, was extraordinarily systematic. It had clearly been planned in advance. Enemies had been demarcated: the active ones, the potential ones, the associates and the sympathisers. Sector by sector, the repression was organised, with a division of labour among the armed forces. The navy seized the Peronists to bring to ESMA. The army went for the Leftists: Communists, Maoists, Trotskyists, Guevaraists and so forth. In ESMA there was even a store labelled The Spoils of War. 'When you were kidnapped the death squads looted your house for what they called booty', said the guide. 'They would take everything – even washing machines and refrigerators.' The authorities even set up their own estate agent to sell the houses of the disappeared. It took 400 people, working in shifts, to staff the torture centre at ESMA alone: military, civilians, nuns and priests.

What could persuade those who had dedicated their life to Christ to work in a torture centre? An attempt at comprehension must begin with the political ideology of the era. Out of the

Cold War there grew, in the United States, the concept of the National Security State. It was conceived within the Pentagon but proselytised by the CIA and spread throughout its sphere of influence in the Americas. The conflict with communism was to be waged as a total war. So the best allies for the US in that would be those right-wing military dictatorships who saw their military and economic interests as identical to Washington's. It was funded through a continent-wide strategy called Operation Condor. A separate building at ESMA was dedicated to the training of the Argentinean armed forces by military advisers from France and the United States sharing expertise in counter-insurgency tactics, including interrogation and torture techniques, learned in wars in Algeria and Vietnam. But it was not just the Argentinean military who were the focus of this preparation. The Church was drawn into the ambit of the strategy seen as defending Western Christian civilisation against atheistic communism.

One of the prime toeholds of Marxism in Latin America was perceived to be Liberation Theology. The years 1973 to 1979 saw the full force of the counter-attack on this theology of empowerment of the poor by the CIA and the Vatican. In this period the CIA created a special unit devoted to working with the Catholic Church. It passed money to a large number of sympathetic bishops and priests. It also supplied information about hundreds of radical priests and nuns who then became the victims of the military dictatorships. In Argentina discussions between the military junta and the Church took place at the highest level. The very day of the coup, 24 March 1976, members of the military junta met for a long time with Adolfo Tortolo, Archbishop of Parana, who was president of the Bishops' Conference of Argentina and Bishop to the Military. Tortolo emerged from the meeting to urge his fellow citizens to cooperate 'in a positive way' with the new government.

Two months later the nation's bishops met to discuss the situation. In 2010 Bergoglio said in his interviews with Rubin and Ambrogetti: 'We have to keep in mind that, like wider society, the church came to realise what was happening gradually. Nobody was fully aware of what was happening at the start.' But that was not true. Declassified documents now reveal that at a meeting on 10 May 1976, ten of the bishops gave chilling details to one another of incidents in their dioceses of persecution, harassment of priests, arbitrary arrest, looting of detainees homes, and even torture. They then took a vote on what to do. Nineteen bishops wanted to issue a public condemnation of the government, but 38 voted against the idea. As a result the meeting issued a statement entitled 'Country and Common Good' which called for understanding towards the military government. The document said it was wrong to expect the security agencies to act 'with the chemical purity' they would in peacetime. This was a national emergency in which people were being killed and kidnapped on the streets. The moment required, the bishops said, that a measure of freedom be sacrificed.

Four of the 57 bishops stepped out of line. They publicly condemned what was going on. One of them, Bishop Enrique Angelelli, was killed in a fake car accident for his refusal to keep quiet. The vast majority of the Church remained silent. Some church leaders were afraid. Others felt it best to retreat into an inner life of worship and wait for better times. But some clearly shared the worldview and anxieties of the military about the need to defend Catholicism against the anti-Church atheist onslaught.

But that was not the worst of the Church's behaviour. Some priests colluded with the military junta and its reign of terror. In the trials which took place after democracy was restored, the former dictator, Jorge Videla said that the Church knew what was happening with the disappeared. He even claimed he consulted with the hierarchy. The former Peronist education minister Emilio Mignone, a devout Catholic who became a leading human rights campaigner after his daughter was seized in front of him by an army snatch squad, asserted in his book *Church and Dictatorship* that Dirty War rules of engagement had been agreed between the military and the military vicar Archbishop Tortolo. He said that it had been agreed that the dictatorship, before detaining a priest, would inform his clerical superior and that some bishops actually took the initiative by sending a sort of 'green light'. This is the accusation that was to be levelled at Jorge Mario Bergoglio.

There is no doubt that some priests and nuns were active collaborators in the terror. One of the techniques of the torturers at ESMA and elsewhere was, after a session of violence was over, to send the victim to see a priest in another part of the prison. One of these was a qualified psychologist as well as a priest. Perhaps the most notorious was the prison chaplain, Christian von Wernich, who actually held the rank of police inspector and frequently visited the regime's secret torture camps. There he encouraged political prisoners to provide information in order to avoid being tortured. One of them, Luis Velazco, revealed at von Wernich's trial how, after a torture session, he had begged the priest: 'Father, please, I don't want to die.' To which von Wernich responded: 'Son, the lives of the men who are here depend on the will of God and the co-operation that you can offer. If you want to stay alive, you know what you have to do.'

Von Wernich was found guilty of complicity in seven murders, forty-two kidnappings and thirty-two instances of torture. He was sentenced to life imprisonment. In another trial a naval captain, Adolfo Scilingo, who confessed to his part in ejecting thirty living people from airplanes over the sea, first having drugged them, told the court that he had been told such activities had been approved by the Church hierarchy, as 'a Christian way to die'. Army and navy chaplains had told the men performing the killings that their actions were justified by the gospel parable of the separation of wheat from chaff. The Church was also involved in the stealing of babies born to 'disappeared' women who had been pregnant when arrested. Both priests and nuns took the babies away to find to 'good Catholic families' who would adopt them. Videla claimed that Catholic bishops endorsed this to prevent the infants being raised as 'a new generation of terrorists'. As many as 500 babies were trafficked this way and their identities changed – and their mothers killed.

The natural outrage against the Church over all this by the victims and their relatives is entirely understandable. But as Bergoglio later pointed out in conversation with Rabbi Abraham Skorka: 'At that time, I was 39 years old and I had been the Jesuit Provincial since 1973. I had a very limited vision of what was happening because it is very different from being a bishop with a jurisdiction.' So to what extent was Jorge Mario Bergoglio complicit in any of it?

**

Three years before Jorge Mario Bergoglio became Provincial Superior of the Jesuits in Argentina his predecessor, Fr Ricardo O'Farrell had given his blessing to the setting up of a new Jesuit community in the Bajo Flores district of Buenos Aires. The four priests – Fr Franz Jalics, Fr Orlando Yorio, Fr Luis Dourrón and Fr Enrique Rastellini – were to live in a new area of social housing known as Rivadavia alongside a shanty town known only by the number given it by some city council bureaucrat: Slum 1.11.14. During the week they would continue their work as university lecturers and writers but at the weekends they would minister to the neglected peoples of the slum next door. Among those with whom they worked in the slum were activists from the *Peronismo de Base* movement, a group with Marxist leanings working among the underprivileged.

This was precisely the kind of activity from which Bergoglio, when he became Provincial in 1973, was determined the Jesuits should end their association. The new Provincial had a double motivation in this. Such work was dangerous, and drew the attention of men of violence towards the Jesuits. But it was also the kind of Liberation Theology which he had been appointed to purge from the order. Using the scriptures to politicise and empower the poor, he felt, was giving scandal to conservative Catholics who saw this 'preferential option for the poor' as subversive and degrading to the traditional Ignatian spirituality. He told the four priests to give up their work in the slum.

A long dispute ensued. Bergoglio was the Superior. But two of the priests, Jalics and Yorio, were not just older than him – Bergoglio was only 36 when he assumed the leadership position – but had been his teachers when he was in his Jesuit formation. Jalics had taught him philosophy and Yorio theology. But after a protracted internal process that lasted more than a year Bergoglio ordered them to dissolve the Rivadavia community. Jalics and Yorio refused. Matters came to a head in February 1976. Bergoglio met the two priests and told them he was getting 'tremendous pressure from Rome and sectors of the Argentinan Church' to dissolve the community. In Italy the Vatican, which was entering its most aggressive anti-Liberation Theology phase, was pressing the Jesuit Superior General to crackdown on theologians who associated with Marxist groups like *Peronismo de Base*. The Superior General in Rome, Fr Pedro Arrupe had told them to choose between the Rivadavia community and the Society of Jesus, Bergoglio told the men. Yorio had his doubts about whether the order came from Rome. A month later, on 19 March 1976, they met again. What happened then is a matter of dispute. Yorio and Jalics thereafter maintained that the Provincial told them they were being expelled; Bergoglio has ever since insisted that the two men had resigned, albeit at his suggestion, as did Fr Dourrón. Bergoglio said that the resignation of Yorio and Dourrón was accepted but that Jalics's resignation could not be, as he had taken his final solemn vows – and only the Pope could release him from those. What seems actually to have happened is that Bergoglio told the men that unless they left Rivadavia they would be deemed to have resigned from the Jesuit order.

There was another point of disagreement. The two men had announced they wanted to start a new religious order and had drawn up rules for it, Bergoglio asserted. They had given him a copy which he had kept. Not true, said Yorio. The document they had given him was not a demand for a new order but a critique of Bergoglio's claim that what they were doing was not compatible with Jesuit practice. It set out, he later said, 'a structuring of religious life in case we couldn't continue in the Society of Jesus', but not a desire to leave the order. Clearly that was, to Bergoglio, a moot distinction. He concluded the meeting with a warning. 'In view of the rumours of an imminent coup d'état,' he said, 'I told them to be very careful.'

Five days later the military junta overthrew the democratically elected government. 'Everyone knew the coup was coming', recalled the human rights lawyer Alicia Oliveira, who has been a friend of Bergoglio since before he was Provincial and is one of those in Buenos Aires with whom he remains in touch as Pope. 'The newspapers, the month before, were speaking about who would be the ministers in the military government. The civilian government was really bad. Most people were happy when the coup happened. But Bergoglio and I weren't happy at all. We both felt that the coup could be really bad.' Both Bergoglio and Oliveira had seen early on what she called the military's penchant for friend/enemy logic – and their dangerous inability to distinguish between political, social or religious activism and terrorist insurgency. 'As we talked in the weeks before the coup I could see that his fears were growing, especially with regard to Yorio and Jalics.' Two years earlier another Jesuit, Fr Juan Luis Moyano, who had been working on literacy programmes with the poor, had been held by the security forces and then deported. And a right-wing Triple A death squad had murdered the slum priest Fr Carlos Mugica. Fellow Jesuits said that Bergoglio was well versed in local politics and would sometimes get tips about pending military sweeps and alert colleagues to avoid them.

'He and I met often and we constantly exchanged with each other all the information we had', Oliveira told me. 'A friend of mine worked with Yorio and Jalics in the slum. She was a catechist. I gave her the same advice Bergoglio gave his priests. I told her to leave. I told her she was not just putting herself at danger but also the poor people she worked with. They could be killed because of her presence. Eventually she listened and she and her husband left. But Yorio and Jalics did not, and we know what happened.'

Someone who did take Bergoglio's advice was the Spanish Jesuit José Caravias, who was active in Buenos Aires in the last months of the democratic government. He had fled to Argentina from

Paraguay four years earlier where he had been imprisoned by the Stroessner dictatorship for his work helping loggers organise a union. In Buenos Aires he worked in the slums. 'Bergoglio came and told me he'd heard that the Triple A had decreed my death and that of Jalics. I felt that it was not worth being a hero. But Jalics was brave and stayed, and it nearly cost him his life. Bergoglio encouraged me to flee to Spain. I think he was relieved when I left; he did not agree with my organising among the poor, and perhaps police reports made him doubt me, but he was noble and helped me.'

Yorio and Jalics, however, were now in a kind of limbo. Their Rivadavia community had been dissolved but they continued to live in the area without any official status so far as the Jesuit order was concerned. What they needed, under church law, was to be attached to another order or placed under the authority of a bishop. The men had approached the Bishop of Morón, Miguel Raspanti, who had participated as one of the Church Fathers in the Second Vatican Council. He agreed to bring them under his jurisdiction so long as their Provincial gave them appropriate references. He even assigned parishes to the priests. Bergoglio promised the men he would provide the necessary references. But when the documents arrived Raspanti became alarmed. They contained allegations which meant the men were not fit to exercise the priesthood. One said that Yorio was a communist who had subverted the members of female religious orders. Yorio went to confront Bergoglio. The Provincial denied it all, saying his references had been entirely favourable. Raspanti was elderly and perhaps confused.

Whatever Bergoglio's references said, the Bisop of Morón was sufficiently concerned to travel to the *Colegio Máximo* to see the Jesuit Provincial in person. A catechist from his diocese, Marina Rubino, who was studying theology at the college at the time, bumped into the bishop as he waited to see Bergoglio. He told her he was very worried. He had had an appropriate reference for Dourrón, who would now transfer to Morón, but he could not accept Yorio and Jalics. Rubino said: 'With the bad references

Bergoglio had given them, he told me, he could not accept them into the diocese.' Both Yorio and Jalics had taught Rubino, who told the bishop they were both fine priests with spotless reputations. That only made the bishop more agitated. 'He was very distressed because he knew that left the two priests stranded without any ecclesiastical authority.' Raspanti told the catechist: 'I've come to ask Bergoglio to withdraw the report saying such very serious things.' Unless that happened, he said, the two priests would be left in the air, without a manager, without hierarchy, and that he was afraid they would disappear. Several days later they did.

But there was another factor which may have played into that. Whether they had resigned or been expelled, Bergoglio regarded Yorio and Jalics as no longer members of the Jesuit community. He informed the Archbishop of Buenos Aires, Juan Carlos Aramburu, who withdrew their licences to say Mass. It was, Yorio later said, based on what he had been told in ESMA, 'like a green light' to the military to move against the two Jesuits. Three days after they lost their licences to say Mass the men were snatched by a naval death squad.

The kidnapping took place at 11 a.m. on Sunday 23 May 1976. The day before, Yorio had telephoned Bergoglio and asked what should they do about the usual Sunday Mass. Bergoglio told them they could say Mass in private at their homes and sent another priest, Fr Gabriel Bossini, to say Mass in the church. As Mass was being said in the church 200 naval storm troops moved into the Bajo Flores area. They snatched the two priests in their homes and also four catechists and two of their husbands. Fr Bossini was left unharrassed. Fr Dourrón, who was cycling round the area at the time, managed to escape on his bicycle. The six people taken with the priests were never seen again.

Bergoglio heard of the kidnapping that day when a resident of Bajo Flores rang him. The men responsible had been from the Navy, he was told. 'The very night I learned they had been kidnapped, I set the ball rolling', he said. He informed the Jesuit Superior General in Rome 'from a phone box on Corrientes Avenue, so as not to use the phone in the Curia'. He rang the church hierarchy. And he contacted the families of Yorio and Jalics to inform them about the actions he was taking. To Yorio's brother Rodolfo he later wrote: 'I have lobbied the government many times for your brother's release. So far we have had no success. But I have not lost hope that your brother will soon be released ... I have made this affair *my* thing. The difficulties that your brother and I have over the religious life have nothing to do with it.' On 15 September 1976, when the two priests had been missing for more than four months, he wrote to Jalics's family in similar terms: 'I have sought in many ways to bring about your brother's freedom, but thus far we have been unsuccessful', began the letter written almost entirely in Latin. 'But I have not lost hope that your brother will be released soon. I have decided that the matter is *my* task.' Alluding to his disagreements with Jalics, he continued: 'The difficulties that your brother and I have had amongst ourselves concerning the religious life have nothing to do with the current situation.' Then, he added, in German: 'Ferenke is a brother to me ... I'm sorry if I started writing in German, but this is the way I think about it ... I have Christian love for your brother, and I will do all in my power to see him freed.'

Those close to Bergoglio insist that the kidnapping caused him great distress. 'Jorge suffered great anxiety in the months after the disappearance of Yorio and Jalics', his friend Alicia Oliveira said. 'He did a lot to try to release them. He visited the head of the junta, General Videla, and Videla told him it had been done by the Navy. So he went to see the head of the Navy, Massera. He talked to the Jesuits in Rome. He talked to the Vatican. He has since constantly reproached himself for not doing enough but he worked like crazy to get them out.'

Bergoglio went twice to see both Videla and Massera. Bergoglio made public details of the meetings when he was in court in 2010, where he was a witness in the trial of 68 individuals accused of nearly 800 crimes against humanity in the ESMA torture centre. He described his first meeting with the army chief, who was the *de facto* President: 'It was very formal. He took notes and he said that he would make enquiries. I told him that it was said that they were in the hands of the Navy. The second time, I managed to find out which military chaplain was going to celebrate mass in the residence of the Commander in Chief. I persuaded him to say he was sick and to send me in his place. That Saturday afternoon, after the Mass, which I said before the whole Videla family, I spoke with him. There I had the impression that he was going to take action, and take things more seriously.'

His meetings with Emilio Massera, the Commander of the Navy, were, by Bergoglio's account, more problematic. 'The first time he listened to me, and he told me that he would look into it. I told him that these priests were not involved in any odd activities. And he said he would give me an answer. But when he didn't answer, after a few months I asked for a second interview. By this time, I was almost certain that the Navy had them. The second interview was very nasty.'

'I've already told Tortolo what I know', said Massera, making curt reference to Archbishop Adolfo Tortolo, president of the Bishops' Conference and Bishop to the Military

'Monsignor Tortolo', corrected Bergoglio.

'Look here, Bergoglio', Massera began to speak, annoyed at being corrected.

'Now you look here, Massera', Bergoglio replied in the same manner, before repeating that he knew where the priests were and he wanted them freed.

The verbatim transcript of their conversation came from Bergoglio himself in a rare interview with the Argentinean journalist Horacio Verbitsky in 1999. At that time Verbitsky had written sympathetically of Bergoglio, then the newly appointed Archbishop of Buenos Aires; he has since become his fiercest critic. 'I never felt this dialogue rang true as it was with one of the most powerful and cruel members of the government, who would have had no scruples in kidnapping Bergoglio', he wrote in 2013.

It took five months for the two Jesuits to be freed. On 23 October 1976 the telephone rang in the Provincial's office in the *Colegio*

Máximo. It was Yorio. Bergoglio later told the court in the ESMA trial: 'I told him: "Don't tell me where you are, and don't move from where you are. Send me a person to tell me where we can meet." At that point one had to take all possible precautions.' Bergoglio then contacted the papal nuncio, Archbishop Pio Laghi, to ask him to accompany Yorio and Jalics to the police headquarters. Laghi played tennis with the head of the navy, Massera. Accompanied by the Pope's chief representative to Argentina, 'nothing bad could happen to them inside there,' Bergoglio told the ESMA trial. It was decided that it would be best if the two Jesuits left the country. Yorio was packed off to Rome to study canon law. Jalics was sent to the United States where his mother was living. Later he went to live in a retreat house in Germany, where he set up a specialism supervising retreats using the Jesus Prayer – *Lord Jesus Christ, Son of God, have mercy on me, a sinner* – since Jalics survived psychologically in captivity by reciting it over and over.

Various accounts were given of why they were released rather than being murdered like most of the 'disappeared'. Bergoglio's friends insisted that it was his intervention which was decisive. The human rights campaigner Emilio Mignone secured the Jesuits' release, his widow insisted, through contacts in Rome who put pressure on the Argentinean regime. Yorio's brother Rodolfo put it down to a deal which secured a meeting between the junta's economic minister and the Vatican that took place within days of the men being freed. But many in Argentina made links with the granting of an honorary degree to the ESMA boss, Admiral Massera. A year after the two Jesuits were released the University of el Salvador, which was run by the Iron Guard to which Bergoglio had links, made Massera an honorary professor. In accepting it, in November 1977, Massera – newly returned from a visit to the Vatican where he had been honoured with an audience with Pope Paul VI – made a bizarre speech in which he lauded the sacred nature of private property, the 'static and inert nature of matter', and called for the exclusion of Marx, Freud and Einstein from the curriculum on the grounds that their Jewishness meant they were not part of the great Western Christian tradition. Bergoglio later denied responsibility for the award, saying: 'I received the invitation to the ceremony, but I did not go. Furthermore, the University is not part of the Society of Jesus and I had no authority there.'

Yet even then the saga was not over. In 1995 Jalics published a book, *Meditation Exercises*, in which he claimed that, before the kidnapping, he had confronted Bergoglio. He wrote: 'Many people who held far-right political beliefs frowned on our presence in the slums. They interpreted the fact that we lived there as a support for the guerrillas and proposed to denounce us as terrorists. We knew which way the wind was blowing and who was responsible for these slanders. So I went to talk to the person in question [Bergoglio] and explained that he was playing with our lives. He promised that the military would know that we were not terrorists. From later statements of an official, and thirty documents which I was able to get hold of later, we saw without a doubt that this man had not kept his promise but, on the contrary, had filed a false report with the military.' Bergoglio must have known, Jalics wrote, that his life and that of Yorio were put in mortal danger by his 'credible libel'. But in the book Jalics said that he had burned the incriminating documents in 1980 to free himself of bitterness and move on. It transpired that Yorio had written to the Jesuit Curia in Rome with similar complaints. Bergoglio's actions, at a time when the junta was trying to 'cleanse' the nation of Liberation Theology, were tantamount to a death sentence on his fellow Jesuits. All they had been doing, Yorio said in his letter to Rome, was entirely in line with Vatican II.

Yorio also told friends that his interrogators had asked questions based on theological information and spiritual confession he thought only his Provincial could have known. He was so upset when Bergoglio was made a bishop in 1992 that he moved to Uruguay, where he lived until his death. In 1996 the Jesuits' new Superior General, Peter-Hans Kolvenbach offered to accept Yorio back into the Society of Jesus. Yorio said he would only accept if he was given access to the documentation in which Bergoglio had filed charges against him. Kolvenbach replied that this could not be done. Yorio died of a heart attack in 2000 after suffering from years of what appeared to be post-traumatic stress disorder. In court at the ESMA trial Bergoglio said that Yorio had been 'conditioned by the suffering that he had to go through'. Whether his evident resentment supports or undermines his testimony is a matter of judgement.

There is one further twist in this tragic tale. In 2005 the investigative journalist Horacio Verbitsky was in the archives at the Argentine Ministry of Foreign Affairs. He was rootling through box after box of old papers in search of a story. He found one. It was in a note bearing the letterhead of the Society of Jesus, with the stamp and the signature Fr Bergoglio, dated 4 December 1979. Jalics was in Germany at this point but the dictatorship was still in power back home. His passport was about to expire – he had been born in Hungary but had become an Argentinean citizen – and he did not think it safe to return to Buenos Aires to renew it. So he asked his old Provincial to do it for him. Bergoglio wrote the requested letter to the Foreign Ministry, asking if the passport could be renewed by post to save him a long and expensive trip. But there was a second sheet in the folder, signed by one Anselmo Orcoyen, the ministry's Director of Catholic Worship. It noted that Fr Francisco Jalics had been involved in subversive activities at female religious congregations provoking conflicts of obedience and that he had been held in ESMA, together with Yorio, on suspicion of contacts with guerrilla groups. What followed sounded as though it might have been the kind of account Bergoglio would have given, for it tallied exactly with his version of events rather than that of Yorio or Jalics. They lived, it said, in a small community that was dissolved by the Jesuit Superior in February 1976; they declined to obey and were asked to leave the order on 19/3; Yorio had been expelled, but not Jalics because he had already taken his final perpetual vows; no bishop in Argentina would accept the two priests thereafter. At the end was a note saying that all this information had been given to Orcoyen by Bergoglio – who admitted in court he had delivered the note by hand. At the same time, Orcoyen's note claimed, he made a verbal recommendation that the passport application be rejected.

To Verbitsky what the two pieces of paper revealed was clear. 'The documents close the case, in my opinion, on Bergoglio's attitude to the junta', Verbitsky wrote. 'He publicly asked for a favour for his priest, Fr Jalics, but behind his back accused him of activities that could cause his death.' What he had done with the passport was clearly what he had done in all his dealings with Yorio and Jalics from the outset, Verbitsky concluded. 'While he seemed to be helping them, he was also accusing them behind their backs.'

The story made a compelling coda to the earlier accusations of bad behaviour by Bergoglio in the Yorio and Jalics case. Within a month of Verbitsky publishing them in his newspaper *Página/12* the allegations were to form the central plank of the Stop Bergoglio dossier which was sent to a large number of cardinals ahead of the 2005 conclave to elect a successor to Pope John Paul II.

Bergoglio offered a clear answer to this in the Rubin and Ambrogetti interviews: 'The civil servant to whom I gave it asked me what had caused Jalics to leave so suddenly. "He and his friend were accused of being guerrilla fighters, but they had nothing to do with any such thing", I answered.' The civil servant made a note of the first part of the sentence but not the second. Why, Bergoglio asked, would he have bothered to intercede for Jalics in the first place if he had been trying to hinder him? 'I wrote the letter making the request. I was the one sticking my neck out for Jalics.'

What all this means is that the only actual evidence on which to make a judgement on Bergoglio's behaviour is a note which is open to several possible interpretations. Perhaps the civil servant was sloppy in his note-taking. Perhaps he misunderstood or over-interpreted what was said. Perhaps he might have been wilfully selective in order to curry favour with his superiors. Perhaps the official could have had other motives. It is hardly conclusive proof on a charge which goes to the integrity of a man who was to become Pope. To find an answer we must look elsewhere.

***

It is beyond doubt that during the years of the Dirty War Jorge Mario Bergoglio did much to protect the victims of the military junta's violence. Indeed he had begun to assist those being persecuted even before the coup. At the Provincial headquarters in Bogotá Street in downtown Buenos Aires he had sheltered individuals on the run from the dictatorship in neighbouring Uruguay. A few weeks before, the military seized power he decided to close down the house, having heard that it was 'marked' by the security forces. Bergoglio transferred the fugitives hiding there to *Colegio Máximo*, more than ten miles away in the suburbs, where he told members of the community that if anyone asked they were to say that the newcomers were undergoing a thirty-day silent spiritual retreat. Bergoglio gambled that the military were less likely to interfere with a Jesuit house of higher learning.

One of the Uruguayans, Gonzalo Mosca, who was not religious, though his brother was a Jesuit, recalled: 'I had novels to distract me, and a portable radio, but it was very tense. I had four days without sleep while Bergoglio made the preparations for me to fly to the city of Puerto Iguazú and then cross from there into Brazil. Bergoglio drove me to the airport and escorted me almost to the plane.' He was both 'personally and institutionally brave', said Mosca, who escaped successfully to Europe. 'The repression in Argentina was very strong. I kept wondering if the priest [Bergoglio] knew what he was playing with.'

If he did not, he soon learned. Within six months of the coup one of the few bishops to speak out against the dictatorship, Enrique Angelelli, was killed in a bogus car crash; Bergoglio took three of Angelelli's seminarians into hiding soon after. They suffered from guilt by association because they had, like Yorio and Jalics, been working in the slums. One of them, Fr Miguel La Civita, spoke out in support of Bergoglio after he became Pope and suggestions began to be made that he had collaborated with the military during the dictatorship. Bergoglio hid La Civita and his friends in *Colegio*

Máximo while documentation was prepared so that they could leave the country. 'This is not something someone told me. I saw it and lived it', La Civita said. 'The Jesuits had an organisation to help people leave the country. Fr Bergoglio acted like a father to us to fill the space that had been left by the death of Angelelli. He took us under his protection at a time when we were being closely watched. Fr Bergoglio never took the time to answer the criticisms of those who said he collaborated. But the reality was the opposite.' Any suggestion that Bergoglio collaborated with the dictatorship, he said, was 'a barbarity that reflects a lack of ethics on the part of the accusers'.

The human rights lawyer Alicia Oliveira offered similar evidence. 'The Jesuits had a retreat house called St Ignatius', she told me. 'Every weekend there, for many many Sundays, Bergoglio invited me. They were often farewell meals for people who had been protected by Bergoglio and who were then being smuggled out of the country. After a small Mass and meal they would leave.' She corroborated the account Bergoglio had given to the interviewers Rubin and Ambrogetti about how he had given his own ID card to a fugitive who looked like the Jesuit Provincial. 'He bought a clergyman's suit and dog collar for the man and gave him his own ID papers,' she said, 'and the man fled to Brazil disguised as a priest.'

Bergoglio did what he could by way of public gestures of support, Oliveira said. She had been a judge before the coup but was sacked immediately when the military took power. That was not all. 'My four-year-old was approached by people who said: "We are going to kill your mother." Two days after someone sent me a bouquet of flowers with a letter saying how good I had been as a judge. It was unsigned but I recognised Bergoglio's handwriting.' He offered her safe haven at the *Colegio Máximo* but she turned him down. Oliveira was a single mother; shortly afterwards Bergoglio made a point of baptising her younger son. It was not public prophetic witness, but it was very supportive personally, she said.

But most of the acts of resistance Bergoglio offered were clandestine, like the time he received a call from his former boss,

Esther de Caragea, asking him to call to give her mother-in-law the last rites. Bergoglio knew that the family were not Catholic but he went anyway. When he arrived de Caragea explained that her daughter had recently been arrested and she feared her house would soon be searched. The security forces would be bound to find a number of books on Marxism. 'Bergoglio took them and hid them in the new library he had had built at *Colegio Máximo*. Among the books was *Das Kapital*', laughed Alicia Oliveira. Later Esther brought another woman to Bergoglio for help. 'She had two sons, who were both communist militant worker delegates who had been kidnapped', Bergoglio himself recalled. 'She was a widow, and her sons were all she had left. How she cried. It was a scene I will never forget. I made some inquiries but got nowhere, and I often reproach myself for not having done more.' Bergoglio resisted in dark places, like the shadowy back staircase at the college he told the students to use to avoid the scrutiny of government agents in the public lobby by *Colegio Máximo*'s main marble staircase.

'It was a very tense time,' recalled Fr Juan Carlos Scannone, a theologian then and now at *Colegio Máximo*, 'you had to be careful of every move you made.' Scannone calls himself a liberation theologian, though of a non-Marxist strain. During the Dirty War he would often show Bergoglio his articles on Liberation Theology before publication 'to protect me from bad interpretations'. Bergoglio asked him to post them from a different address because he suspected the military were scrutinising the Jesuits' mail, but he made no attempt to censor Scannone's writing. And he advised Scannone and others doing work in poor neighbourhoods to avoid travelling back alone after dark to evade government kidnappers.

But he felt very limited in what he could do publicly, he told Oliveira, who was later Human Rights Ombudsman for the City of Buenos Aires. She urged him to speak out during the dictatorship. 'He was anguished', she recalled. 'But he said he couldn't, that it wasn't an easy thing to do.' It is important to take into account the limitations Bergoglio faced at the time, said Scannone: 'He wasn't even a bishop yet, and could act only in his capacity as head of the country's Jesuits. His job was to protect the Jesuits, and all of the Jesuits made it through the period alive, which tells you he did his job.'

***

There is one other grave accusation that must be addressed in making a judgement on how Bergoglio acquitted himself during Argentina's Dirty War. Among the tens of thousands who disappeared there were around 500 pregnant women. They were held in places like ESMA until they could give birth. As soon as the baby was born it was taken from the mother and given to priests and nuns, who disposed of the tiny infants to 'good Catholic families' – a euphemism for those sympathetic to the right-wing junta. One of the women who had their babies taken in this way was Elena De La Cuadra. The 23-year-old was five months pregnant when she was kidnapped in 1977.

Elena's father, Roberto Luis De La Cuadra was well connected. He got Elena's brothers to visit Pedro Arrupe, head of the Jesuit order in Rome, to appeal for help. Arrupe asked his Provincial in Argentina to assist the family. In 1977 Bergoglio met Elena's father twice and gave him a diplomatically worded letter to take to Mario Picchi, the auxiliary bishop of La Plata who had contacts in the military. It said simply of Mr De La Cuadra: 'He will explain to you what this is about, and I will appreciate anything that you can do.' Several months later the bishop told the family that Elena had given birth to a daughter who had been christened with the bitterly ironic name of *Ana Libertad* – Anna Freedom. The child was 'now with a good family', the bishop said. The situation was 'irreversible', the family were told. Elena's body was never found.

In 2010, during Argentina's crimes against humanity trial, Cardinal Jorge Mario Bergoglio was asked to testify as a witness. He told the court that it was only about ten years earlier that he had heard of babies being stolen and their mothers killed. Really, said one of the prosecutors, ten years ago? Well perhaps it was twenty-five years, Bergoglio said. But it was after the return of democracy. So what about the case of Elena De La Cuadra whose family had a photocopy of Bergoglio's hand-written letter dated 1977? Horacio Verbitsky promptly accused the cardinal of lying under oath.

Once again the evidence is inconclusive. The letter does not mention Elena or that she was pregnant. It simply asked the bishop to speak to Mr De La Cuadra on a matter which Mr De La Cuadra would explain. 'He told me that his daughter had been kidnapped', the cardinal told the court. 'I don't recall him telling me if his daughter was pregnant.' And yet copious numbers of press reports in the late 1970s show that the issue of the 'stolen babies' was well in the public domain. It was inconceivable, Elena's sister Estela told the court, that Bergoglio couldn't have known.

This is a charge which many feel Bergoglio has not satisfactorily addressed. Fellow Jesuits have talked about how well-informed he was as Provincial in the 1970s, with intelligence from his friends in the Iron Guard and the tip-offs he seemed to receive about impending military sweeps. His friend Alicia Oliveira admitted: 'He always seemed to know more than me when we met to exchange information.' Fr Michael Campbell-Johnston, the assistant Arrupe dispatched to Buenos Aires in 1977 to pull Bergoglio into line over the work of the Jesuit social institute (see Chapter 3), returned to Rome to receive 'a copy of a letter addressed to the Pope and signed by over 400 Argentinean mothers and grandmothers who had "lost" children or other relatives and were begging the Vatican to exert some pressure on the military junta'. And Alicia Oliveira told me: 'The Jesuit retreat house called St Ignatius was right across the road from a secret maternity hospital where kidnapped women who were pregnant were taken to have their babies – the babies that were then taken away from them and the women "disappeared".'

The evidence proves none of these surmises. Even so, many in Argentina agree with Lisandro Orlov, a leading Lutheran theologian in Argentina – who, in all other aspects, defends Bergoglio's record during the Dirty War – who said this is the area in which Bergoglio has most questions to answer. 'None of us who were around in those years can say we didn't know what was going on. He can't sustain the argument that he didn't know about the missing children.'

The issue goes to a wider point. Many of the families of the victims of the Dirty War have asked why Bergoglio did not speak out later when he could, as a bishop, archbishop and cardinal. Only as Pope has he agreed to meet the Grandmothers of the Plaza de Mayo who regularly, and always fruitlessly, petitioned him to meet them when he was in Buenos Aires, requesting that he open the church's archives to help trace the stolen babies so they could be put back in touch with their blood relatives. It may have been prudent to decide that, during the dictatorship, it was too dangerous to confront the military openly. Look what happened to Angelelli. But what is the explanation for his reticence, once the dictatorship was over, in condemning the wrongdoing by priests who were so closely involved in the illegal incarceration of political prisoners and even their torture?

It did nothing for his reputation that when he was asked to testify at the 2010 ESMA trial Cardinal Bergoglio refused, exercising a provision in Argentine law allowing senior church officials to decline a summons to court. When the court duly decamped to the Archbishop's office, prosecuting lawyers repeatedly expressed their frustration at Bergoglio's minimalist answers. One of the prosecutors, the human rights lawyer Myriam Bregman, accused him of avoiding giving straight answers. 'Bergoglio's reticence and the brevity of his replies', she said, 'was consistent with the Church hierarchy's attitude of silence and concealment during the whole post-dictatorship period, systematically refusing to hand over files or documentation.' Anyone watching videos or scrutinising transcripts of his evidence would be hard put to disagree that his performance looked evasive. He also admitted that when Jalics and Yorio were released they told him that there were still kidnapped people in ESMA, yet he did nothing about it. For all that Germán Castelli, one of three judges in the trial, later insisted: 'It is absolutely wrong to say that Jorge Bergoglio delivered these priests.

We've heard this version, analysed the evidence presented and concluded that his actions had no legal involvement in this case. If this was not the case, we would have charged.'

In the end, diligent examination of Bergoglio's conduct leaves unanswered questions. But if there is, finally, a shortage of definitive facts, there is no lack of opinion among those most intimately involved. Yorio died convinced Bergoglio was a duplicitous traitor. The devout Catholic establishment man Emilio Mignone agreed. Yet Jalics, who once thought the same, has resiled from that view. He announced in March 2013 that years after his grim ordeal he and Bergoglio had met and concelebrated Mass together and shared what Jalics called 'a solemn embrace', after which he was reconciled with Bergoglio. When Bergoglio's critics pointed out 'you don't pardon somebody that didn't offend you', Jalics issued a categorical statement which said: 'I myself was once inclined to believe that we were the victims of a denunciation but ... after numerous conversations, it became clear to me that Orlando Yorio and I were not denounced by Fr Bergoglio.'

Those on the periphery are similarly divided. Bergoglio's only surviving sister, María Elena, said she could not conceive that her brother would have colluded with the junta, betraying everything his father had taught them about the need to resist the fascism he had fled Italy in 1929 to escape. Bergoglio's former Jesuit driver, Miguel Mom Debussy, who is largely critical in his memories of his old Provincial, has conceded: 'During the Seventies I saw his attitude as repressive but looking back I think he was trying to protect us.' The Vatican, not unexpectedly, has insisted: 'There has never been a credible, concrete accusation against him', and talked of slanders on the new Pope's past by 'anti-clerical left-wing elements' used by the Kirchner government in Argentina to attack the Church. The investigative journalist Horacio Verbitsky has countered by pointing out that the first accusations were levelled by Mignone in 1986 when Bergoglio was largely unknown outside Argentinean church circles – and that Verbitsky himself began to investigate Bergoglio long before the Kirchner government, which he supports, came to power. Verbitsky is convinced that Bergoglio, while far from the worst of the church leaders colluding with the junta – 'the degree of complicity of the highest hierarchy of the church at that time was enormous' – the man who went on to become Pope is guilty of lying and 'a duplicitous *modus operandi*'. To which Alicia Oliveira, who was once both friend and lawyer to Verbitsky, shrugged her shoulders and said: 'Each of us is in charge of our own madness.'

Opinion is fragmented too in Argentinean society and the wider Church. The leading Jesuit theologian Fr José Ignacio González Faus has insisted: 'Franz Jalics has written things about him that cannot be overlooked, particularly since these things were written in a very respectful way. And when they met each other, many years later in Germany, they fell into each other's arms crying.' And Fr Eduardo de la Serna, co-ordinator of the Movement of Priests for the Third World has said: 'Bergoglio is a man of power and he knows how to position himself among powerful people. I still have many doubts about his role regarding the Jesuits who went missing under the dictatorship.' By contrast Fr Angel Centeno, the current Secretary of Religious Matters in the Argentinean Jesuit headquarters, has said: 'It was a very difficult time for the Society but if he had not been at the forefront the difficulties would have been much worse.' And Adolfo Perez Esquivel, who was awarded the Nobel Peace Prize for the defence of human rights in Argentina, said: 'There were bishops that were accomplices to the dictatorship, but Bergoglio was not one of them [though] I think he lacked the courage to accompany our struggle for human rights in the most difficult times.' 'Maybe, as a pastor, he didn't do enough to protect those priests', said Fr Ignacio Rafael Garcia-Mata, who has been Provincial of the Jesuits since Bergoglio. 'But he couldn't imagine what was going to happen. You can say the same against me or any other priest. Maybe we didn't have the courage to express our rage against the dictatorship.' 'All of us', concluded Lisandro Orlov, 'could have done more during the dictatorship.'

Bergoglio the church politician has picked a very careful path through all this, choosing his words with great precision in the set of interviews he gave to Rubin and Ambrogetti. 'It's true that there were some more perceptive pastors who took great risks', he said. 'There were others too who immediately began to take strong stances in defence of human rights. There were others who did a lot but spoke out less. And, finally, there were a few who are naive or lazy. On the other hand, sometimes, subconsciously, an individual doesn't want to see things that could become unpleasant. Any organisation has both saints and sinners. There were also men that are a mix of both of those characteristics. There were Catholics who justified their actions with the argument that they were fighting against communism, there were Christians [who] killed as guerrillas, Christians who helped save people and repressive Christians who believed that they were saving the mother country. It cannot be assumed that there was a simplistic complicity.'

Yet what this kind of careful diplomacy does not address is the clear fact that the pastoral relationship broke down between Bergoglio and the priests in his care. Emilio Mignone understood that back in 1986 when he asked: 'What will history say about these pastors who allowed the enemy to take their sheep without defending them or rescuing them?'

Argentine society was polarised during the Dirty War. Many on the Left were not just secularist but very anti-clerical and anti-Church. By contrast the Right espoused Catholicism. For a churchman of traditional spirituality, as Bergoglio very much was in those days, it undoubtedly seemed natural to side with the worldview of the Right, if not with its tactics. His links to the Peronist Iron Guard movement will undoubtedly have reinforced that. So will his antipathy to Liberation Theology and the crackdown the Vatican was, in those years, beginning to impose upon those who saw the empowerment of the poor as a key part of the Gospel mission. Yet a Jesuit of his intelligence ought to have seen the danger of allying his opposition to Liberation Theology too closely with support of the military's anti-communist agenda. Being politically astute, and also well-informed about the tactics and even occasionally the timing of the military's repressive behaviour, he ought to have realised in May 1976 the danger that Yorio and Jalics were in.

Obedience is a key virtue for Jesuits. It is one of their prime vows, along with poverty, chastity and particular loyalty to the Pope. Bergoglio was clearly outraged by the refusal of Yorio and Jalics to obey his order as Provincial to end their work in the slums. When he told them the order had been reiterated by Rome, and they still resisted, he locked horns with them. Disobedience for a Jesuit was a cardinal offence. To this was added the affront to what we have found was, in those days, a deeply authoritarian streak within his leadership style. The idea that they wanted to set up a new order, as he saw it, deeply offended him. It is hard not to suspect that all this coloured his judgement and made him reckless of the level of risk to which the men were being exposed.

There is no evidence that Bergoglio informed the military that he had disowned Yorio and Jalics but he informed other clerics, including officials in the archdiocese of Buenos Aires. The military will have known how to read Bergoglio's views, without being told, once they heard that the Archbishop of Buenos Aires had withdrawn the two Jesuits' permission to say Mass. The anxieties of Bishop Miguel Raspanti, who was prepared to offer alternative ecclesiastical supervision in his diocese of Morón to the dissenting Jesuits, add to the doubts as to the propriety or wisdom of Bergoglio's actions in the volatile political climate of the day – of which, indeed, he had warned Yorio and Jalics. A man of Bergoglio's intelligence, political acumen and contacts ought to have known what he was doing.

Whether he had a duty to speak out publicly is more problematic. Many have recently, from the comfort of their armchairs, looked back to the example of Oscar Romero in El Salvador who confronted a similarly brutal right-wing dictatorship. Romero was shot at the altar for it. But martyrdom is not a calling to which all Christians are summoned, nor do the rest of us have a right to expect that.

Closer to home, Bergoglio had before him the example of Enrique Angelelli. The Bishop of La Rioja met his death within weeks of denouncing the military for abducting two of his priests; the men were found shot dead in response and within a month Angelelli was dead too. Bergoglio may well have felt that he could achieve more working secretly behind the scenes while keeping his public lines open to the government. And he had limited influence; he was the Provincial of a religious order, not a bishop or Cardinal Archbishop. That is not a judgement which it is apt for those who sit in safety to overturn in hindsight.

Yet if Bergoglio the politician has delivered one verdict, Bergoglio the priest has offered another more penitential one: 'I don't want to mislead anyone – the truth is that I'm a sinner who God in His mercy has chosen to love in a privileged manner', he told his interviewers Rubin and Ambrogetti. 'From a young age, life pushed me into leadership roles – as soon as I was ordained as a priest, I was designated as the master of novices, and two and a half years later, leader of the province – and I had to learn from my errors along the way, because, to tell you the truth, I made hundreds of errors. Errors and sins. It would be wrong for me to say that these days I ask forgiveness for the sins and offences that I might have committed. Today I ask forgiveness for the sins and offences that I did indeed commit.'

Whatever judgements others have made of the role of Jorge Mario Bergoglio, they probably do not match the one he has made of himself before God in prayer. His conduct in the Dirty War, along with the deeply divided legacy he had left the Jesuits in Argentina, were just two of the knots with which the exiled priest wrestled as he sat before the Marian painting which so moved him in the church of St. Peter am Perlach in Augsburg in 1986. The theme of mercy and forgiveness, which was so dominant in his homilies in his early days as Bishop of Rome, speaks of something far more personal than many supposed.

5

The Bishop of the Slums

The slum was not even graced with a name. The locals called it by the number which the unimaginative bureaucrats of Buenos Aires city had designated it. Welcome to Villa 31. Villa comes from the term *villas miserias*, which translates as 'misery villages'. The taxi driver would only take us to the edge. The potholes in the alleyways between the ramshackle houses, built of crudely cemented terracotta breezeblock, would have ruined his suspension. Or perhaps worse. Police cars would not enter here either. There was a fortified building on the periphery, but the security guards there looked more concerned with keeping any crime or gang violence from spilling outside the shanty town rather than tackling the problems within. This was a place where the law was as crooked and chaotic as the townscape of criss-crossed water pipes, dangling electricity cables and lanes down which open sewers run like streams when the rain comes.

But Sunday 12 May 2013 was a fine and sunny autumn morning here south of the equator – and the weather matched the mood of the people of Villa 31 who were spilling out of their homes and crossing the bridge over the railway which cut though the slum. They were making for the church. But they did not go inside. There were too many of them for that. Instead they gathered on a grassy bank that rose to the motorway flyover under which their homes squatted. Before them, on a stage in the yard before the church, was a makeshift altar on which seventeen of the twenty-four priests who serve the slums of Buenos Aires assembled. They had come to celebrate a murder – not one of the slum's routine gangland killings, but the death thirty-nine years ago that weekend of the first of the *curas villeros* (slum priests) to be martyred. Fr Carlos Mugica was killed by a right-wing paramilitary terror group, the *Alianza Anticomunista Argentina*, in 1974 outside the church where he had just finished celebrating Mass and was talking to a young couple about their forthcoming wedding. In 1999 his remains were transferred here, to the tiny church of *Cristo Obrero* (Christ the Worker) in the slum where he spent his priesthood. At that ceremony Jorge Mario Bergoglio, by then Archbishop of Buenos Aires, had prayed 'for Fr Mugica and all those involved in his death – for his actual killers, for those who were the ideologues of his death, for the complicit silences of most of society and for the times that, as members of the Church, we did not have the courage to denounce his assassination, Lord have mercy.'

And yet the anniversary of Carlos Mugica's death was a cause for celebration rather than sadness for the sons and daughters and grandchildren of the slum-dwellers the martyred priest had served. Mugica had left a legacy. It had brought the faith back into their daily lives, restored a self-esteem to people who had felt marginalised by society and energised them to do battle with the city authorities to improve the basic living conditions in the *villas,* like clean drinking water, electricity and improved sanitation. In recent years all this had been accelerated by Jorge Mario Bergoglio, the man who had, twenty years earlier, recalled priests from the slums for doing exactly that work. After he became Archbishop of Buenos Aires the number of priests working in the slums of the vast city had quadrupled, though that is still not many to serve the needs of the estimated 700,000 poor people who pack into around 110,000 makeshift dwellings in the cramped slum where the only way to build is up – so that new rooms are piled on top of one another, like stacked containers at a port, in precarious teetering towers within sight of some of the most desirable residential areas in the Argentine capital. Slum landlords demand exorbitant rents for these basic facilities.

Behind the open-air altar was a giant banner bearing the name of the dead priest and two huge portraits. At one end was a black-and-white photograph of Mugica, blond-haired and Seventies film-star handsome. To the left was a colour portrait of Papa Francisco, the first pope of the Americas, in papal yellow and white. Between them a chequerboard flag of different colours represented all the different nationalities living in the slum, economic migrants and refugees from Paraguay, Peru, Bolivia and Brazil. Propped against the front of the altar was a poster of Mugica bearing the legend: 'A priest has died, who dares to follow him.' And another quote from the murdered man: 'Nothing and nobody will prevent me from serving Jesus Christ and his Church, fighting with the poor for their liberation. If the Lord offers me the privilege, which I don't deserve, of losing my life, I am at his disposal.'

Behind the altar, facing the huge crowd on the grassy bank, stood a priest with long hair, a dark beard and a shy smile. Quietly, through a hand-held microphone, he said: 'You are all welcome here, all you in the slums and all those who want a better society.' The crowd hushed, hanging on his every word. There was an extraordinary charisma about him, even if you did not know that he had been working here in the slums for twenty-seven years. His name was Father Jose-Maria de Paola, though everyone called him Padre Pepe. One of the other priests took the microphone. 'What he won't tell you,' he told the crowd, 'is that it's his birthday. And he's 51!' There was a huge cheer and the crowd began at once to sing Happy Birthday.

The music was from Bolivia and Peru and Paraguay as well as Argentina. A band of acoustic guitars of many sizes and shapes shifted from the song into an opening hymn and then a Gloria in which there was much call and response and rhythmic clapping. Faith in Villa 31 is a two-way process. During the prayers of intercession, after Padre Pepe had led the formal prayers, the congregation shouted out prayers in the names of their favourite saints. Religion here is immediate and about everyday life. Faith is strong and of the people.

A younger priest in his early 30s stepped forward to give the sermon. It was about how Jesus had a simple faith like the people in the slums, a faith nourished by the Virgin and protected by St Joseph. The slum-dwellers stood enrapt, a motley collection: some looked well, others pinched and unhealthy; some too thin, others too fat; some in clothes washed translucently threadbare, other city-smart in stylish pants, glitzy sunglasses and high boots.

The sermon continued. 'Faith is not selfish or individual', the priest said. 'It must be shared with everyone, including immigrants. We have to develop things for ourselves. We have to cut through the bureaucracy. We have to fight against *paco* [the cheap cocaine of the poor]. This is the faith of Jesus. It is the faith of Fr Mugica – the same faith he felt in his heart and that made him offer his life to be a martyr for our people. It is the faith Pope Francis will renew by asking for a poor Church for poor people.'

Paco is the bane of life in the slums. It is the chemical residue left over from the processing of the high-quality cocaine which is sent to Europe and the United States and the lower-grade coke which is sold to the affluent of Buenos Aires. Once it was thrown away. But then in the economic crisis which hit Argentina in 2001 someone had the idea of mixing the residue with kerosene, rat poison or even crushed glass and selling for a dollar a dose to the people of the slums. It is so addictive that one day's free supply is enough to get people hooked, creating a very short-lived high followed by an intense craving and then paranoia and hallucination. The dealers targeted adolescents and children.

Padre Pepe led other slum priests in a campaign against *paco* which was far too effective for the liking of the drug dealers. The priests set up *Hogar de Cristo*, an addicts' recovery centre for addicts, and two farms where recovering addicts could live and work. Even more disturbingly for the drug dealers, in slums where 44 per cent of the residents are under the age of 16, they launched an education campaign, a church Scout group called the Explorers, and an apprentice scheme to give kids an alternative to aimless unemployment; instead they could train to become electricians, stonemasons, car mechanics, metalworkers, tailors, cooks or bakers. Suddenly *parroquia* (the parish) looked an alternative to *paco*.

'Then one evening in 2009, when Padre Pepe was coming home to his church in Villa 21 and 24, on his bicycle, he was stopped by a well-dressed stranger and told that if he did not stop his anti-drugs activities, '*vos vas a ser boleta, te la tienen jurada*' – 'they have their knives out for you, you're doomed'. The frightened priest contacted his archbishop. They met, just the two of them, in Bergoglio's room in the archdiocesan offices. Padre Pepe recalled: 'He told me "If someone has to die, I would prefer it be me". He said that to me personally. He didn't say it somewhere else in order to look big. He just said it to me.'

Bergoglio showed up in Pepe's parish unannounced. He walked slowly through the entire slum and chatted to people, blessed them and drank *mate* (Argentina's national tea drink) as he often did. He said nothing, but the message was clear: 'if you touch him, you touch me'. He even offered to sleep in Padre Pepe's house in the slum. 'Bergoglio showed great courage when Padre Pepe was threatened', said Fr Pedro Velasco, who took over as chaplain in Slums 21 and 24 when Pepe was moved to another slum parish.

The next day, the archbishop held an outdoor Mass in the Plaza de Mayo, the city's main gathering point between the cathedral and the Presidential Palace. Television crews had been briefed that Archbishop Bergoglio had something to say. When he reached the sermon Bergoglio delivered a bold denunciation of the drug traffickers and their death threats. He called them *los mercaderes de las tinieblas*, the merchants of darkness. In defiance he elevated Padre Pepe to a new position as Vicar for All Slums. 'At that time we were all afraid,' said Velasco, 'and when it was time to celebrate Mass, the fear was still very present. Just like the Bible says, if a pastor is hurt, the flock will disperse. Bergoglio understood this and the fact that he said the Mass spoke volumes.'

Padre Pepe is in no doubt that he could not have done what he has without Bergoglio. 'My relationship with Bergoglio is very deep', he said, eschewing the past tense. 'We spoke every week and he came a lot to this slum. When we started he would show up by surprise. But then he left us to work freely. He didn't impose things.

He let us get on with things as we saw fit. He felt comfortable here.'
The archbishop would wander the alleyways alone, talking with
people, drinking tea and eating biscuits in the villa's homes, posing
for photographs when requested. Bergoglio was, the locals said,
campechano (matey). Some called him, instead of Father, *El Chabon*
(The Dude). He was at home with those he felt had been tossed on
what one of his aides said he referred to as life's 'existential garbage
pile'.

'He came and washed the feet of the kids who were addicted to
paco', recalled Padre Pepe. 'We wrote two important documents
here in the slums and Bergoglio included them in the official
magazine of the Church. He was trying to show that the slums were
not just important for the people who live here but for the whole
Church. The documents said that the culture of the slums and the
people who live here have to be respected. The state and the local
city authorities should not just impose changes on what the people
here have decided. The people here need not to be helped but to
help themselves. Our theology is not theoretical. Its main idea
is to respect people's choices. Liberation has to start, not with an
ideology nor with charity, but with people.'

Yorio and Jalics and the other Jesuits whom Bergoglio once
ordered out of the slums for saying such things would have been
astonished to hear that, almost forty years on, the same man would
not just be tolerating such sentiments but endorsing and blessing
them.

***

It had been two decades earlier that Jorge Mario Bergoglio, then
aged 55, had arrived in the slums of Buenos Aires. It was 1992 and
he had just left behind the community life of the Jesuits and arrived
back in Buenos Aires as one of five auxiliary bishops chosen by
the Archbishop of Buenos Aires, Cardinal Antonio Quarracino.
The canny old veteran had chosen five different assistants to help
him manage the twelve million people who lived or worked in the

Born in Flores, a suburb of Buenos Aires in 1936, Jorge Mario Bergoglio (*left*) was the eldest of five children. He is pictured here with his brother, Oscar in the early 1940s.

Bergoglio attended the *Wilfred Barón de le Santos Ángeles* primary school in Greater Buenos Aires until he was aged 13.

Bergoglio, *circled*, with his classmates, *c.* 1951.

Bergoglio poses for a family portrait in 1958: (*back row, from left*) his sister Maria Elena, mother Regina, brother Alberto, Jorge Mario Bergoglio, brother Oscar, sister Marta, and Marta's boyfriend Enrique. (*Front row, from left*) His grandfather Juan, grandmother Rosa – the woman responsible for Bergoglio's spiritual upbringing – and father Mario.

While studying in Germany, Bergoglio saw the painting *Mary Untier of Knots* (*top*) at the St Peter am Perlach Church in Augsburg (*bottom*); it so spoke to the turmoil in his life, after presiding over a deep rift among Argentina's Jesuits, that he took copies of the painting back to Argentina where a cult has since developed around the image of Virgin as the solver of problems.

Bergoglio came out of years in the wilderness to be made a bishop in 1992 and then Archbishop of Buenos Aires. He changed his leadership style to allow consultation and participation, particularly among the poorest people. He quadrupled the number of priests in the shanty-towns and earned himself the title 'Bishop of the Slums'.

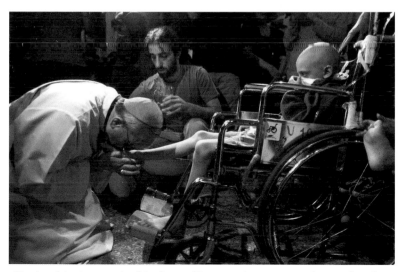

During his time as Archbishop of Buenos Aires, Bergoglio made it his custom to celebrate the Holy Thursday ritual by washing the feet of the poor or the marginalised including drug addicts and people with AIDS; he is pictured here at a hospital in Buenos Aires.

Jorge Mario Bergoglio was made cardinal by Pope John Paul II (*above*) in February 2001. Five years later, the Argentine attended the funeral of the Polish Pope but a Stop Bergoglio campaign was launched to prevent him being elected Pope and he was the runner-up in the conclave which made Joseph Ratzinger (*below*) Pope Benedict XVI.

Following Benedict XVI's retirement, Jorge Mario Bergoglio was elected Pope on 13th March 2013, becoming the 266th head of the Roman Catholic Church and the first to take the name Francis.

(*Above*) Old adversary, Argentina's president Christina Fernandez de Kirchner, was the first politician Francis met as Pope.

Francis returns to pay his bill at the hotel he used before he became Pope – one of the bold early gestures of humility and integrity with which he signalled that major change must come in the Vatican.

Argentine capital. Bergoglio was given Flores, the area where he was born. 'That's where I met him', recalled Guillermo Marcó, the man who would later be Bergoglio's close aide for eight years. 'I was the curate to a parish priest who was a friend of his. He'd come to our parish a lot and he would ask me to walk home with him so, he said, he could get to know his diocese and what a young priest like me was thinking.' From the outset his style was markedly different from that of other bishops. In addition to fulfilling the tasks given him by the Archbishop, he acted on his own initiative to get to know the priests and people on his patch. And his first approach was to listen and consult. He gave the impression that the views of the ordinary clergy and laity counted. And the slums in his area were his first focus. When he visited more affluent parishes he invariably asked them what they were doing to help their poorer neighbour in the villas. Everywhere he ended his visits by asking people to pray for him. Something had happened which had changed utterly the man who had been so self-certain and domineering with the Jesuits.

'Quarracino was a very different man', remembered Marcó. 'He wasn't humble or austere like Bergoglio.' When he went to Rome he would stay in the best hotel. But he liked Bergoglio, who was very faithful and loyal to Quarracino. So much so that within a year he named Bergoglio as his vicar general, which put the Jesuit in charge of the day-to-day administration of the diocese. After four more years Quarracino, whose his health was failing, decided that he wanted to choose his own successor and decided upon Bergoglio, whom he felt had been outstanding as a bishop in all departments: pastoral, administrative and financial. Outgoing archbishops usually leave such appointments to the Vatican, but Quarracino flew to Rome and told the Congregation for Bishops, which makes the selection, that Bergoglio was the man. He asked for him to be made coadjutor of the diocese, which would give him automatic right of succession when Quarracino retired or died. The powerful Curia officials said No. Since they also controlled Quarracino's access to the Pope, it seemed that was that. But the wily old cardinal, was had been born in Italy, was not defeated. He then wrote a letter of appointment for the Pope to sign and went to see the Argentinean ambassador to the Holy See, Francisco Eduardo Trusso, who was an old friend. 'Give the Pope this when you next see him', the cardinal told the diplomat. As Quarracino knew, Trusso was due to see Pope John Paul II quite soon; when he did, he gave the Pope the letter. He signed it there and then and gave it back to Trusso, who sent it on to Quarracino. The Vatican bureaucrats were furious. But the deed was done. In June 1997, Bergoglio was appointed coadjutor. Eight months later, on 28 February 1998, Quarracino died of a heart attack and Bergoglio, aged 61, became Archbishop of Buenos Aires.

It was from this point that the reputation of Bergoglio began to grow outside Church circles. The main residence of the Archbishop of Buenos Aires was an elegant house in one of the capital's most exclusive neighbourhoods, Olivos, close to the presidential estate. But instead of moving there, Bergoglio chose to remain in the four spartan rooms – an office, bedroom, library and chapel – he had occupied in the archdiocesan office next to the cathedral in downtown Buenos Aires. In part, his decision was pragmatic. It was fourteen miles from official residence to the city. Archbishops had a chauffeur-driven limousine but the traffic jams in Buenos Aires were, and are, horrendous. But Bergoglio also knew the symbolic significance of rejecting the palace and chauffeur. He had the building turned into a hostel for priests and nuns and the driver was redeployed to other work in the diocese. Bergoglio used public transport – the subway and then the bus – for his visits to parishes around the city. In his apartment he cooked his own meals and he wore a normal dark clerical suit and dog collar in preference to an archbishop's purple. His personal belongings were so few that when someone gave him a gift of some CDs he asked a friend to record them to cassettes, as he did not have a CD player. When he was made a cardinal in February 2001 he refused to order new robes but had his predecessor's garments altered to fit him. When as an archbishop people addressed him as Your Grace, or as a cardinal Your Excellency or Eminence, he asked them instead to call him Fr

Jorge. Those who wanted to fly to Rome to see him elevated were told by him to save the money for use among the poor at home.

Within the Church his priests were finding him unusually accessible. He woke each day around 4 a.m., without an alarm clock, to pray. After breakfast he would read the papers and then from 7 a.m. to 8 a.m. he would sit by a landline to take calls from any priest in his charge. 'There was no secretary', said Marcó. 'They would get straight through to him. Every priest in the diocese was given his number.' After a morning of meetings and a frugal lunch at 12.30 p.m., he would take a forty-minute siesta and then visit parishes. Back home he would often have just an apple and tea for dinner – 'he avoids invitations to dinner', said Marcó – and then listen to classical music on the radio before bed around 11 p.m. 'He's always been quite a solitary person. He looks after his interior life and doesn't really have a social life.' But his days were flexible. He would spend nights in any parish attending to a sick priest if necessary. One of the Jesuits with whom he kept in contact from his old days at *Colegio Máximo*, the theologian Fr Juan Carlos Scannone, recalled how as auxiliary bishop Bergoglio travelled 250 miles on one occasion to be by the side of one of his priests who had gone to Mar del Plata and fallen ill, so that the man was not alone. 'He would make himself available till late in the evening', said Padre Pepe, who talked endlessly with the Archbishop when the young priest had a vocational problem. 'Bergoglio wasn't preaching a particular message', he recalled. 'I was in a crisis. He just listened and gave me the space to make my own decisions.'

Bergoglio was revolutionary when it came to administrative matters too. He put an end to the traditional system of young priests starting in poor parishes and then being promoted with the years to larger and wealthier ones. 'Nor did he like the idea that the best priests would go off to jobs in Rome', said Marcó. 'He saw that as careerism. It had a downside though. He put young priests in their 20s and 30s with no experience in important places. It was not a good idea. They found it difficult to manage. It also meant there was a generation of older priests you were stuck with in smaller parishes. Bergoglio was never a parish priest so he didn't understand that.' Perhaps he did, and did not care. For all the administrative disadvantages, he could undoubtedly see the symbolic importance the gesture sent to ordinary members of the Church – and the message it sent to priests about where their priorities should lie. Where previous archbishops had left the pastoral care of priests to auxiliaries, Bergoglio insisted on doing that job himself. 'He didn't delegate much to his auxiliaries,' said Marcó, 'so everyone went straight to Bergoglio. He's a man with a strong sense of power.' He also kept very well informed. 'He would sometimes ring you and chat away asking innocent questions,' one Buenos Aires priest told me, 'and then when you had said everything was OK he would ask the killer question which showed that he knew all along what your problem was.' Priests who were not toeing the line were offered a chance to change but then could be sent packing.

In other matters he was more collegial. He delegated a lot of admin and finance work to his six auxiliaries, with whom he held fortnightly meetings. All the detailed public affairs work was delegated to Guillermo Marcó, though the pair would speak daily about policy and strategic issues. At the twice-monthly meetings Bergoglio would routinely go around the table and solicit advice. He considered it carefully but when it came to decisions, said Marcó, 'he would do that himself'. There was no vote. When he was facing a tough call, said Federico Wals, a layman who succeeded Marcó as the archbishop's PR man, 'he'd pick up the phone and ask opinions from different people and get different points of view, and then he'd make his own decision'. But auxiliaries, priests and the laity were all involved. 'The way he implemented change was consultation, long process, participation – parishes, priests, deaneries', said Augusto Zampini, a Buenos Aires diocesan priest. 'At the beginning people didn't believe it. He made it clear he did not want to impose; he wanted things to emerge.' And new emphasis was given to the ordinary people in the Church. 'It wasn't just about priests doing the job', said Wals. 'He was also concerned with getting the laity active inside these movements, and letting them take charge. Priests were just one leg of the stool, along with the religious and the laity. He felt that if you didn't do it that way, you would end up with a Church that's too focused on itself. It's not just about what priests do, but above all the laity.'

Yet Bergoglio also knew when unilateral executive action was necessary. When he took over as Archbishop the diocese of Buenos Aires was facing not just a financial crisis but a banking scandal. His predecessor, Cardinal Quarracino had been very close to a prominent family of Argentinean bankers, the Trusso family – of which the Argentine ambassador to the Holy See (see page 102 above) was a member. 'Quarracino was very dependent on the Trusso family for money', said Marcó. 'At one point there was a run on the Trusso family bank. So one of the sons went to an insurance company and said the Archbishop wanted to borrow $10 million.' The company was the *Sociedad Militar Seguros de Vida* – an insurance company for military veterans – and the loan was under-written by the Trusso family bank, the *Banco de Crédito Provincial*. 'When the lenders went to see Quarracino to get him to confirm this, and get the necessary paperwork signed, the Archbishop's secretary, Mgr Roberto Marcial Toledo, told them Quarracino was busy. He took the paperwork and said he would get the Archbishop to sign it. He came back a few minutes later with the signed papers. But out of sight he just forged Quarracino's signature.' When the *Banco de Crédito Provincial* became insolvent and the military veterans asked the archdiocese to return the money, it turned out there was no money in the Church accounts. A year later, after the *Banco de Crédito Provincial* went bust, it was discovered that the bankers had been paying Quarracino's credit card bills, and taking advantage of the churchman's political influence. More than that, $700,000 had been transferred from the archdiocese's account to the bank – without being registered in the archdiocese's records. Toledo and two of the Trusso sons went to prison.

'Bergoglio immediately called in the international accountants Arthur Andersen to get to the bottom of the affair,' said Marcó. 'The judge in the case tried to make political capital out of it all in an attempt to embarrass the Church. But Bergoglio's thoroughness in the paperwork he handed over to the court meant his reputation was enhanced by the way he handled the whole affair.' The new Archbishop did not leave matters there. He then sold off the archdiocese's shares in several banks in order to sever any inappropriate links and placed the Church funds in normal commercial banks in which the Church held no shares. This abolished the grey area, said Federico Wals, by which the archdiocese was a partial owner of the banks and allowed to borrow on favourable terms – discouraging fiscal indiscipline. 'It was a black hole, so there were basically no limits on what we could spend', Wals said. Bergoglio acted swiftly and brought in outsider bankers to help sort out the archdiocese's chaotic finances.

***

But money matters were never at the top of Bergoglio's agenda. 'His vision was for the Church to reach out,' said Wals, 'to those for whom society didn't seem to care, such as single mothers, the poor, the elderly, the unemployed.' But if they were his top priority from the outset, Archbishop Bergoglio was keen to reach out to the widest possible range of groups outside the Catholic Church which, in a metaphor to which he returned again and again, he felt was sick from spending too long turned in on its own interior sacramental spirituality when it ought to be reaching out to the world. 'A Church that stays in the sacristy too long gets sick', he repeatedly said.

Bergoglio was admirably comprehensive in those he tried to include in his reaching out – from Christians of other denominations and believers of other faiths to those who were none of those. His relations with Argentina's Anglicans were so good that their leader, the Archbishop Gregory Venables, described him, in a back-handed compliment, as not so much a Catholic as 'more of a Christian, Christ-centered and Spirit-filled'. He was 'a friend to Anglicans', who made clear that he thought Benedict XVI's

Anglican Ordinariate – set up to attract disaffected members of that Communion into the Catholic Church – was unnecessary because the wider world needed the diversity of the Anglican witness. Similarly, he reached out to Evangelical Protestants, whom many in the Catholic Church treated suspiciously as the rivals who were enticing away the faithful to more colourful and charismatic styles of worship. Bergoglio took the opposite view and went to pray with them. He particularly outraged Catholic traditionalists when he asked a stadium full of Protestant evangelists to pray for him. 'Archbishopric of Buenos Aires *sede vacante*', roared the headline from an ultra-traditionalist Catholic magazine the following week, using the Latin phrase to indicate that a bishop has died or retired leaving the episcopal chair empty. To make matters worse, apparently, he had knelt down to receive the blessing for everyone to pray for him. 'What's the problem?' Bergoglio shrugged in response. Bergoglio is no Protestant. He is deeply Catholic in the colour, richness and sacramentality of his being in the world; one of his favourite films is *Babette's Feast*, in which a severe Puritan community is confronted by a meal which is a metaphor for the staggering cornucopia of gifts God has provided for the world. Bergoglio had always intuitively comprehended that there are deeper poetic qualities to religion which go beyond belief. But over the years he had become a man intent on seeing the good in others, and their common ground, rather than defining himself by the singularity of his religious identity.

He made particular efforts with other religions too. He held several inter-faith gatherings in his cathedral. He visited both a mosque and an Islamic school and he took part in several Jewish ceremonies in synagogues. In the cathedral he commemorated the anniversary of Kristallnacht. He even produced a book of conversations with one of Argentina's leading Jewish scholars, Rabbi Abraham Skorka, *Sobre el cielo y la tierra* (On Heaven and Earth). In it Bergoglio said: 'Dialogue is born from a respectful attitude toward the other person, from a conviction that the other person has something good to say. It supposes that we can make room in our heart for their point of view, their opinion and their proposals. Dialogue entails a warm reception and not a pre-emptive condemnation. To dialogue, one must know how to lower the defences, to open the doors of one's home and to offer warmth.' Bergoglio might have been talking about himself, Skorka later told me. 'He's very open-minded', the rabbi said. 'He can dialogue with anyone who speaks with honesty and respect even if he does not agree with them. He'll listen to a woman tussling with abortion and suffer with her. He has empathy. He has a very important listening capability. That doesn't mean he will change his mind. He is a conservative priest. But he's not got a dogmatic attitude. So he will dialogue too with opponents.'

Skorka and Bergoglio ranged across God and the Devil, through Death and Old Age to Communism and Globalisation. 'We had a good dialogue because the roots on which we stand are the same roots. Our ethics are the ethics of the Prophets of Israel. Bergoglio has a special feeling for the Synoptic gospels and when you analyse Jesus' words there you find many parallels between them and the principles developed by the Prophets.' They even agreed on the controversy around Pope Pius XII and Europe's Jews during the Holocaust. 'There are two views', Rabbi Skorka said. 'One is he did all he could to save Jews without confronting the Nazis which could have accelerated the killing of Jews. The other view asks how could Pius XII stay silent and not shout to all the winds: "Stop killing innocent people." Bergoglio said: "We must open the Vatican archives and find out the truth." Now he has the chance to do that. I'm confident he will.' Again right-wing Catholics in Argentina protested at Bergoglio's openness to inter-faith dialogue; they particularly complained about a display in the cathedral, near where Cardinal Quarracino is buried, containing fragments of Hebrew prayer books saved from the different concentration camps along with other documents relating to the Holocaust. Bergoglio ignored them and called the Jews 'my elder brothers'.

But it is to those outside the traditional religious convention that Bergoglio showed himself most anxious to reach. Sometimes at 11 p.m. he was to be found in the Plaza de Flores talking to the prostitutes who worked there. Occasionally he would even hear a confession sitting on a park bench. 'No doubt I will one day appear in the newspapers', he joked to a colleague. He went out of his way to embrace those marginalised by society, using the symbolism of Christ's washing his disciples' feet which the Church celebrates each year on the Thursday of Holy Week. In 2001 he surprised the staff of Muñiz Hospital in Buenos Aires by asking for a jar of water and then proceeding to wash the feet of twelve patients hospitalised with AIDS-related complications. He then kissed their feet. In 2008 he celebrate the Holy Thursday Mass of the Lord's Supper in the *villas miserias*, where he washed the feet of twelve youths from the *Hogar de Cristo* rehabilitation centre for drug addicts. And Bergoglio also sought to offer greater acceptance to those marginalised within the Church. While not departing from the Church teaching that remarried Catholics should not take Communion, he went as far as he could to reach out to them, saying: 'Divorced members who have remarried … are not excommunicated – even though they live in a situation on the margin of what indissolubility of marriage and the sacrament of marriage require of them – and they are asked to integrate into the parish life.' He went out of his way to protect theologians under investigation by Rome, like Marcelo Gonzalez and Gustavo Irrazabal, even where he didn't agree with what they had said or written.

His befriending of the widow of Jerónimo José Podestá was particularly bold. Podestá was a progressive Catholic bishop from the 1960s whose radical teachings had irritated the Vatican. He was exactly the kind of priest Bergoglio would have condemned at the time. He made outspoken attacks on the Government's economic policies, made stirring speeches at trade union rallies, and enthusiastically supported the reforms of the Second Vatican Council which the conservative Catholics in Argentina's hierarchy so doggedly opposed. Rome found the perfect opportunity to get rid of him when he began a relationship with his secretary Clelia Luro, a single woman with six children, in 1967. Worse than that,

Clelia, a feminist as radical as was imaginable on the Catholic spectrum, used to concelebrate Mass with her husband. He fled Argentina after death threats from the *Alianza Anticomunista Argentina* and returned in 1983 after the overthrow of the military dictatorship, but by the time of his death in 2000 he was poor and living in obscurity. He had continued to be president of the *Federación Latinoamericana de Sacerdotes Casados* (Latin American Federation of Married Priests), however, and on his deathbed, on impulse, he contacted Archbishop Bergoglio to talk about the movement. Bergoglio not only received him but was the only Church official to have any contact with the disgraced bishop before his death. Indeed Bergoglio visited the dying cleric in hospital to give him the last rites and hold his hand as he neared death. For the rest of the Church hierarchy Podestá was, like anyone who left the priesthood, to be ostracised. For Bergoglio it was a pastoral issue; Podestá was, like everyone else, a child beloved of God. And Bergoglio was confident enough in his own faith to be able to reach out pastorally to his widow.

Sitting in a grand colonial house with pink colonnades which had seen far better days, his feisty widow, now aged 87, told me that over the thirteen years since her husband's death Bergoglio had become a close friend. 'After Jerónimo's death he kept in touch', she said. 'Whenever I had a problem he would help – with economic issues, with the house, and my pension, because everything was complicated for me. At nights when I couldn't sleep I would write letters to Bergoglio and every Sunday, faithfully, he would call me. He did this every week until he left for Rome, and he has rung me from the Vatican too. We talk about all manner of things. He was very respectful of our marriage, of myself, of women in general. I told him: "Celibacy is a law that has to be changed. It's a law made by men, not by Jesus." Bergoglio said to me: "It's a cultural issue; change may well be accepted at some point." '

On gay marriage too, Bergoglio acted from a perspective of pastoral inclusion. Like other bishops in Argentina, he was opposed to the concept of marriage being applied to same-sex partnerships.

But when in 2010 Marcelo Márquez, a gay rights leader, devout Catholic and a former seminary theology professor, delivered a critical letter to him on the subject, he was surprised to hear the phone ring within the hour and find Cardinal Bergoglio on the other end of the line. The men met twice. 'He listened to my views with a great deal of respect', said Márquez. It was not perhaps what he expected. This was a Church in which Bergoglio's predecessor as Archbishop of Buenos Aires, Cardinal Quarracino, had said that homosexuals should be 'locked up in a ghetto'. Bergoglio took a very different tone. Despite the strong public criticisms Church officials had been making for months of the Government's plans to legalise same-sex marriage, privately Bergoglio revealed that 'homosexuals need to have recognised rights, including civil unions, but not same-sex marriage'. A political row inside the Church broke out over Bergoglio's stance (see page 121 below) but here again dogmatic principle did not overcome pastoral concern.

The same approach governed Bergoglio's position on a wide range of subjects. Some of his toughest criticisms were for conservative legalists who put obedience to Church rules above everything else. 'There are sectors within the religions that are so prescriptive that they forget the human side', he said. He once said of Catholics obsessed with sexual ethics that they wanted to 'stick the whole world inside a condom'. He excoriated priests who refused to baptise the children of unmarried mothers, calling them hypocritical clericalists who were hijacking baptism in a kind of sacramental blackmail. When it comes to the confessional, he told his priests to be neither too severe nor excessively indulgent. '"And so Father what should we do", they ask me. And I tell them: "be compassionate"'. In confession, Bergoglio admitted, he is more likely to ask parents whether they are too busy with work to play with their children; it is not the kind of sin they are expecting to be quizzed about. Once a mother who lived in a slum rife with crime, unemployment, drugs and poverty apologised to him for the fact that her son had stopped going to church. He replied: 'Is he a good kid? That's what matters.' Or as he put it elsewhere: 'The most important thing is the person in front of you.'

In all this the Church must go to people and not expect the people to come to the Church, Bergoglio insisted. 'He used to say that we need to learn from the model of the Evangelicals, meaning that we have to knock on doors and talk to people', said Federico Wals. 'He wanted to make the Church visible outside its buildings, which is why Buenos Aires developed some very interesting outdoor events. For instance, the Via Crucis procession during Holy Week moves through the entire city, going on for miles and miles. There are also lots of open-air Masses. The most important Masses here don't take place inside the cathedral, but in the square.' It was why Bergoglio, who in his earlier years had been an avid fan of San Lorenzo football team, would go to say Mass in the club's stadium on special occasions.

But it was more profound than that. When fire swept through the Cromañon nightclub in Buenos Aires in 2004 Bergoglio was one of the first on the scene, arriving before many of the fire engines. Some 175 people had died, with the tragedy being compounded by the fact that the club owners had locked the emergency exits to keep freeloaders out. Bergoglio accompanied the grieving relatives to the morgue. He said nothing. 'He was quiet and respectful', recalled the father of one of the victims. 'But he was one of the few authorities that was with us that day. He accompanied us with his presence.' In the face of a cruel death, Bergoglio later said: 'I stay silent. The only thing that occurs to me is to remain quiet and, depending on the trust they have in me, to take their hand. And to pray for them because both physical and spiritual pain are borne from within where no one can enter … What people need to know is that someone is with them, loves them, respects their silence and pray that God may enter into this space that is pure solitude.' What Bergoglio showed that night, wrote Alberto Barlocci of the Buenos Aires monthly magazine *Ciudad Nueva*, was that the Church wanted to accompany people in this moment of sorrow: 'For many his close presence was a consolation; for some it was nothing less than the rediscovery of a faith they seemed to have lost. For all it was an encounter with a Church that is near, like a friend, a sister and mother.'

***

There were two groups with whom confrontation rather than inclusion was the dominant model of Bergoglio's years as Archbishop. With both the government and the conservatives in the hierarchy of the Catholic Church relations were more problematic. Bergoglio had not cast a vote in a political election since the late 1950s during the mid-term of the government of Arturo Frondizi which was overthrown by the military in 1962, but throughout his life he has been a highly political animal. When he became Archbishop of Buenos Aires the president of Argentina was the Peronist Carlos Menem. On May 25 each year, to celebrate one of Argentina's two national days, the President traditionally attends an annual Te Deum and Mass in the capital's cathedral at which the Archbishop of Buenos Aires preaches. In his first year Bergoglio spoke from the pulpit about Argentina as a society where all sat at the table but only a few benefited and where the social fabric was being destroyed. Menem's face registered clear discomfort at the words. It was only the start of Bergoglio's robust interaction with the political class. Menem's successor as president, Fernando de la Rúa, was told that under him 'the system has fallen into a period of dark shadow'.

But it was under a later president, Néstor Kirchner, that Bergoglio's relationship reached its nadir. At the 2004 Te Deum Kirchner had to sit and listen to the nation's most senior cleric criticise political exhibitionism and slander, intolerant populism and propaganda and the bastardisation or elimination of institutions as part of 'a long list of stratagems which conceal and protect mediocrity'. The next day, when the press asked if Bergoglio had been referring to Kirchner, the Church's spokesman, Fr Guillermo Marcó replied: 'If the shoe fits, wear it.' Kirchner riposted that 'the Devil also reaches everyone – those who wear trousers and those who wear cassocks'. The President refused ever again to attend a Te Deum where Bergoglio was preaching. By 2007 a US diplomat in a cable to Washington was describing the Archbishop of Buenos Aires as the 'leader of the opposition' to the government.

Relations hardly improved when Néstor Kirchner was succeeded in that year as President by his widow, Cristina Fernández de Kirchner. In 2008 when Bergoglio called for national reconciliation during disturbances in the country's agricultural regions, Mrs Kirchner interpreted his words as support for anti-government demonstrators. The two went on to fight further political battles. Bergoglio had already objected to government plans in 2006 to legalise abortion in some cases and in 2010 he unsuccessfully sought to oppose Mrs Kirchner's plans to legalise gay marriage (see page 121 below), a position she derided as 'medieval', while he continued sharp criticisms of the government's failures to address corruption and poverty. The latter particularly rankled. Kirchner is a Peronist who projects herself as pursuing left-wing policies on social justice – though critics attack her government for crony capitalism and economic mismanagement. Bergoglio's criticisms of her bolstered that, for they came not from the right but the left, saying that Kirchner's policies did little for those in extreme poverty.

Not all Bergoglio's interaction with politicians has been oppositional. As Archbishop he had good relations with many in the government and has been active in dialogue with politicians of all parties. 'In truth,' said Federico Wals, 'there were plenty of government ministers who came here to talk to Bergoglio about human trafficking, about poverty, about trying to channel government funds for urban development through Catholic charities because they know it would be done well.' The idea that the whole government was at war with the Church was a considerable exaggeration. Bergoglio once lamented to Wals that politicians from the right complained about him being on the left but that those of the left saw him as right-wing. 'He said, "I'm trying to be a bishop of the centre, who talks to both parties and takes the best from each".' The reality, Wals said, is that Bergoglio is much more interested in concrete situations than ideological theories. 'As part of that, he was always open to talking with anyone.' Bergoglio often took the initiative of approaching politicians himself, though Mrs Kirchner, it is said, turned down the offer of meeting with Bergoglio no fewer than fourteen times.

One area where they did find a measure of agreement was over the thirtieth anniversary commemoration of the invasion of the Falklands Islands – or the Malvinas, as they are known in Argentina. Mrs Kirchner marked the occasion with an international appeal for the Argentinean claim of sovereignty over the islands to be upheld. Critics abroad rebuffed the idea, saying that it was an attempt by Mrs Kirchner to divert the attention of the voters of Argentina away from her mismanagement of the country's economy. But Bergoglio attended a ceremony marking Argentina's defeat in the Falklands War and said: 'We come to pray for those who have fallen, sons of the homeland who set out to defend their mother, the homeland, to claim the country that is theirs and that was usurped.' Such sentiments led Mrs Kirchner, who changed her attitude to Bergoglio markedly once he was elected Pope, to hope that he might intervene from Rome in the sovereignty dispute. But those hopes were quashed by Vatican officials, who announced, after a meeting between the Argentinean president and pontiff, that the Pope would be remaining neutral on the Falklands issue.

Perhaps the most significant dimension of Bergoglio's interaction with politicians in his time as Archbishop of Buenos Aires has been the way it focused his attention on the issue of poverty in a different way. The man who was once the scourge of Liberation Theology began to see, as national leader, that there was weight to aspects of the liberation theologians' analysis that sin could reside in structures as well as in the bad behaviour of individuals in positions of power. The great Argentinean economic crisis of 2001 was perhaps a turning point.

During the 1990s Argentina's constantly changing political classes had done what they could to reverse the decline in the economy and build-up of national debt that had taken place under the military dictatorship. Some 400,000 companies of all sizes went bankrupt under the junta. Reforms recommended by the International Monetary Fund included privatisation, deregulation and trade liberalisation, but Argentinean politicians pursued these without success. Throughout the years which followed, the Argentinean economy staggered from one crisis to another. A decision to peg the currency, the peso, to the US dollar to control inflation proved disastrous when the dollar was revalued internationally in 1997. Argentina had got stuck in a spiral in which higher interest rates constantly increased its national debt and the cost of servicing it until, in December 2001, the country announced it would stop paying the interest on the $94bn it owed. It was the biggest debt default in world history.

The impact on ordinary people was devastating. Banks closed, accounts were frozen, the value of wages was slashed, one in four people lost their jobs, the savings of millions of people were wiped out, more than half the population was plunged below the poverty line (compared with just 7 per cent before the dictatorship), a quarter of the Argentinean people were destitute and hungry and the economy suffered its sharpest decline since the Great Depression. Riots broke out in Buenos Aires. Angry Argentinians took to the streets marching, protesting and looting. President Fernando de la Rùa resigned and was followed by four presidents in eleven days. More than twenty-seven people were killed as the police responded so brutally that, overlooking one riot from his window, Archbishop Bergoglio rang the Minister of the Interior protesting that the police, who were beating people outside his window, seemed unable to distinguish between looters and ordinary people who only wanted to withdraw their savings from the bank.

In his pleas to the public throughout the crisis Bergoglio urged the people of Argentina to avoid violence. Later he castigated the rich as those who wanted to keep their 'privileges, their rapacity and their share of ill-gotten gain' even as the country was 'on the verge of national dissolution'. But he also turned his attention to the need for structural change: 'In becoming involved in this common attempt to overcome the crisis in Argentina, keep in mind what is taught by the tradition of the Church, which regards oppressing the poor and defrauding workers of their wages as two sins that cry out to God for vengeance', he warned. And he said on behalf of the bishops who had responded to the emergency by opening a network of parish food programmes for the needy: 'We are tired of systems that produce poor people so that then the Church can support them.'

It was a theme he was to continue to explore at the milestone meeting of all of Latin America's bishops at Aparecida in 2007, where he noted that they lived in 'the most unequal part of the world, which has grown the most, yet reduced misery the least', where the 'unjust distribution of goods persists, creating a situation of social sin that cries out to Heaven and limits the possibilities of a fuller life for so many of our brothers'. In 2009 he developed the same line of thinking, condemning 'extreme poverty and unjust economic structures' as violations of human rights. What changes all this wrought in Jorge Mario Bergoglio is something we shall consider in the next chapter.

The other significant group with whom Bergoglio had problems throughout his fifteen years as Archbishop of Buenos Aires was to be found, ironically perhaps, within his own church. For all his growing sense of the need for social justice, Jorge Mario Bergoglio was doctrinally orthodox and mainstream. But that placed him, in the words of one informed outside observer, the prominent Argentinean Lutheran theologian, Lisandro Orlov, 'on the left in what is a deeply reactionary and right-wing collection of bishops'. Almost all the serious opposition to Bergoglio in his time as Archbishop came from the right rather than the left in the Catholic Church.

In some areas, of course, there was no division. When Néstor Kirchner's government in 2006 proposed that abortion be legalised in certain cases, the Argentine Episcopal Conference was of one mind in its opposition. It was a delicate political atmosphere, for there was rising public concern over the rapes of two mentally disabled women. Both had been denied abortions after pressure from religious organisations. The health authorities then demanded a change in the law and the government proposed abortion should be made legal in some circumstances. Opinion polls suggested that 76 per cent of Argentineans supported abortion being legalised for the victims of rape. Bergoglio intervened robustly, describing it as an attack on the Catholic values of the Argentinean people. When the Supreme Court ruled, in 2012, that abortion is legal in the case of rape or where a woman's life is threatened, Bergoglio spoke for all the bishops when he condemned it as a 'backdoor attempt' to bring abortion to Argentina. 'Abortion is never a solution', he said. 'We listen, support and offer understanding from our place to save two lives: respect a human being small and helpless.'

But in other areas there were tensions inside the Bishops' Conference, where the hardliners were led by Héctor Rubén Aguer, the Archbishop of La Plata, a cleric widely linked in Argentina to Opus Dei. One central issue which Bergoglio was never able to resolve because of the factionalism within the Conference was the extent to which the Church should respond to its collusion with the military dictatorship during the dark days of the Dirty War. At the turn of the millennium Pope John Paul II called upon the Church worldwide to examine its conscience and make apology for its historic sins in preparation for the Jubilee that was held in 2000. The bishops of Argentina responded with a statement in which they acknowledged that the Church needed 'to put on garments of public penance for the sins committed during the years of the dictatorship'. It continued: 'We share everyone's pain and once again ask the forgiveness of everyone we failed or didn't support as we should have. We were indulgent towards totalitarian positions. Through actions and omissions we discriminated against many of our brothers, without exerting ourselves sufficiently in defence of their rights. We beseech God to accept our repentance and to heal the wounds of our people.' It was a big step forward, but many in Argentina were not satisfied, pointing out that the Church was not taking responsibility for institutional complicity but instead placing the blame on the mistakes of individual Catholics.

The situation was compounded in 2012 when the unrepentant ex-dictator General Jorge Rafael Videla gave a rare interview to the Spanish political magazine *Cambio16* in which he claimed: 'My relationship with the Church was excellent. It was very cordial, frank and open. Don't forget that we even had military chaplains assisting us, thus not allowing our partnership and friendship to falter ... The Argentine Church in general, thankfully, was not carried away by the leftist Third World tendencies of other churches of the continent. Even though certain members of the Argentine Church fell for this game, they were a minority group that was hardly noticeable.' The attitude of the Argentine church was in stark contrast to the Church leadership elsewhere. 'There was much clearer leadership in Brazil,' said Professor Jeffrey Klaiber, author of *The Church, Dictatorships, and Democracy in Latin America*, 'where Dom Helder Camara, Aloisio Lorscheider, and Paulo Arns of Sao Paulo were very vocal and took a strong stance, denouncing the military. The Catholic Church in Argentina was the black sheep of Latin America in the passive way they dealt with the military dictatorship.'

But Bergoglio insisted the picture was not so black and white. 'In the Church there were Christians from different groups', he said in 2010. 'There were Christians who killed as guerrillas, Christians who helped save people and repressive Christians who believed that they were saving the Homeland. There were different types of clergy ... We have to do a significant investigation. But it cannot be assumed that there was a simplistic complicity.' Even so, Bergoglio was instrumental in organising another apology from the bishops, which was released in 2012 after he had ceased to be chairman of the Episcopal Conference. It expressed sorrow to all those who had been let down or felt unsupported by the Church. But critics expressed the same reservations as before, saying the apology was woolly and unspecific.

Delivering an apology deemed adequate by the families of the victims defeated Bergoglio. Lisandro Orlov said he thought he knew why. 'People have asked why did it take so long for Bergoglio to get the Catholic Church to apologise', he said. 'But the fact is that it was not up to Bergoglio alone. There had to be a consensus within the Bishops' Conference of the Church. He had to negotiate with people who wanted to remain silent. The more progressive elements were in a minority. So they never apologised as a Church but just asked forgiveness for the behaviour of individuals.'

This view was emphasised by the fact that five years after the former police chaplain Christian von Wernich was sentenced to life in prison for complicity in seven homicides, forty-two kidnappings and thirty-two instances of torture during the Dirty War, he has still not been penalised by the Catholic Church. In 2010 a Church official said that 'at the appropriate time, von Wernich's situation will have to be resolved in accordance with canonical law'. But it did not happen and von Wernich was allowed to continue to celebrate Mass in prison. Professor Fortunato Mallimacci, a researcher on Catholicism at the University of Buenos Aires, believes that is because 'the great majority of the bishops believe von Wernich has not committed any crime' but simply 'fulfilled his role as a priest, which at that time was to support the military during a terrible time caused by the attack from Marxist subversives'.

The Archbishop of La Plata had more than a theological disagreement with Bergoglio. The two men had both been auxiliary bishops to Cardinal Quarracino at the same time; indeed Aguer, though younger in years, was the senior bishop by a few months. The younger man had wanted to be Archbishop of Buenos Aires after Quarracino and had thought he had the better chance. He was a favourite of Cardinal Angelo Sodano who, as the papal nuncio in Chile, had become a friend of the Chilean dictator Augusto Pinochet. He had a strong influence on Latin American affairs at the Vatican, where he was Secretary of State under Pope John Paul II. Aguer was also smiled upon by the Argentine cardinal Leonardo Sandri, who was Sodano's deputy. In Bergoglio's circle it was assumed that it was through the influence of these men that whenever Bergoglio made a recommendation to Rome on who should be a created a bishop in Argentina his suggestions were repeatedly ignored. His appointment of the Rector of the Catholic University of Buenos Aires was blocked for two years, and was only unblocked when Bergoglio became Pope.

'Bergoglio didn't get along with Opus Dei', said his longtime friend, the human rights lawyer Alicia Oliveira. 'It was people associated with that group who spread the slanderous stories about Bergoglio in the 2005 conclave. There were all kinds of murky dealings about money-laundering and the Vatican Bank.'

'There were certain bishops in the Episcopal Conference who were always complaining to Rome behind Bergoglio's back', said Guillermo Marcó, who was one of Bergoglio's closest aides as Archbishop for eight years. One regular gripe was that vocations to the priesthood had fallen in Buenos Aires in his time, where they were rising in other dioceses. But in 2010 the conservative faction saw a much greater opportunity to unseat Bergoglio, who would be 75 in December 2011 and therefore obliged to tender his resignation to the Pope. The Pope did not have to accept it, but if pressure could be applied by Bergoglio's enemies there would be a chance for Aguer to succeed to Buenos Aires and become the nation's senior churchman. It was at this point that Argentina's politicians decided to introduce a law permitting same-sex couples to marry. Various conservative bishops and rabbis protested. 'Bergoglio kept out of it', said Alicia Oliveira. 'He was angry at the shocking things the conservatives were saying, linking homosexuality with paedophilia. When the law was issued he started talking about it. But he left it too late.'

Bergoglio went to the Bishops' Conference with a strategy. The Church should offer to back same-sex civil unions as the 'lesser of two evils' so long as gay marriage was ditched. He persuaded a prominent evangelical parliamentarian, Congressional Representative Cynthia Hutton, to make the same proposal in the legislature.

'Bergoglio was against same-sex marriage but in favour of a law for equal rights for gays', revealed Marcó. 'The hard-line conservatives were in the minority but they were supported by the papal nuncio and by Rome. The nuncio was at the meetings every week. The hard-line traditionalist bishops and Opus Dei had complained to Rome about Bergoglio.' It looked as though the bishops would say No to Bergoglio's proposal. To regain some ground Bergoglio embarked upon a dangerous tactic. A month before the parliament was due to vote he wrote a letter about gay marriage, taking the orthodox line and using vivid language, and sent it to a closed order of Carmelite nuns, asking them to pray for the right outcome in the vote. It said:

'Let us not be naive: this is not a simple political struggle; its intention is to destroy God's plan. It is not merely a legislative project but rather a move by the Father of Lies who wishes to confuse and deceive the children of God.'

'He thought a closed order would not make the contents public but that he could send a copy of it to Rome to show he was doing what was required', said Marcó. 'But it was published. The strategy backfired on him. He lost the vote among the bishops. The law was passed. And the traditionalists denounced him in the Vatican for not speaking out soon enough.' In the six years that Bergoglio was president of the Bishops' Conference it was the only time he was unable to broker consensus.

But Aguer had not done enough to unseat Bergoglio, just as his supporters in Rome were not able to land him the job he craved as the Vatican's chief doctrinal watchdog, the head of the Congregation for the Doctrine of the Faith when its Prefect, Cardinal William Levada, stood down in 2012. Aguer, the man who had posted bail of one million dollars for the release of the disgraced banker, Francisco Trusso – who had been jailed in the fraud Bergoglio had exposed when he took over as Archbishop of Buenos Aires – had played out his career in the shadow of Bergoglio. 'He had been a thorn in Bergoglio's side', as Clelia Luro claimed she had learned from her weekly conversions with Bergoglio. 'He was a constant problem.'

Aguer had been so piqued by his rival's election as Pope that he instructed that the bells of his cathedral in La Plata should not be rung, as was traditional for the announcement of a new pontiff – and justified it by telling the congregation that there was no need to have a sort of 'soccer stadium celebration' just because a fellow Argentinian was elected. Pope Francis responded by magnanimously granting an early papal audience to his old nemesis.

But all this politicking, both secular and ecclesiastical, was merely an irritant to Jorge Mario Bergoglio, those close to him said. His main concern was to turn the Church outward to those who needed to hear the Good News rather than allowing it to remain turned in on itself and its own spirituality. To him, one of the defining moments of his time as Archbishop of Buenos Aires was the meeting of all the bishops of Latin America at Aparecida in Brazil in 2007 (see Chapter 1, page 17 above). It encapsulated his conviction that his duty was 'to proclaim the Gospel by going out to find people, not by sitting [around] waiting for people to come to us'. More than that, there was a *sensus fidei* (sense of the faith) among the everyday lives of ordinary men and women which helped them grasp the reality of the faith with more clarity than that of many specialists, theologians and priests. 'To remain faithful we need to go outside', Bergoglio concluded. 'That is what Aparecida says at bottom. That is the heart of the mission.'

There is a deep irony in the fact that one of the places where Jorge Mario Bergoglio best detected that in his days as Cardinal Archbishop of Buenos Aires was in the very slum that he instructed Yorio and Jalics to leave all those years ago. Today Villa 1–11–14 at Bajo Flores is one of Buenos Aires' largest and most dangerous slums, though the risks now come from drugs and gang warfare rather than military death squads.

The slum priest at *Santa María Madre del Pueblo* (Holy Mary, Mother of the People) is Fr Gustavo Carrara, another of 'the Bergoglio generation' of hand-picked, dedicated, strong young priests who do not just visit the slums but live and work here, sharing the lives of the poor. 'It was Fr Bergoglio who suggested

I came here', Carrara said, 'and it has been a great experience.' He works long hours, seven days a week hearing confessions, giving communion, baptising children, visiting the sick and conducting funerals. But his day is also filled with the practicalities of life among the unemployed and hungry: soup kitchens, health centres for teenage mothers, job training for unemployed youth, even running community radio to give the people a voice.

'Bergoglio was in a way like my father', Carrara said. 'He was very close to me. He trusted me. He let me do things my own way. And he was always there when I needed him. I could visit or call in whenever I wanted. He'd always return the call immediately. "Hi, this is Bergoglio, how can I help?" Once I wanted to set up a project to help kids who are drug users. I found a good place but told him I needed $180,000 to buy it and set it up. He said, OK, and a few days later the money arrived. He would come here whenever he could, incognito, travelling on the bus. He doesn't like fuss but he loves talking to the ordinary people.'

'The poor are the treasure of the Church and we must care for them', Bergoglio said in his conversations to Rabbi Abraham Skorka. 'If we lose this vision of things, we will have a lukewarm, weak and mediocre Church. Our true power must be service. We cannot adore God if our spirit does not include the needy.'

In that service the religious and the political are indivisible to the slum priests like Gustavo Carrara. 'The biggest problem we face is marginalisation of the people', he said. 'Drugs are a symptom, violence is a symptom, but marginalisation is the disease. Our people feel marginalised by a social system that's forgotten about them and isn't interested in them. Popular faith is very important to them. It is the culture of the people that religion is not just for one day a week. God has to do with all life, and vice versa. When there's a market in the slum you can take the Virgin there. People will ask in the marketplace to be blessed, for a visit to the sick at home, to bless holy water. This is our life, everyday things like lobbying the city authorities to provide better water pressure in the neighbourhood and blessing holy water.'

Priests and people alike will miss their Bishop of the Slums, said Carrara, 'but we were having to get used to the idea of missing him anyway'. When he turned 75 in December 2011, Bergoglio submitted his resignation as Archbishop of Buenos Aires to Pope Benedict XVI as required by canon law. It had not, at the time of the 2013 conclave, been accepted, but Bergoglio had already selected his room in a priests' retirement home in the place of his birth, Flores. 'He'd started to give away his books and to say goodbye', Carrara said. In his spartan set of rooms in the archdiocesan office he had begun throwing out papers, saying: 'I want to leave as little as possible behind me when I take my leave from this world.'

He left it behind. But not in the way he expected. 'He has gone to Rome, but at least,' said one woman happily in the *villa miseria*, 'he takes the mud of the slums with him on his shoes.'

6

What Changed Bergoglio?

There are books on Liberation Theology for sale in the foyer of the *Colegio Máximo* today. To the side of the grand entrance, with its stone arches, marble floor with diamond squares and heavy smell of polish on the dark mahogany, is a glass-fronted case containing titles like *Labour and Capital* and *Democracy, Human Rights and the Political Order* and *The Theology of Liberation and the Social Doctrine of the Catholic Church*. They would not have been allowed there when Jorge Mario Bergoglio was Provincial Superior of the Jesuits or Rector of the college. But if the *Colegio Máximo* has changed, so has the authoritarian conservative who has been transformed from the scourge of Liberation Theology to a Pope for the Poor. What brought about such a metamorphosis?

The extent of the change took many people by surprise, and not just those who had not been paying attention. Hebe de Bonafini is one of the leaders of Mothers of the Plaza del Mayo, whose members for years protested in the square between Buenos Aires cathedral and the Casa Rosada, the official residence of the President of Argentina. It was a public witness to the disappearance of their children and grandchildren at the hands of the death squads of the military dictatorship in the years from 1976 to 1983 – and to the lack of information which was forthcoming from the files of official organisations including the Catholic Church. Priests and nuns were involved in the disappearances of their victims and the children they bore in captivity. Hebe de Bonafini once famously left a bucket of urine in the cathedral, accusing Bergoglio of being in league with fascism. But after his election as Pope she wrote to him:

'Fr Francis, I did not know about your pastoral work; I just knew that a top leader of the Argentinean Church lived in that cathedral. When we marched and passed by the cathedral we used to scream: "You kept silent when they were being taken away"'. But since, she said, she had found out about his commitment to the slums and was overjoyed at the prospect for change in the Vatican. And even one of Bergoglio's former Jesuit pupils, Fr Rafael Velasco, who is now rector of the Catholic University of Córdoba, said: 'Bergoglio was so very conservative that I was rather shocked years later when he started talking about the poor. It wasn't something which seemed at the top of his agenda at the time but clearly became so as a bishop. Something changed.'

Those who deal with him at a more intimate level agreed. 'He has changed. He was pretty conservative', said Fr Michael Campbell-Johnston, who in 1977 was sent by Jesuit headquarters in Rome to pull Bergoglio into line with the social justice agenda of the order throughout the rest of Latin America. He added: 'he has clearly grown in his witness for the poor.' Fr Humberto Miguel Yáñez, who was received into the Jesuits in that same year by Bergoglio and who is now the head of moral theology at the Gregorian University in Rome, has watched Bergoglio over almost four decades. 'He did change', Yáñez said. 'It was mostly when he was a bishop and an archbishop. But it was not a sudden change, so much as a gradual evolution. Being outside the tensions and complex atmosphere of the Society [of Jesus] he possibly became more open to dialogue and more open generally. Looking at him now I recognise he's the same person; he's always had a strong personal authority. But his relationship to the poor has deepened.'

The change goes wider than that, according to Rabbi Abraham Skorka, with whom Bergoglio had a series of conversations for a book and television series. 'Bergoglio has changed over the years', the Jewish leader said. 'He's a very dynamic person. He's a person who is learning from life. He's very sensitive and has great empathy. He has changed according to his life's experience.' Bergoglio himself, talking to Skorka, added this gloss: 'Religious truth does not change, but it does develop and grow. It is like with the human being, we are the same as a baby and in old age, but in the middle there is a whole journey. In this way ... something that was once seen as natural, is not seen like that, today.'

In the middle there is a whole journey. Bergoglio's own words – and the testimony of those who know the new Pope well, and over many years – hint at how deeply Bergoglio's experiences have affected him and how profound has been the change they have wrought. But it is his own words, definite but slightly opaque, which are intriguing enough to want to unpack more explicitly. In the middle there is a whole journey.

What changed Bergoglio? External events played their part. So did regular contact with the poorest of the poor in the slums of Buenos Aires. So did a growing understanding of the theology of liberation which he found too disturbing as a young man. Ironically, forty years on, he found he had arrived at a similar understanding of social justice to that of Yorio and Jalics, the two Jesuits he had cut off because of their work in the slums in 1976, leaving them exposed to the violent predations of a military torture squad. But most of all, what really changed Jorge Mario Bergoglio was something which happened deep within his soul.

**

History has been a major factor in the transmutation of Bergoglio, for the world has changed significantly around him. His opposition to Liberation Theology was very much rooted in the mindset of the Cold War and the fear that atheistic Soviet-style communism would supplant both capitalism and Catholicism in Latin America, with Cuba as its toehold. But then the Berlin Wall came down. The Soviet Union and its empire collapsed. A new international *realpolitik* was ushered in. It was not quite 'the End of History' predicted by the American academic Francis Fukuyama, but the globalisation of the world's economy prompted Bergoglio to think differently about extreme poverty. To recognise the exploitation of the poor, or their wilful marginalisation, was no longer to risk being seen to side with the forces of an anti-religious Marxism. Rather it began to sound like a form of solidarity which was part of bringing the good news to the poor. Similarly, the end of the military dictatorship in Argentina, the steady awful revelation of the details of its brutality, and the extent of the collusion of prominent figures in the Argentinean Church created the emotional and intellectual space in which Bergoglio could re-evaluate all that – and examine his conscience over his own role in it. Even those with no sins of commission were forced to face up to sins of omission in the decades since democracy returned. And the final contextual factor was that as a bishop, and particularly as an archbishop, Bergoglio – who had been very much rooted in Argentina for most of his life – travelled more and had more contact with international figures which brought home to him, as Jeffrey Klaiber said in the last chapter, how out of step the Church had been in Argentina by comparison with the prophetic witness it had offered against military dictatorships elsewhere in Latin America.

But there was not just change in the outside circumstances; there was change within Bergoglio too. Looking back on his earlier days as a schoolmaster, Bergoglio recognised, in conversation with Rubin and Ambrogetti in 2010, how much he had learned from his students. 'I thank them for all the good they did me,' he reflected, 'particularly for the way they taught me how to be more a brother than a father.' Something similar happened to him when he first became a bishop. He learned from the poor in the same way a good teacher learns from his students. 'In Buenos Aires he came across more concrete problems', said Fr Augosto Zampini, a diocesan priest from the city. 'When you're working in a shanty town 90 per cent of your congregation are single or divorced. You have to learn to deal with that. Communion for the divorced and remarried is not an issue there. Everyone takes Communion.' Bergoglio never altered his doctrinal orthodoxy on such matters but he did not allow dogma to overrule the priority of pastoral concern. 'He was never rigid about the small and stupid stuff,' said Fr Juan Isasmendi, the parish priest in Villa 21 slum, 'because he was interested in something deeper.' Bergoglio's visits to the slums brought him into contact with a huge number of ordinary people in their everyday situations. Over his eighteen years as bishop and archbishop in Buenos Aires, one *villa* priest estimated, Bergoglio must have personally talked to at least half the people in the slum in visits where he would just turn up, wander the alleyways, and chat to the locals and drink *mate* tea with them. 'It is when we are involved in ministry that we discover who we are', Michael Campbell-Johnston said of him. And the man who was Bergoglio's close aide for the first eight years of his episcopal ministry had no doubt about that either: 'He doesn't see the poor as people he can help but rather as people from whom he can learn', said Fr Guillermo Marcó. 'He believes the poor are closer to God than the rest of us; they have a very personal experience of him.'

All this developed a new openness in Bergoglio. As he said in *El Jesuita:*

> 'I don't have all the answers; I don't even have all the questions. I always think of new questions, and there are always new questions coming forward. But the answers have to be thought out according to the different situations, and you also have to wait for them. I confess that, because of my disposition, the first answer that comes to me is usually wrong. When I'm facing a situation, the first solution I think of is what *not* to do. Because of this I have learned not to trust my first reaction. When I'm calmer, after passing through the crucible of solitude, I come closer to understanding what has to be done ... You can do a great deal of harm with the decisions you make. One can be very unfair.'

Clearly he was there looking back to the *modus operandi* of the younger Bergoglio. As a young priest in powerful leadership positions he did not have maturity he needed to cope in the 1970s with the competing pressures of the Jesuit Curia in Rome, the Vatican and a ruthless military dictatorship. He had only taken his final Jesuit vows months before he was thrust prematurely into the

top leadership role among Argentina's Jesuits. His experience led
to some bad judgements. 'To tell you the truth, I made hundreds
of errors', he told Rubin and Ambrogetti. 'When you're young, you
believe you can change the world, and that is good, that's the way
it should be. But later, when you seek this change, you discover the
logic of patience in your life and the lives of others ... A good father,
like a good mother, is one who intervenes in the life of the child
just enough to demonstrate guidelines for growing up, to help him,
but who later knows when to be a bystander to his own and others'
failures, and to endure them.' Shortcomings, he concluded, act as a
springboard for growth.

A key part of Bergoglio's growth has been in the development
of an understanding that what the poor need is not charity but
justice – an insight at which Yorio and Jalics had arrived two
decades earlier. The quality of Bergoglio's commitment to help
alleviate the consequences of poverty was never in doubt from the
outset; his establishment of soup kitchens in the 1970s, even as
he was expunging Liberation Theology from the Jesuit province,
was testimony to that. But in the early days his concern for the
poor never went beyond the impulse of gospel-inspired philanthropy. Some of that impulse survived into his years as a bishop
and archbishop. If only the rich would behave with more decency
then things would be much better for the poor. Thus in Argentina's
massive economic crisis in 2001, which plunged half the population
into poverty, he castigated the rich for 'rapacity' in attempting
to maintain their privileged position as the rest of the nation
descended into an economic maelstrom. A year later in a sermon he
chastised golden-mouthed politicians who were making unrealistic
promises to voters to fix the nation's economy. 'Go and fix yourself',
he told them 'Have a change of heart. Get to confession, before
you need it even more!' *The Wall Street Journal*, not unreasonably,
concluded of Bergoglio that 'his Christianity is less political than
personal'.

But in 2001 an economic crisis forced Argentina to tell the world
that it would refuse to pay the $94bn it owed to foreign banks

and investors. What happened next sowed seeds in Bergoglio's mind which would change the personal into the political. The economy spiralled uncontrollably and life became incredibly tough for ordinary Argentineans. In the years that followed, the International Monetary Fund did its job as the guardian of world financial stability, but the austerity its medicine imposed fell cruelly upon the poorest people in the land. Bergoglio began to be highly critical of the economic formularies of neo-liberalism; he was particularly critical of how it creates speculative financial markets which damage the real economy. He attacked the way that the cost of the debt-restructuring process was the cutting of services on which the poor depended. He began to make use of the insights of Liberation Theology with regard to economic structures which were so corrupt that they constituted structures of oppression which were themselves sinful. He attacked 'unbridled capitalism [which] fragments economic and social life'. What was needed instead, he said, was a solidarity which brought people together. The 'unjust distribution of goods' creates 'a situation of social sin that cries out to Heaven and limits the possibilities of a fuller life for so many of our brothers', he lamented. 'Unjust economic structures' were violations of human rights. Ever-rising national debt on the back of restructuring of the original 2001 debt default was 'immoral, unjust and illegitimate'. Homelessness he described as 'structural slavery'.

More radical liberation theologians, like the Argentinean Lutheran Lisandro Orlov, were unconvinced as to how far Bergoglio really understood the concept of sin residing in structures. 'He talks about the imperialism of money and the tyranny of the market, but that's not liberation theology, it's just Catholic Social Teaching', said Orlov. 'It's strong on analysis, but without real proposals or programme for an alternative. Bergoglio does not go onto the next step – the empowerment of the poor. He stops halfway, as Catholic Social Teaching does. It's all about goodwill, we need more solidarity etc – but there is no paradigm for the new society. Bergoglio has moved from the right to the middle not the left.'

This is unfair. Bergoglio directly addressed the issue of helping poor people to take control over their own lives in his conversations with Rabbi Skorka. He said:

'In the Social Doctrine of the Church it took quite some time to assimilate the concept of social justice, though now it is accepted everywhere. When someone takes up the manual of the Social Doctrine of the Church, they are astounded by the things it denounces. For example, the condemnation of economic liberalism. Everyone thinks that the Church is against communism, and yet it is as against communism as it is against the wild economic liberalism we see today. We have to seek equal opportunities and rights and strive for social benefits, dignified retirement, vacation time, rest, and freedom of unions. All of these things build social justice. No one should be dispossessed and there is no worse dispossession – and I want to emphasise this – than not being able to earn one's own bread, than being denied the dignity of work.'

Throughout the slum parishes of Buenos Aires he and his priests put that into action. A strong example of that, said Bergoglio's spokesman Federico Wals, was his work supporting the *cartoneros* – some of the poorest people in Buenos Aires who make a living sorting through the city's garbage each night to find and sell recyclable materials. 'Bergoglio helped them to form a union and to turn this work into something from which they can make a decent living', said Wals. 'He wanted to help them to protect their rights.' This was exactly the kind of work for which two decades earlier he had condemned Yorio and Jalics. It was only one of many similar schemes Bergoglio introduced, working with government, city authorities and a variety of community organisations.

***

Bergoglio's thinking was more sophisticated on Liberation Theology than many credit. From the outset he was vehemently opposed to the Marxist analysis and the talk of class war adopted by some theologians. Yet he embraced the notion of the preferential option for the poor – though he viewed it from a distinctly Argentine perspective. Fr Humberto Miguel Yáñez, head of moral theology at the Gregorian University in Rome and also an Argentine Jesuit, explained: 'Liberation Theology in Argentina is not as it is understood elsewhere in Latin America. Those who embraced aspects of Marxist thinking saw elements like culture and religion as tools of alienation rather than liberation and had difficulty accepting elements of popular culture and religion. In the more distinctly Argentinean strain, both philosophically and theologically, there was a strong appreciation of culture, in particular the culture of popular religiosity.'

The key thinker in this different approach was Fr Juan Carlos Scannone, a Jesuit who was a theologian at *Colegio Máximo* when Bergoglio was Provincial and Rector there. Scannone's work emphasised all the qualities of folk religion – the rosaries, processions and novenas – which Bergoglio so valued from his upbringing. For Scannone, local culture was an essential part of what he called the Theology of the Poor. He told me: 'Some people think Argentine Theology of the Poor isn't Liberation Theology at all and class it just as popular theology. But others see it as a current within Liberation Theology; the father of this theology Gustavo Gutiérrez and I wrote an article to that effect in 1982.' The Vatican crackdown in the 1984 document entitled *Instruction on certain aspects of the 'Theology of Liberation'* did not object to all Liberation Theology, Scannone emphasised, but only that which used a Marxist analysis of society and history. 'Argentine People's Theology does not use Marxist analysis, but a historical and cultural one. It pays attention to social structures, but it does not consider class struggle as the main principle.' Rather it concerns itself with how to change culture in line with gospel values, but also with how the gospel should be read differently in different cultures.

Scannone saw the folk religion which Bergoglio so valued (see Chapter 2) as playing a key role in his theology. He too believed that it was best preserved 'by the poor and simple people'. What

Scannone and his peers were fighting was a view handed down from Argentina's colonial masters, which saw local culture as 'barbaric' in contrast to European culture, which it presented as 'civilisation'. So the core tension came not from class war so much as culture war. It was for this reason, said Yáñez, that Bergoglio insisted on Jesuits novices developing a close knowledge of Argentine and Latin American literature and history. Bergoglio grew increasingly alive to this debate towards the end of his time as Rector at *Colegio Máximo*. In 1985 he and Scannone jointly organised an international conference on the relationship between faith and culture. They combined it with a large popular mission to local communities in greater Buenos Aires to commemorate the 450th anniversary of the arrival of the Jesuits in Argentina. 'The story was about contact with poor people and re-establishing the popular piety', recalled Yáñez.

This was the vision which Bergoglio tried to make good, more than a decade later, when he encouraged priests like Padre Pepe to move in greater numbers into the slums of Buenos Aires. When Pepe arrived in a villa where most of the occupants were from Paraguay, the young priest decided he needed some symbol of the people's popular faith to ignite interest in his mission. With funding from Bergoglio he sent a group of local people to Paraguay to bring back an icon of that country's patron saint, Our Lady of Caacupé – an image originally carved by a Guarani Indian and credited with miraculous properties. Pepe then paraded the icon around the alleyways of the shanty town. Cheering crowds gathered on such a scale that Bergoglio held a special Mass for the people of the slum – but invited them into the city's cathedral to celebrate it. As the children of the slum clambered all over the formal high-backed chairs normally occupied by Argentina's elite, Bergoglio said delightedly: 'Look how far the children from the *villa* have come!' When the people paraded back to their slum with the icon, Bergoglio, wearing a poncho, slipped surreptitiously in among the procession. The arrival of the icon of the Virgin created a new mood in the shanty town. Amid a new sense of common heritage among the slum-dwellers the fierce fighting between rival gangs reduced.

Co-operation on schemes to improve the neighbourhood increased. In part, what Padre Pepe had done was in the tradition which the French theologian Charles de Foucauld called *presence* – being present among the poor and sharing their lives with great emphasis on symbolic gesture. To that Pepe had added an affirmation of local culture by bringing the statue of the Virgin to the slums. But he also set about tackling the causes of poverty and improving life for ordinary people.

Padre Pepe was just one of a new generation of *curas villeros* – slum priests – whom Bergoglio sent to work among the poor. What they, and Bergoglio, discovered was that learning was a two-way process. The slum priests were changed by the simple devotion of those they had arrived to help. Fr Jorge Vernazza, one of the slum priest pioneers, who died in 1997, wrote a book on his experiences in which he confessed 'our ignorance about the real feeling of the people' when he and his peers arrived expecting that 'authentic faith' would be defined more by evangelical think tanks than by 'the richness of the devotion of the people'. The reality of life in the slums brought them to do battle with what Pepe called the 'misunder-stood progressivism' of liberation theologians educated in Europe, who arrived 'from outside to give lessons' and looked askance at the statue-kissing, processions, and the like. The slum priests, by contrast, had 'seen and followed the faith of the people, their way of living it and expressing it' and been changed by it. 'Liberation has to start with people, not an ideology and not with charity', Pepe said. Augusto Zampini, a diocesan priest who has taught at the *Colegio Máximo* where Bergoglio was once Rector, went further: 'To disregard popular faith', he said, 'is, in a way, to disregard the option for the poor.'

That said, over his years in the slums, Bergoglio came to see the value of what had been done by the followers of the Liberation Theology of which he had once been so afraid. With the ideology of the Cold War drained away, Bergoglio's distrust slowly evapo-rated. He began to respect and pay homage to the sacrifice of those of whom he had once been so suspicious. In 1999, just a year after he became Archbishop of Buenos Aires, on the twenty-fifth anniversary of the murder of Fr Carlos Mugica, Bergoglio gave instructions that the remains of the priest should be disinterred and brought back to the district where he had exercised his ministry. The cardinal celebrated Mass on the occasion, and made his prayer for 'the complicit silence' of the Church at the time. In 2005 he authorised a request for the beatification of six members of the Pallotine community murdered in the shrine they served by a military death squad. In 2006 he travelled to La Rioja to say Mass for the anniversary of the death of Bishop Enrique Angelelli who died in a fake car crash and, for the first time, publicly acknowledged that Angelelli had 'preached the Gospel, and shed his blood for it'. At the service Bergoglio quoted Tertullian's maxim that the blood of the martyrs is the seed of the Church. In 2011 Bergoglio authorised the process to recognise as a saint Fr Carlos Murias, a priest killed under the military dictatorship, despite reservations among conservative Argentinean bishops against canonising priests who were killed for 'social' causes.

'History has its ironies', Bergoglio began when he went to the Faculty of Theology in Buenos Aires in 2012 to honour the memory of Rafael Tello, one of the founders of Liberation Theology, who was in his day silenced by the Church. Tello, Bergoglio now confessed, had made 'one of the most important contributions' to the Church in Argentina. 'Nobody who has opened up new paths leaves without scars on his body', he observed wryly.

Then, not longer after becoming Pope, Bergoglio privately got in touch with one of the liberation theologians most reviled by Rome – the former Franciscan priest Leonardo Boff, who was condemned to 'obsequious silence' and suspended from his religious duties by the Congregation for the Doctrine of the Faith for his theology. It is a measure of the extent of his turnaround that Pope Francis asked Boff to send him his writings on eco-theology in preparation for a major encyclical Francis is considering on environmental matters.

'Getting involved in politics is a Christian duty', Pope Francis told an audience of young students in June 2013 in Rome. 'We

Christians cannot be like Pilate and wash our hands clean of things. We need to get involved in politics because it's one of the highest expressions of charity. It takes the common into consideration. Lay Christians must work in politics. That's no easy task you might say. But it isn't an easy task becoming a priest either! Politics is dirty but the reason it has become dirty is that Christians didn't get deeply enough involved in the evangelical spirit. It's easy to find excuses for this … but what do I do? Working for the common good is a Christian duty.'

In Bergoglio is to be found a figure who bridges one of the great divides in Catholicism, said the 2012 Nobel Peace Prize nominee and Argentinean social activist Juan Carr. The faith is split, he said, between 'a Church completely focused on the spiritual side' and 'a Church that's completely committed to the social issues but without addressing the devotional needs of the people. Bergoglio is a rare figure who transcends that divide.'

What shines through all this change is that Bergoglio is a pragmatist rather than an ideologue. In his more conservative younger years he adopted pre-Vatican II styles of worship, discipline and theology because he thought they worked better, said his 1975 student Humberto Miguel Yáñez. But as a bishop and archbishop he embraced many of the central doctrines of Liberation Theology – especially those relating to poverty, inequality and economic justice – because they now fitted his changed priorities. His contact with the popular piety of ordinary people had knocked out of him any tendencies towards the Tridentine which may have seemed attractive when he was Jesuit Provincial in the 1970s and hankered after those pre-conciliar liturgical and academic styles. In his later years he saw clearly that worship in the vernacular, with guitars, clapping and in the liturgical reforms of Vatican II, appealed more directly to the plain people who became his priority in his later years. Anyone who doubts that should watch the videos of his inter- active, almost pantomimic *porteño* style of preaching in his Masses in the slums or scrutinise the homeliness of his papal homiletics.

As Provincial in the 1970s he was severe in his instructions to his Jesuits that they must serve only in parishes and not in Liberation Theology's smaller bottom-up base communities where lay men and women took the place of priests and the poor learned to read and interpret the Bible for themselves. Yet as Archbishop he reversed his earlier attitude, giving the exact opposite instructions. When religious sociologists discovered that a parish had a zone of influence which typically radiated 700 metres around its church, Bergoglio told his priests – knowing that Buenos Aires churches were on average 2,000 metres apart – to set up something in between the churches:

'If you can, rent a garage and find some willing layman, let him go there, do a little catechesis, and even give Communion', he instructed his priests.

'But if we do this people won't come to Church any more', one priest replied.

'Do they come to Mass now?' Bergoglio inquired pointedly.

The new Bergoglio would have shocked the old Bergoglio with the scathing critique he delivered in 2010 of a clericalism which puts the clergy at the centre of the Church in a way which infantilises the ordinary people where they need empowering. 'Priests and bishops [are] falling into clericalism, which is a distortion of religion', he told Rabbi Skorka in one of their conversations. 'The Catholic Church is the entire People of God, including priests. When a priest leads a diocese or a parish, he has to listen to his community, to make mature decisions and lead the community accordingly. By contrast, when the priest imposes himself, when in some way he says "I am the boss here", he falls into clericalism.'

In his years in Buenos Aires Bergoglio was anxious to put that into practice. 'He was also concerned with getting the laity active,' as his aide Federico Wals has said, 'and letting them take charge.' This was in line with the classic Liberation Theology vision of all the Latin America bishops assembled at Puebla in 1979 that the poor should be agents and not merely recipients. Bergoglio wanted it to become a permanent feature of the Church that it should not depend on whoever happened to be in charge at any given time for

the Church to act out its mission in a way in which all had a part
to play.

That sense was underscored by his experiences with Rome.
Bishops around the world were treated in the same infantilising
manner by the Vatican that many priests imposed upon the laity.
Though Jesuits swear a special oath of loyalty to the Pope, Bergoglio
became increasingly disillusioned with the way that the Pope's
underlings in practice restrained the autonomy bishops should
properly possess. He was unhappy with Rome's response to what he
saw as constructive criticisms of Benedict XVI's ill-judged remarks
about Islam at Regensburg. He resented the Curia's repeated
refusal to accept his nominations for new Argentinean bishops. He
was irritated by the high-handed advice of what his former aide
Guillermo Marcó called 'Italians with emptying churches telling
bishops in countries with growing congregations what they should
and should not be doing'. He resented the way some in Rome
colluded with the ultra-traditionalists in the Argentinean church
who, like school sneaks running to the headmaster, persistently
complained to the Vatican about him behind his back. All this
instilled in him the importance of the Church being run more
collegially, so much so that he stuck to the principle of collegiality among the Argentinean bishops during his six years as their
president – even when their decisions were not ones he agreed with,
as over civil unions for same-sex couples.

***

But something more significant than all this happened to Jorge
Mario Bergoglio which changed him dramatically. It was much
more than changed circumstance or learning from experience. All
that might have changed his head. But something also changed his
heart. Many years after Fr Franz Jalics and his fellow slum priest
Fr Orlando Yorio had been released from their illegal detention, in
Germany there was a meeting between Jalics and Bergoglio, who
was by then the Archbishop of Buenos Aires. After Bergoglio was

elected Pope a statement was issued by Jalics from behind the closed walls of his Bavarian retreat house. It said that the two men had met and concelebrated Mass together, ending with what Jalics called 'a solemn embrace'. What an eyewitness says actually happened was that the only time the two men met, many years later in Germany, they fell into each other's arms and cried. There was more than a change of politics about the encounter. It was the visceral intermingling of relief, remorse and repentance. The change within Jorge Mario Bergoglio, it seemed, sprang from deep within his soul.

When the new auxiliary bishop of Buenos Aires arrived back in the city after his exile in Córdoba in 1992, he came having made a key decision. It was that he would begin as a bishop in an entirely different way to how he had acted as the leader of the Argentine Jesuits. Bergoglio had lost none of his steely sense of purpose. But his style was consultative, delegatory and participative. And his manner was distinctly different. From the outset humility was his watchword.

Humility is a much-misunderstood quality in the contemporary world, where it is a quality in short supply. It is not, as is often assumed, some kind of synonym for shyness, reticence, bashfulness or lack of ambition; humility is not a character trait with which some are born, rather it is the orphaned virtue which our age has publicly forgotten how to embrace. For Bergoglio in 1992 humility was more like an intellectual stance than a personal temperament. 'He's worked out that to be a good Shepherd he needs to be humble', said Augusto Zampini. 'It's calculated. That's not to suggest it's fake but it is thought-through.' More than that, it has been nurtured, suggested Bergoglio's friend Rabbi Abraham Skorka: 'he's developed it through spiritual exercises.' Bergoglio's humility is a religious decision, according to Bishop Jorge Eduardo Lozano of Gualeguaychú, who was Bergoglio's auxiliary in Buenos Aires for six years. His humility and simplicity are 'actually an expression of his magisterium'.

Bergoglio's critics have claimed there is something cynical in the change. Too humble is half proud, as the Yiddish proverb has it. Bergoglio's nemesis, the investigative journalist Horacio Verbitsky has gone so far as to suggest that the series of interviews Bergoglio gave in 2010 to Rubin and Ambrogetti for *El Jesuita* were a Machiavellian attempt by Bergoglio to clean up his image after the dossier at the 2005 conclave had so damaged his chances of rivalling Joseph Ratzinger for the papacy. Bergoglio's political opponents in Argentina have seen many of the great gestures he has made since becoming Pope as gimmicky or even hypocritical PR stunts.

This is too conspiratorial. Pope Francis's decision to take the bus with the cardinals after his election, instead of taking a chauffeur-driven official limousine, was just a reprise of his routinely taking Linea A on the Buenos Aires subway for years. Sitting in his papal white in the back row in the Vatican church of Santa Anna merely continued his longstanding habit as a bishop of always taking a seat in the lowest place. Bowing his head for the blessing of the people of Rome at his first appearance on the balcony of St Peter's was no different to kneeling for a blessing from a stadium full of Argentinean evangelical Protestants.

Certainly Bergoglio in all phases of his life has been a shrewd politician, but there has been more to that than sheer ambition. Throughout his career Bergoglio has shown significant courage. It was a bold tactic to ask a priest to feign illness so Bergoglio could gain access to the leader of the military junta during the Dirty War. It took strength of character to stand by Clelia Luro, the widow of the ostracised bishop Jerónimo Podestá, when no other bishop would, after her husband died. There were repeated examples of his personal bravery smuggling out victims of the military dictatorship, standing up to the drug gangs in the slums and sticking to his principles on interfaith dialogue despite accusations of heresy, apostasy and disloyalty by ultra-traditionalists in Argentina and Rome. At the same time it is clear that his decision to embrace radical humility was something of a struggle against his own personality with its dogmatic and authoritarian streaks. There is evidence of that in a whole range of incidents. At its most trivial was the row over the cakes in the Jesuit residence on his return from Germany.

At its more grave was his unco-operative and even evasive performance in the witness box during the ESMA trials where he appeared to put the defence of the institutional Church before the pursuit of the full truth – the opposite of the strategy he has embraced on sex abuse in the Church. On the Church and the Dirty War he clearly felt that the collusion in the dictatorship by members of the Church, to a very senior level, was so deep and wide that individual accusations and recriminations would damage, rather than help, wider Argentinean society. Some things are best left buried, be believed, because too many people are guilty in some degree. Many suspect that he is wrong about that. He may yet change his view. As Pope he has already had a brief meeting with representatives of the Grandmothers of Plaza de Mayo who are hopeful he will instruct that the records of the Argentinean Church be opened to outside scrutiny, even as Rabbi Skorka hopes he will do the same with the Vatican archives on the role of Pius XII. The journey from Bergoglio to Francis may mean that change is not yet complete.

For the change in Jorge Mario Bergoglio may not have been triggered by an event so much as a process. Bergoglio's key decisions are all made during his long sessions of daily prayer. It is difficult to overstate the importance of prayer in his life, says his former close aide Guillermo Marcó: 'He liked to wake at 4.30 a.m. to 5 a.m. every morning to pray. He makes decisions while he prays.' Prayer, Bergoglio has said, 'should be an experience of giving way, of surrendering, where our entire being enters into the presence of God'. In *El Jesuita* he said: 'This is where dialogue, listening, and transformation occur. Looking at God, but above all sensing that we are being watched by Him. This happens, in my case, when I recite the rosary or the psalms or when I joyfully celebrate the Eucharist. But the moment when I most savour the religious experience is when I am before the tabernacle. Sometimes I allow myself to fall asleep while sitting there and just let Him look at me. I have the sense of being in someone else's hands, as though God were taking me by the hand.' In Buenos Aires he often prayed for two hours before the start of his day.

It was because prayer was so important to him, said Marcó, that he would rarely accept invitations to dinner as Archbishop of Buenos Aires. 'He knew that if he accepted invitations for evening events he wouldn't get up early. And he did not want to miss that prayer time. He has a very strong relationship with God. He doesn't have very many friends. He's a solitary man. In the eight years I worked with him I only ate with him about five times though I saw him every day. He's always been, I'd say, monkish in his lifestyle. His main relationship is with God.'

The many people with whom Bergoglio stays in touch, particularly those in Buenos Aires who still receive weekly phone calls from him, might be surprised to hear Bergoglio described as a solitary man. But Marcó is adamant. 'He has a pastoral care for people', his former aide said. 'He keeps dates and numbers in his little work book and rings people on their birthday, on the anniversary of a loved one's death, or with a few people every Sunday afternoon. He keeps in touch. He has an interest in people. He worries about them. But it's a kind of pastoral concern rather than friendship. If you define friendship as having fun with people then he has no friends. Friendship is a symmetrical relationship. His relationships are not like that. People believe they are his friends but he never goes to dinner at their homes. He doesn't even see his family at Christmas. He is quite happy after the Christmas service to go to cook for priests and people in the slums and then go home to his room on his own. He is quite content. It's the life he has chosen. It's not mawkish. In his own time he wants to be alone.'

Except that he is not alone. He is with God. 'Prayer is talking and listening', Bergoglio has said. 'Prayer is an act of freedom but sometimes it emerges as an attempt at control, which is the same as wanting to control God.' Yet there are also 'moments of profound silence, adoration, waiting to see what will happen'. In prayer, 'this reverent silence coexists together with a sort of haggling'. In the end what Bergoglio does, he said, is 'put myself in the presence of God and, aided by His Word, go forward in what he desires'.

In prayer Jorge Mario Bergoglio is struggling against his own personality to become the person he believes God wants him to be. Over the years the Ignatian exercises at the heart of Jesuit spirituality have honed and refined his instincts in this. It is this which most opened Bergoglio's capacity to change. Examination of conscience, exercises in empathy, and a cultivated process of discernment are at the heart of Ignatian spirituality. The founder of the Jesuits, St Ignatius of Loyola, devised a series of Spiritual Exercises which are meditations and contemplations whose aim is 'to conquer oneself and to regulate one's life in such a way that no decision is made under the influence of any inordinate attachment'. The goal is to create a spiritual detachment or indifference to an individual's own 'likes, dislikes, comforts, wants, needs, drives, appetites and passions' so that they may be able to discern what is God's will for them.

If it is impossible for us to see into another's soul, the exercises have made Jorge Mario Bergoglio see further into his own. And the clues to what he has seen over the years, and continues to see, have been evident in what he has said as well as done. Of the errors he committed as Provincial, he said in his interviews with Rubin and Ambrogetti: 'It would be wrong for me to say that these days I ask forgiveness for the sins and offences that I might have committed. Today I ask forgiveness for the sins and offences that I did indeed commit.' Guilt, Bergoglio said in his conversations with Rabbi Skorka, can be just a psychological feeling which is not a religious experience. 'Guilt by itself … is just another human resource. Guilt, without atonement, does not allow us to grow.' He returned to the subject in *El Jesuita*. 'There's no clean slate', he said. 'We have to bless the past with remorse, forgiveness, and atonement.' Regret is not sufficient; there has to be change. By changing his style of spiritual leadership so radically Bergoglio is saying to the world that he has made a change of heart and a change of behaviour is its fruit. Just before he left for Rome and the conclave Bergoglio penned what turned out to be his last Lenten message to the people of Buenos Aires. Morality, he said, is not a 'never falling down' but an 'always getting up again'. And that is a response to God's mercy.

Mercy has been the greatest of his themes as Pope. It was the subject of his homily on the first Sunday after his election as Pope. 'Mercy is the Lord's most powerful message', he told the congregation in the little Church of Saint Anna located within the Vatican. 'It is not easy to trust oneself to the mercy of God, because [God's mercy] is an unfathomable abyss – but we must do it.' From Jesus, he said, we will 'not hear words of contempt, we do not hear words of condemnation, but only words of love, of mercy, that invite us to conversion. "Neither do I condemn you. Go and sin no more!"... The problem is that we get tired of asking forgiveness. Let us never get tired. He is the loving Father who always forgives, who has that heart of mercy for all of us.' Bergoglio has changed, is the message, but changes will continue for Francis too. The man who is now Pope remains, he is telling us, a work in progress.

7

Francis – A Man to Change History

'He can't go in those shoes', said one of the priests in the Metropolitan Cathedral at Buenos Aires to a colleague. Cardinal Jorge Mario Bergoglio was about to set off for Rome and the conclave to elect a successor to Pope Benedict XVI. On his feet was an extremely shabby pair of plain black shoes. He had had them for years but he liked their simplicity with their smooth toe and no decorations. They were exceedingly comfortable. And who needs, he said, more than one pair of shoes? But it would be embarrassing if the Archbishop of Buenos Aires turned up in the Vatican wearing those, the priest said, and persuaded several friends to club together to raise the cash to buy their cardinal a new pair. Bergoglio was duly grateful. 'Thank you very much', he said, and promptly put the new shoes away and set off to catch the bus to the airport wearing his old ones.

The Vatican had sent him a first-class ticket, but he refused to use it and travelled in economy for the thirteen-hour flight to Rome. The only concession to comfort he made was to request a seat by the emergency exit where there was more legroom. He had a bad knee and hip, he explained. On a previous trip to Rome the journey had provoked an attack of sciatica so bad he had to stay in bed and miss the meeting he had gone for. He did not want that to happen this time. The Alitalia crew put him in Row 25 and he settled in for the long flight.

He arrived in Rome one day before the date that Pope Benedict XVI had designated that his resignation would take effect and the See of Rome would become vacant. Bergoglio had booked a room, as he always did, at the international clergy hostel, the *Domus Internationalis Paulus Sixtus* in Via della Scrofa, whose occupants were still coming to terms with the first resignation by a Pope in 600 years – and already indulging in speculation about who were the likely candidates to succeed him. The Italian press were pretty clear that the next Pope would be Cardinal Angelo Scola of Milan. He had as many as 50 votes already in the bag, said *Corriere della Sera*. And only 77 were needed to reach the necessary two-thirds majority. And Joseph Ratzinger had coasted to the papacy last time after reportedly starting with 47 cardinals backing him in the first ballot of the conclave.

The talk in Rome was that Pope Benedict wanted one of two cardinals to succeed him, and had shown this by how he had recently promoted them. The first was the Canadian cardinal Marc Ouellet, whom he had transferred in 2010 from the Archdiocese of Quebec to the Vatican to run the Congregation for Bishops. As the man in charge of the appointment of new bishops, that post would mean he would have cardinals from all over the world vying for his attention. He would make the necessary contacts. The second man was Cardinal Scola. Benedict broke the usual conventions by moving him from the prestigious post of Patriarch of Venice in 2011 to become Archbishop of Milan, which for centuries had been seen as a staging post to the papacy. The three popes before Pope John Paul II had all come from Milan or Venice. Many saw it as the anointing of a successor for, surely, after a Polish then a German pope it was time to return to an Italian. Both Ouellet and Scola had in earlier days worked on *Communio*, the journal Ratzinger had founded to stem the liberal spirit unleashed by Vatican II.

The Italian press was sure it would be Scola. They all agreed he had dozens of votes in the bag. But to make the race sound more interesting they tossed in a few other candidates. As well as Ouellet there were Odilo Scherer of Brazil, Peter Turkson of Ghana, Francisco Robles Ortega of Mexico and Luis Antonio Tagle of the Philippines. Longer shots were said to be Sean O'Malley of Boston, Timothy Dolan of New York and Christoph Schönborn of Austria. Some even floated Francis Arinze of Nigeria even though he was over 80 and not eligible to vote for the new pope. In the days before the conclave began, various cardinals were being quoted in the Italian newspapers saying there were half a dozen to a dozen possible candidates. It was going to be a long conclave, they suggested.

Hardly anyone even mentioned Jorge Mario Bergoglio. Some did not realise he had been the runner-up last time. Of those who did, some shrugged that you didn't get a second chance at the papacy or just said that, at 76, he was too old, since many cardinals had said that, after Pope Benedict's age-increasing infirmity, they would not vote for anyone over 70. Bergoglio was so off the radar of the media that when he slipped into the Synod Hall for the first of the cardinals' pre-conclave meetings he went largely unnoticed. Anyone who had been reckless enough to put a bet on him would have got odds of 30 to 1 against him being elected.

The international media read the election so poorly because they tend to take their lead from the seemingly well-informed Italian journalists. The problem was that, with a few exceptions, the resident press got most of their information from Italian cardinals, which created an entirely misrepresentative picture.

Inside the hall were gathered most of the 115 cardinals who would vote. Also there were a significant number of cardinals over 80, and thus ineligible to vote, but able to make a contribution in the seven pre-conclave assemblies known as General Congregations. These would not discuss individual candidates but would explore the general issues thought to be facing the Church. Two cardinals were noticeably absent: Julius Darmaatmadja, from Indonesia, was too ill and the disgraced Keith O'Brien from Scotland had stayed away after being accused of sexual misconduct towards priests.

The Church's maladroit handling of the scandal of sex abuse by priests – and the hierarchy's bungled attempts to cover it up – was one of the issues uppermost in the mind of the cardinals. But that was only part of what was widely seen as a dysfunctional Vatican bureaucracy in which various Curia departments were operating in an autonomous and high-handed manner, issuing instructions to bishops around the world with the authority of the Pope but without his knowledge. The Vatileaks scandal – which saw the leaking of confidential documents Pope Benedict had marked to be destroyed – had only made public what individual bishops abroad knew from personal experience. By the morning of the first General Congregation there was already a clear consensus that the new Pope needed to be a strong administrator – and probably a Vatican outsider – to clear up the mess.

Usually the first days of a pre-conclave General Congregation are taken up with organising the funeral of the pope who has just died. After a long papacy, like that of John Paul II, there is a need for cardinals, many of whom have not met before, to get to know one another. But this time was different. Some cardinals had to resort to Googling one another, but 50 of the 115 cardinal electors had been present at the 2005 conclave and knew one another and also had views on how things should be done. Pope Benedict had put into their minds a new possibility: that a pontiff could resign. That altered many cardinals' thinking about the age of the next pope; an older man could be elected because he could resign if he became too infirm to do the job. And because the previous pope was not dead, and there was no mood of grief, so it became easier for the electors to scrutinise the previous papacy without emotion. They concluded for all Benedict XVI's strengths as shepherd and teacher he had been lamentably weak as a governor. Some unusually frank public discussions followed.

There was a pointed exchange of views on the running of the Roman Curia, the Church's central administration. The Brazilian cardinal João Bráz de Aviz was widely applauded after criticising Benedict XVI's *de facto* prime minister Cardinal Tarcisio Bertone, the outgoing Secretary of State, for his poor management, inept diplomacy, inadequate supervision of the Institute for Works of Religion (the official name of the Vatican Bank) and general lack of coordination. Some senior cardinals had gone to Pope Benedict a few years earlier and asked him to sack Bertone, but the Pope had refused; now they said in public what Benedict XVI had refused to heed in private. The report of the three cardinals commissioned by Benedict to investigate the Curia in the light of the Vatileaks scandal was, one cardinal told me, 'like an additional elector in the room'; its contents were not available to cardinals – Benedict XVI had locked it away in a safe for the eyes of his successor only – but the three authors of the report, all cardinals over the age of 80, were in the Congregations and made themselves available for some discreet one-to-one conversations with their peers as requested. Other cardinals used more coded language about the need for the new pope to govern in a more collegial manner, but beneath the cautious language, as Cardinal Cormac Murphy O'Connor told me, 'everyone knew what the message was': the Curia should have less say and bishops round the world should have more.

There was a second key area around which consensus began to emerge among many electors. It was a shared sense that the Church needed to leave behind the old-fashioned culture wars over which Benedict XVI had presided in his attempts to reinforce Catholicism's identity, particularly in its historic home, Europe, following the collapse of the Church's influence in the face of a rising and sometimes aggressive secularism. The German pope had tried to foster in Catholics a siege mentality in which a 'creative' remnant of the Church would nurture a purer doctrine to resist the tide of secularism across the Western world. 'Cardinals felt that after Benedict they wanted to press the reset button and go back eight years', another insider said. The speakers were not openly critical of Benedict, but were clear on the areas in which they thought he had been deficient.

Cardinals had begun to divide into two main camps. One wanted a pope who would reform the Vatican. The other wanted to defend the Curia and keep it in the hands of a Roman insider. But who should be the champion of each cause? This was where Cardinal Scola began to run into difficulties. There were cardinals on one side claiming that he would be an effective reformer because he knew well how the system worked. And there were electors on the other side insisting he would defend the interests of the status quo. Geography proved not to be so much a factor in the election as some had predicted. There were twenty-eight cardinals from Italy and eleven from the United States compared with just nineteen from the whole of Latin America, the region with the world's largest Catholic population. But the Italians were not united behind a single candidate. And Cardinal Odilo Scherer, the Archbishop of São Paulo in Brazil was widely seen not as a candidate to unite the developing world so much as a representative of the curial old guard, since he had worked for many years in the Vatican and was of German extraction. He defended the Curia when his fellow Brazilian João Bráz de Aviz attacked it. A number of cardinals began to become convinced that the next pope should come not only from outside Europe but also be among those who had not spent years working in Rome. Some electors began to look to Cardinal Luis Antonio Tagle of Manila in the Philippines, a media-savvy intellectual with a man-of-the-people touch, but he was just 55 and a very new cardinal and ruled out as too young, this time.

The eleven cardinals from the United States had a particular influence on events. In part this was because they were the biggest single bloc outside the disunited Italians; in part it was because of their savvy use of the media. They held daily press conferences until they were stopped, apparently on the instructions of Secretary of State Bertone. But that development only further strengthened the general agreement for reform. It was symptomatic of the problems with the Vatican that transparent communication was curbed, leaving the Italians to carry on their backdoor briefing and leaking.

The man assumed to be the front-runner, Cardinal Scola of Milan, however did not shine in the Congregations. His complex Italianate way of speaking made little impact. But one speech did. It was from Jorge Mario Bergoglio. Towards the end of the week Bergoglio took the podium and, speaking in Italian, offered a short contribution in which he made one simple point in several striking phrases:

The only purpose of the Church is to go out to tell the world the good news about Jesus Christ, the cardinal from Argentina said. It needed to surge forth to the peripheries, not just geographically but to the existential peripheries where people grappled with sin, pain, injustice, ignorance and indifference to religion.

But the Church had got too wrapped up in itself. It was too navel-gazing. It had become 'self-referential' which had made it sick. It was suffering a 'kind of theological narcissism'. When Jesus said: 'Behold I stand at the door and knock' people assumed he was outside, wanting to come in. But sometimes Jesus knocks from within, wanting to be let out into the wider world. A self-referential Church wants to keep Jesus to itself, instead of letting him out to others.

The Church is supposed to be the *mysterium lunae* – the mystery of the moon is that it has no light but simply reflects the light of the sun. The Church must not fool itself that it has light of its own; if it does that it falls in to what Henri De Lubac in *The Splendour of the Church* called the greatest of evils – spiritual worldliness. That is what happens with a self-referential Church, which refuses to go beyond itself.

Put simply, there are two images of Church: a Church which evange-lises and comes out of herself or a worldly Church, living within herself, of herself, for herself. The next Pope should be someone who helps the Church surge forth to the peripheries like a sweet and comforting mother who offers the joy of Jesus to the world.

The speech lasted just three-and-a-half minutes – instead of the five allotted to each cardinal – but it electrified the synod hall. 'Bergoglio was the first man not to be introspective about the problems of the Church but to be outgoing,' said Cardinal Cormac Murphy O'Connor, 'he was more spiritual and more theological' – and, as several cardinals said in the same shared phrase afterwards, 'he spoke from the heart'. It was very simple, very spiritual, and it touched on the urgent necessity for renewal. Cardinal Schönborn turned to a neighbour and said: 'That's what we need.'

The Archbishop of Havana, Cardinal Jaime Ortega y Alamino, was so struck by the force of the speech that he asked Bergoglio for the text. Bergoglio had spoken only from a few scribbled notes but overnight he transcribed from memory what he had said and gave the text to Ortega. The Cuban asked if he could distribute it and, when Bergoglio gave his consent, Ortega put it on his diocesan website. Cardinals found the text repaid study. The *mysterium lunae* was a concept which originated with the Church Fathers: '*fulget Ecclesia non suo sed Christi lumine* – the Church shines not with its own light, but with that of Christ', St Ambrose had said. But it was an image which had been used by both Popes John Paul II and Benedict XVI. It spoke of both continuity and change. There was a rich ambiguity too in a phrase like 'the periphery', which in Italian had resonances of the *periferia* – the parts of Europe's cities where the poorest residents, including the immigrants, live. The echoes of the indignities of poverty and the needs of social justice were clear. It was a speech, said Ortega, which seemed 'masterful, enlightening, challenging and true'.

In the final days, as Congregations gave way to conclave, the discussion moved, Cardinal Cormac Murphy O'Connor told me, 'from just the need for good governance to the need for a Pope deeply rooted in the gospel – a new style in the Church and a new style of papacy'. The Bergoglio candidacy began to take shape. Cardinals began to examine his background. The liberals highlighted a personal lifestyle which rejects the modern consumerist vision of life. The conservatives that his family background and culture made him 'Italo-compatible'. As a cardinal who never worked in the Roman Curia, with a track record of criticising careerism and ambition, Bergoglio appealed to those who saw reform of the Vatican bureaucracy as a top priority. The more assiduous looked into the 2007 Aparecida document, produced following the Fifth General Conference of the Latin American and Caribbean Bishops' Conference, which Bergoglio had the main hand in writing. They found it spoke of the same themes of taking the gospel out to where people were instead of waiting in vain for them to come to the Church. It was also strong, they noted, on collegiality, which was a repeated theme of the pre-conclave Congregations, with the idea being floated that perhaps the new pope needed to create a group of cardinals that he could consult with regularly as a sort of 'council of elders'. (Pope Francis was to set this up within his first month.) Bergoglio maintained a low profile, as had long been his habit, but in the meetings, lunches, dinners and coffee breaks that followed his name became part of the wider conversation.

Yet, despite all this, the talk in media circles was still of Scola as the man who could attract votes from both camps. What the press failed to pick up was that leading European moderates Cardinals André Vingt-Trois of Paris and Walter Kasper, the man previously in charge of promoting Christian Unity for the Vatican, had begun lobbying their peers – who counted for 15 to 20 votes – saying Bergoglio was the man. Among the Latin Americans Cardinal Oscar Rodríguez Maradiaga of Honduras, who had once himself been considered a contender to be pope, was briefing on behalf of Bergoglio.

Bergoglio began to suspect that he would be going into the conclave on Tuesday 12 March as a candidate. Two days before, he was walking through the Piazza Navona, not far from the clergy house in the Via della Scrofa, when he met Fr Thomas Rosica, a Canadian broadcaster who helped out in the Vatican press office when times were busy. The Argentine, Roscia said later, looked agitated. Bergoglio stopped and grabbed Rosica's hands. 'I want you to pray for me', the cardinal told the priest. 'Are you nervous?' Rosica asked. 'A little bit', Bergoglio confessed.

Next morning Bergoglio was up early for Mass in the Domus. It was the last day of the General Congregations. The conclave would start twenty-four hours later. It was 6.30 a.m. A young priest was preparing to say Mass in the chapel. Bergoglio did not pull rank and take the altar. The priest said the Mass with the man who would next day be Pope as his altar server.

There was just one vote on the afternoon of the first day of the conclave. Black smoke coming out of the Sistine Chapel's chimney indicated that the first ballot was inconclusive. Cardinals in a conclave are sworn to secrecy but enough reports eventually emerge, via non-voting cardinals and well-informed Vaticaniste journalists, to piece together a good idea of what transpired. Inside the front-runner Scola had not done anywhere near as well as the Italian press had anticipated. He had topped the poll, but only with 35 votes, it was said. Bergoglio had 20 votes and Ouellet 15. The 28 Italians, it turned out, had split over Scola. Big figures like Angelo Bagnasco of Genoa, president of the Italian bishops, and Carlo Caffarra of Bologna had backed him. But Bertone and the Dean of the College of Cardinals, Angelo Sodano had rallied significant numbers of the Italians to an 'anyone but Scola' stance. The Italian contingent were in chaos, with some seeing Scola as a threat to the vested interests of cardinals serving in the Curia and others insisting he was too close to the centre of power to initiate thorough-going change. There was talk of 'betrayal' in the Italian camp as the conclave ended for the day and the cardinals went off for dinner.

Over the tables of the Casa Santa Marta, and afterwards in huddles over coffee or smoking outside on the patio, the chief theme was that Scola could not make it. The Brazilian Scherer, who had been the preferred candidate of Bertone and many in the Curia, had performed far more weakly than anyone expected. His candidacy had been adversely affected by his defence of Bertone in the final Congregation after the attack on the Italian by Scherer's fellow Brazilian Braz de Aviz, who reportedly had a quite vocal spat with Bertone during the last day of General Congregations, on Monday. Many expected Scherer to tell his followers to now back Scola, but over dinner it was said Scherer was directing his support to Bergoglio. The reform camp had already begun to coalesce about Bergoglio. In the American camp the moderate Archbishop of Washington, Donald Wuerl began pressing the eleven cardinals from the United States, some of whom had voted for Cardinal Timothy Dolan of New York in the first round, to swing behind Bergoglio.

Next morning, when the second ballot was counted, Scola's candidacy had stalled and support for Dolan had fallen. Votes started to converge around Ouellet as the conservative candidate and Bergoglio for reform, though Scola still retained a significant number of electors' support. By the third ballot it looked as though Bergoglio might be the next pope. When they broke for lunch Bergoglio seemed 'very weighed down by what was happening', said the Archbishop of Boston, Cardinal Sean O'Malley, who sat by him. In the dining room over lunch Ouellet told his supporters to back Bergoglio. So did Scola, whose support had remained steady until the third ballot but who could by then see he had entirely lost momentum. By the fourth ballot, the first after lunch, Bergoglio took the lead in the voting and was not far off the required two-thirds majority. With each round his vote had grown. As the fifth ballot was being cast, and then counted, Bergoglio sat looking serious and slightly dazed. At his side his old friend Claudio Hummes, the former Archbishop of São Paulo, sat supportively.

The votes were counted by three cardinals randomly chosen to act as Scrutineers. As the votes were unfolded each Scrutineer read the vote and made a record of each individual result on a tally sheet. The final Scrutineer read the name each time aloud. When the vote was read which meant that Cardinal Jorge Mario Bergoglio, the Archbishop of Buenos Aires, had passed the 77 votes required, applause broke out in the Sistine Chapel. When the final vote was read aloud Bergoglio had 90 of the 115 possible votes. The Catholic Church had a new Pope.

Finally, when the tally had been made, the assistant Cardinal Dean, Giovanni Battista Re approached Bergoglio.

'Acceptasne electionem de te canonice factam in Summum Pontificem?' he asked. Do you accept your canonical election as Supreme Pontiff?

'Accepto' is the normal response. But Jorge Mario Bergoglio said: 'I am a great sinner, trusting in the mercy and patience of God in suffering, I accept.' Even at this moment, or perhaps especially now, the remorseful awareness of his past was in his consciousness.

'Quo nomine vis vocari?' What name do you take?

'Vocabor Franciscus.' I will be called Francis.

At the name the cardinals cheered. But no Pope had ever taken the name Francis before. Some eyebrows were raised. More than a few wondered what they had let themselves in for.

It did not take them long to begin to work it out. Over the centuries a comparatively small list of standard papal names has evolved. At one time popes simply used their baptismal name but when a pagan convert to Christianity became Pope in 533 he changed his name from Mercury to John II. Over the years John has been taken 23 times, Gregory and Benedict 16 times each, Clement 14, Leo 13, Pius 12, Stephen 9, and Boniface, Alexander and Urban eight times. Not since the tenth century has a pontiff – Pope Lando – ventured right outside this nominal mainstream and since the eleventh century only two Popes have not changed their names on election. Over those years the choice of name has come to represent either an indication of intended direction or a gesture of continuity, gratitude or respect to their predecessor. John Paul I chose his as a joint tribute to his two predecessors – John XXIII and Paul VI – and added the numeral I to his name, something Francis has chosen not to do. He will remain plain Pope Francis until some successor might chose to become Pope Francis II. The Polish pope, Karol Wojtyla, who it is said had to be dissuaded from taking the name Stanislaus after the eleventh-century Polish martyr bishop, took John Paul II to honour the untimely death of his predecessor who was Pope for just thirty-three days. Bergoglio, by choosing Francis, indicated that he intended the trajectory of his pontificate to be a radical break with the past. Not many of the cardinals would have read his book of conversations with Rabbi Abraham Skorka. Had they done, they would have known that he once said of St Francis of Assisi: 'He brought to Christianity an entire new concept about poverty in the face of the luxury, pride and vanity of the civil and ecclesial powers of the time. He changed history.'

A few days later Pope Francis gave a clear indication of his programmatic intent when he explained his choice of name to the media. 'Some people wanted to know why the Bishop of Rome wished to be called Francis', he said. 'Some thought of Francis

Xavier, Francis de Sales, and also Francis of Assisi. I will tell you the story. During the election, I was seated next to the Archbishop Emeritus of Sao Paulo and Prefect Emeritus of the Congregation for the Clergy, Cardinal Claudio Hummes: a good friend, a good friend! When things were looking dangerous, he encouraged me. And when the votes reached two-thirds, there was the usual applause, because the Pope had been elected. And he gave me a hug and a kiss, and said: "Don't forget the poor!" And those words came to me: the poor, the poor. Then, right away, thinking of the poor, I thought of Francis of Assisi. Then I thought of all the wars, as the votes were still being counted, till the end. Francis is also the man of peace. That is how the name came into my heart: Francis of Assisi.'

But when the white smoke ascended from the chimney of the Sistine Chapel at 19:06 (Rome time) on 13 March 2013, announcing that a Pope had been chosen, the huge crowd gathered in the heavy rain in St Peter's Square were unaware of the name. They cheered rapturously at the smoke and waved flags from all around the globe as the great bells of the basilica rang out. *Habemus papam* – we have a Pope – the crowd began to chant, happy that there was a new Pope even if they did not know who he was.

Inside the Vatican they were beginning to learn exactly who Bergoglio was. The new Pope was led by the Papal Master of Liturgical Ceremonies, Mgr Guido Marini, to the robing area in a small sacristy to the left of the High Altar just off the Sistine Chapel. The vestibule is known as the Room of Tears. It is the first place a new Pope is accorded a degree of privacy after the long and public process of the conclave. It is in this time and space that the burden of the high office can make itself felt. Bergoglio saw papal vestments in three different sizes hanging from a rail and red papal shoes resting in tissue-papered boxes in five different sizes. The rest of the world was waiting, thinking of a new chapter in the history of the Church. But the thoughts of the new pontiff often cling to the old life they realise they have left behind. Bergoglio will have known that he might never again see the little room in Buenos Aires that had been his spartan home for eighteen years with his modest music collection of classical music, tango and opera; his poster of his beloved San Lorenzo football team signed by all the players; his individual photographs of recovered drug addicts from the slums; and the crucifix of his Grandma Rosa hanging over the simple wooden bed. He would not deliver the sermon he had prepared for Easter Sunday which was lying on his desk there. He would never use the return portion of the airline ticket on which his journey home had been booked for 23 March.

At the rail of papal vestments Pope Francis changed from his scarlet cardinal's robes into a plain white cassock with a watered silk sash. Then the Master of Ceremonies offered the new Pope the traditional ceremonial elbow-length red velvet cape, trimmed with ermine – the *mozzetta*. Benedict XVI had been keen on papal fashions. He wore violet copes, blue chasubles and a furry white paschal mozzetta not seen since the days of Pope Paul VI for the spring season. He rediscovered the stripey papal collar known as the *fanon* and a faintly preposterous hat called the *camauro*, dating back to the twelfth century but which would look at home on one of Santa's gnomes. In the days after the Pope's election a story began to circulate in Rome that Francis had spurned the mozzetta, when it was offered by Marini, with the words: 'No, thank you, Monsignore. Carnival time is over.' What he actually said was: 'I prefer not to.' Humiliating a papal servant is not Bergoglio's style. But the message was the same. 'He doesn't like the trappings of monarchy that surround the papacy', his old friend Rabbi Skorka told me. 'He rang the other day. He's feeling very at peace with himself.'

The other signals to the papal courtiers were clear. He declined a jewel-studded gold pectoral cross and pulled on the old pewter-coloured cross he had worn since he became a bishop in Argentina. There would be no papal cufflinks. Then an assistant asked his shoe size and pointed to the boxes of red shoes which represented another tradition Benedict XVI had revived. Red shoes for the papacy go back to the Byzantine era and a time when only three individuals were allowed to wear red footgear: the Emperor, the Empress and the Pope. Francis looked down at his dilapidated old black shoes. 'These are fine with me', he said. The papal outfitters were to have no more success than the friends back in Buenos Aires cathedral who had given him their new pair.

Outside St Peter's Square was thronged, despite the wind and rain. A great cheer went up as the long red curtains on the balcony opened and Cardinal Jean Tauran, Protodeacon of the College of Cardinals, emerged onto the loggia. Blinking in the bright lights, he proclaimed the ancient '*Habemus Papam*' – We have a Pope. The crowd roared once again but fell silent as he announced the identity of the 266th successor of St Peter:

'*Eminentissimum ac Reverendissimum Dominum, Dominum Georgium Marium Sanctae Romanae Ecclesiae Cardinalem Bergoglio qui sibi nomen imposuit Franciscum*.' The most eminent and most reverend Lord, the Lord Jorge Mario, Cardinal of the Holy Roman Church, Bergoglio, who has taken the name Francis.

A sudden silence fell upon the drenched revellers. Who was he? The name sounded Italian. And the Jesuit cardinal from Buenos Aires had been on hardly any of the lists of Vatican-watchers' *papabili*. The crowd began asking one another: Who is he? Where is he from? On television channels across the globe, commentators began Googling his Wikipedia entry. Jorge Mario Bergoglio had taken the world by surprise.

But though few apart from Argentineans knew the name Bergoglio, everyone seized upon his chosen name: Francis. No pope had ever before taken the name of the great saint of the poor, Francis of Assisi. Any new pope, like any New Year, prompts within the faithful a renewed sense of promise and optimism, but this was a new departure. Might it mean that the era of the institutional Church, with its power and pageantry, scandal and silk-brocaded vestments, was over – and that one bearing the Franciscan virtues of poverty, simplicity, humility, charity, obedience and wisdom was being ushered in? Among the crowd smartphones and radios were being used to check out the new man. The excitement mounted as the word went round of the number of precedents being broken: the first non-European pope for a thousand years, the first pope from the Southern hemisphere, the first Jesuit pope, the first pope from the Americas where more than half of the planet's 1.2 billion Catholics live. It was, said one US citizen in the crowd, 'an Obama moment – the arrival of the first pope from the Third World was like the arrival of the first black President in the White House'. A new chapter in the history of the Church had begun.

Inside the Apostolic Palace the College of Cardinals was beginning to discover what that might mean. They lined up in the *Sala Clementina* to offer their congratulations and pledges of fealty to the new pontiff in the traditional manner. But as they did, they found that Francis had determinedly declined to sit on the papal throne which is a centuries-old symbol of a past in which the papacy saw itself as the equal of imperial power, purloining temporal trappings like the triple crown tiara and the highest pagan religious title *Pontifex Maximus*. This new pope would not even stand on an elevated platform when fellow cardinals approached, but greeted them, one by one, on equal footing. Gone was the notion of Pope as Prince in the pyramid model of spiritual authority which destroyed the unity between the East and West of Christendom. It was the first sign many of the cardinals had that change was really now afoot. Francis was saying: the old model of autocratic feudal monarchy has gone, this pope will gain his status as a first among equals, collegiality has returned. He addressed them as 'brother cardinals' rather than 'Lord cardinals'. He offered to greet them with a hug and when one insisted on bending to kiss his ring, he bent to kiss the ring of the man paying homage.

That done, he made his way to the upper corridor of St Peter's façade to address the waiting crowd. But first, he decided, he would ring his predecessor in Castel Gandolfo. An aide put a call through to the residence of the man who had styled himself Pope Emeritus. There was no reply. It turned out that Benedict and his entourage were glued to the television, waiting for the new Pope to appear on the balcony, and were ignoring the phone in case they missed his emergence. Eventually an aide answered and the new Pope spoke to the old, exchanging good wishes and assurances of mutual prayer. Then the red velvet curtains parted on the central balcony.

What happened next was, in the richness of its symbolism, like a programme for the new papacy. When the figure in white appeared on the balcony, he was not wearing the traditional scarlet and ermine cape which is a symbol of pontifical authority. Nor did he raise both arms as Benedict XVI had done in 2005, clasping his hands together above his head like a victorious boxer. Pope Francis stood there, arms straight by his sides, and made a simple blessing with his right hand towards the 150,000 people crowded in the piazza below. He looked dazed, which he may have been; he had once said that his mind went blank after any shock, good or bad. Or he may have intended his actions to look as simple as possible. On his chest was the old metal cross he first used as a bishop in Buenos Aires.

He spoke in Italian, in a halting Spanish accent which was modestly engaging rather than hesitant. He was the Bishop of Rome presenting himself to the people of Rome and he spoke their language. He had also, of course, chosen the name of perhaps the most famous of Italian saints. At his side he brought with him the Vicar of Rome, Cardinal Agostino Vallini. Here was the Bishop of Rome speaking to his diocese before addressing the world. He began with the most quotidian words possible: 'Buona Sera' - Good Evening. The greeting sounded refreshingly informal, even intimate, for this most momentous of occasions. Then he made a gentle joke. 'You know that the task of the conclave was to give Rome a bishop. It seems my brother cardinals went almost to the ends of the earth to find one.' His voice was quiet and gentle too, and yet somehow more compelling than had he spoken with physical power or energy. The world seemed to lean forward to listen. It was the first indication of the power that resides inside humility.

He prayed first for his predecessor, pointedly referring to him not as Pope Emeritus but as the emeritus Bishop of Rome. He prayed the prayers best known to Catholics in all languages: the Our Father, the Hail Mary and the Glory be. And then he said:

'Now let's begin this journey, bishop and people, this journey of the church of Rome, which is the one that presides in charity over all the churches – a journey of brotherhood, love and trust among us.' Only the church scholars would have realised that 'presides in charity' was a quotation from the first-century saint Ignatius of Antioch in a way which, decoded, amounted to a call to restore collegiality inside and between the churches. 'He is undermining a thousand years of papal monarchy', said Fr Timothy Radcliffe, the former Master of the Dominicans. 'He is adopting a more Trinitarian church – a mutuality of listening. It's not just about the reform of the Curia; it's about a shift in our understanding of Church. The community which presides in love: that is putting the Pope back in the college. It is ecclesiastically radical. He has thought through what he is doing. It is the product of the many years of practical theology.'

What was more immediately evident to the ordinary listener was the extraordinary mutuality in his next gesture. He said: 'Let us pray for one another', and he meant it. Tradition has it that a new Pope offers a blessing, *urbi et orbi* – to the city and the world. But before he did that he said to the people: 'First, I need to ask you a favour. Before the bishop blesses his people, he asks that you pray to the Lord to bless me.' Another departure. And he asked them to do it in silence. Yet another. Then he lowered his great head towards the balcony rail and bowed down to the people of God for their prayer, a new and unprecedented gesture: a bishop asking for the prayers of his people, reasserting the fundamental relationship of the bishop to the community of the baptised: that they should pray for one another.

Italian crowds are notoriously noisy, but the silence was complete. It was as if, a commentator later said, for a few precious seconds a desperately needed spiritual silence had fallen upon our frenetic and distracted world. So powerful was the silent prayer that, the tale was later told, the technicians in one TV studio momentarily panicked, thinking they had lost the sound feed. The story walked the line between urban myth and parable.

When the blessing came, the Pope placed a rich red embroidered stole around his neck and spoke, though he did not sing, in Latin. But the blessing was addressed not just to the Church but to 'all people of good will'. This was the language of Vatican II. It sent out another ripple of shock after the retrenchments of Popes John Paul II and Benedict XVI. And then, at the end, more demotic language for the plain people. 'Brothers and sisters, I'll leave you. Thank you so much for the welcome. Pray for me. We'll see each other soon. Good night and sleep well.' In a few short moments, packed with symbolism of so many kinds, Pope Francis had set out a whole programme of governance in miniature and signalled that things were going to be rather different from now on.

So they were. After his first public appearance the official papal limousine – registration SCV1, for Stato della Citta del Vaticano – was waiting to take the new Pope to dinner. The Pope declined to use it and climbed aboard a minibus taking his fellow cardinals back to the Casa Santa Marta. 'We have come together, we go together', said Francis. The papal limousine drove away empty. After the meal the Pope responded to a toast from the cardinals by saying: 'May God forgive you for what you have done.' They laughed.

Back in Buenos Aires there were tears among the cheers as crowds thronged the streets, car horns hooting in delight, to greet an Argentine Pope. Héctor Aguer, the Archbishop of La Plata, who knew he would now never ascend to the post of Archbishop of Buenos Aires which he had so coveted, instructed that the bells in his cathedral be not rung as is traditional to greet a new pontiff. There was no need to have a sort of 'soccer stadium celebration' just because a fellow Argentinean was elected, he later told his congregation grumpily. In a little corner cafe in Argentina, Bergoglio's friend of forty years, the human rights lawyer Alicia Oliveira, had watched it all on the television behind the bar. 'When I saw the white smoke on TV and I heard it was Bergoglio I burst into tears', she said. 'Someone in there asked me why. I said: "he's my friend and I'm missing him already". I was thinking of myself. Real friends like him are very few. I'm lucky to have had such a great friend. He is a very good man. I'm very happy he's running the church, and I am happy for him. He wanted to be Pope. He tells me he's having a great time. But I'm sad too because I won't see him any more.'

Bergoglio will miss Argentina too. The evening before his installation a huge crowd began to gather in the main square of Buenos Aires, Plaza de Mayo, where four huge screens had been erected to carry the live broadcast from Rome. They spent a sleepless night, apart from the young children who dozed in their parents' arms, but the atmosphere was joyous and buoyant. Through the night the screens displayed the first images of the new Pope with extracts from the most famous of his past homilies. Priests and rock singers took to the stage to keep the crowd company. Amid the throng priests wandered chatting and even hearing confessions. Suddenly at 3:32 a.m. – which was 7:32 a.m. in Rome – the loudspeakers crackled with a long-distance call. Bergoglio had phoned the Rector on his mobile phone and an enterprising TV technician who was nearby patched the call through to the loudspeakers in the square. A huge wave of cheering and applause swept the crowd as they recognised the voice from the other side of the world. It was Papa Francisco. He spoke:

'Dear sons and daughters, I know you have gathered in the square. I know that you are saying prayers, I need them very much. It is beautiful to pray because we look to heaven and know that we have a good Father who is God.

'I want to ask a favour of you. I want to ask for us to walk together, to care for one another, for you to care for each other. Do not cause harm. Protect life. Protect the family; protect nature; protect the young; protect the elderly. Let there not be hatred or fighting. Put aside envy. *No le saquen el cuero a nadie* [don't take the skin off anyone's back with your gossiping tongue – the crowd laughed affectionately at his use of *porteño* slang]. Talk with one another so that this desire to protect each other might grow in your hearts. And draw near to God. God is good. He always forgives and understands. Do not be afraid of him. Draw near to him and may the Virgin bless you. May she, as a mother, protect you. And don't forget that this bishop who is far away loves you very much. Pray for me.'

The whole square broke into riotous applause. At the other end of the phone Francis could hear them. 'Now be silent and pray,' he said, 'and I will bless you.'

'Through the intercession of Mary, ever Virgin, and each of your guardian angels, the glorious patriarch St Joseph, St Therese of the Child Jesus, and each of your protector saints, may God Almighty Father, Son, and Holy Spirit, bless you.'

As the Pope departed to prepare himself for Mass in Rome and the applause in Buenos Aires died away, a priest from the city's slums took the microphone and said: 'There is still extreme poverty and slavery here; people take advantage of others, of children and make money by forcing women to give up their dignity and sell their body. Change needs to come from within us, if we really want it.' In the crowd a young woman wrapped in an Argentinean flag, with tears in her eyes and a smile stretched across her face, told a local reporter: 'I'm also happy to share this man with the rest of the world because he is the change our Church needs.' He was Argentina's gift to the world. Dawn came just after Communion had been given and received, in Rome and Buenos Aires alike, but the crowd remained in the square. No one wanted to leave.

Bergoglio was by no means finished with his phone calls to Argentina. He rang, and continues to ring, friends like Alicia Oliveira, Rabbi Abraham Skorka and Clelia Luro, the widow of the former bishop to whom no one else in the church hierarchy would speak. 'When he left for Rome I told him: you won't be back', Luro recalled. 'When he called me after he had been elected he laughed and said: you're a witch. He didn't want to be Pope in 2005. He didn't want the power. But I think he's very happy now. He's very serene, quiet, happy.' He also rang his newsagent to cancel his paper order and his dentist to say he wouldn't be making his appointment there. And he rang the man who made those battered old black shoes. 'He wanted to know if I could repair them', said 81-year-old Carlos Samaria, who had for the previous forty years made shoes specially to suit Bergoglio's bad knee and hip. The cobbler said he would try but that he would also send him some new ones. Reluctantly Jorge Mario Bergoglio saw sense. 'But not red ones,' he insisted, 'make them black, like usual.'

8

A Pope of Surprises

He could not sleep the night he was elected Pope. After a celebratory dinner in the Casa Santa Marta his brother cardinals, as he had continued to call them, retired to their beds. But not long after they had settled down for the night Francis opened the door to his room and stepped into the corridor. He had changed from his papal white and was wearing the black trousers and black overcoat he habitually wore to travel the subway in Buenos Aires. Startled officials found themselves being asked if there was a car available. The new Pope wanted to go for a drive, he said. A driver was summoned and, in a small unmarked car, the man who hours earlier had pointedly styled himself only as Bishop of Rome, toured the streets of that city watching the celebrating crowds.

The next morning, at 5.45 a.m. he emerged from his room for a second time, in black pullover, trousers and shoes. He made his way to the chapel of the Vatican hostel. Security staff looked on bemused. Where was his papal garb? Perhaps he had forgotten he was Pope? He had not. Rather he had embarked upon a process by which the staff of the Vatican would have to learn that the Pope now did what Bergoglio had always done. And Bergoglio's day began with up to two hours' prayer before the tabernacle. After prayer, and a breakfast with six other early-rising cardinals, he again took an ordinary car – rather than the papal limousine – to arrive just before 8 a.m. at the fifth-century Basilica of Santa Maria Maggiore. He carried a small wreath of yellow and white roses. There, in the oldest church in Rome dedicated to the Virgin Mary, Francis prayed for the people of the city, as he had promised them from the balcony the night before that he would. He stopped first before the Byzantine icon of the *Salus Populi Romani* – Protectress of the Roman People. He prayed too at the altar where the founder of the Jesuit order, St Ignatius of Loyola celebrated his first Mass and at the tomb of Saint Pius V, the Dominican pope who established the tradition that the Pope should wear white because he would not give up his Dominican religious habit. When the security officers tried to close the church to the public, Francis protested: 'Leave them alone. I am a pilgrim too.' But behind his back his security officials ushered the public away. The Vatican machine will not end its old ways without a fight. As he left the church, he met the priests about to hear confessions and urged them: 'Be kind. Be merciful, the souls of the faithful need your mercy.' He stopped finally at a nearby schoolyard to greet the children who thronged to see him.

On the way back to the Vatican, Francis asked his driver to stop at the *Domus Internationalis Paulus VI*, the hostel for visiting foreign clergy in the centre of Rome where he stayed for the two weeks before the conclave. Alighting in the arc-cobbled courtyard of the gold-stuccoed building he climbed the few stairs, past the copper-green bust of Pope Paul VI, to the mahogany desk in the reception and asked for the housekeeping staff. He wanted to thank them all for their kindness over the previous two weeks, he said. Then he handed them a credit card to pay for his stay. 'Don't forget to add on the phone calls', he said. The flummoxed staff protested that, as Pope, it was unnecessary that he should pay. 'On the contrary,' said Francis, 'that is precisely why I must set a good example.' While they prepared his bill, he said, he would just go upstairs and pack his things. And then he asked a man behind the desk if he had a bulb for the bedside lamp which, he recalled, had blown. A bulb was produced. When staff went up to the room after Francis had descended with his battered black suitcase and old briefcase, paid his bill and returned to the Vatican, the bulb had been changed.

When he got back to the Vatican the new Pope was given the keys to the papal apartments in the Apostolic Palace, just to the right of

St Peter's basilica. In accordance with tradition the rooms had been sealed after the departure of Benedict XVI. Francis broke the seals on the door in order, the papal courtiers assumed, to take possession of his new home, as every Pope had done throughout the century since Pius X moved there in 1903. The papal apartments accommodated offices for the Pope and two private secretaries, a chapel and living quarters for the pontiff, his secretaries and household staff – four consecrated women from the lay movement *Comunione e Liberazione* had run the place in Benedict's time. Francis shocked Vatican staff by his response. As he looked around he said: 'There's room for 300 people here. I don't need all this space.'

He provoked a similar response among some cardinals later in the day at the Mass for the closure of conclave that evening in the Sistine Chapel. In his homily he told them: 'If we walk without the Cross ... then we are not our Lord's disciples. We are worldly people. We may be bishops, priests, cardinals, popes. But we are not disciples of the Lord.' Cardinals were not used to anyone suggesting, particularly not the Pope, that they were not proper disciples of Christ. It was not just his words which ruffled some. He had had the freestanding altar moved in the Sistine Chapel so that he would say Mass facing the congregation. Pope Benedict had, in recent years, reverted to the old practice of saying Mass there *ad orientem*, with his back to the congregation, as was the norm in the days before the Second Vatican Council. Francis made plain that this practice had been overturned for good reason, to make the people feel more included in the Church's liturgy. If he had ever doubted that he had learned its truth in the slums of Argentina.

Francis used the occasion of his first public Mass as Pope to send other signals. He carried Benedict's pastoral staff, as a sign of continuity, but declined one of his elaborate mitres in preference to a simple one trimmed in brown, in honour of St Francis. Most strikingly he set aside the homily in Latin which the Secretariat of State had prepared for him (in accordance with another old tradition) and spoke off-the-cuff in Italian, reflecting on the Gospel passages that had just been read – and did so from the lectern, as any parish priest would do, instead of from the papal throne as previous popes had done.

The days that followed gave an insight into what would be the priorities of the new papacy. On the Friday, two days after he had been elected on Wednesday 13 March, he rang the Superior General of the Jesuits, the order in which he was formed. Rome, and the rest of the world, had to accustom itself to the precedent of a pontiff who made his own phone calls. The receptionist at the Jesuit house in Borgo Santo Spirito was disbelieving when a voice came on the line saying: 'Good morning, this is Francis, the Bishop of Rome, here. I would like to speak with the Father General.' The Pope was ringing in response to the letter of congratulation which he had just received from the head of the Jesuits, Fr Adolfo Nicolás. He had written to the Pope with particular warmth in an attempt to assign to the past the tensions between the order and the man who had become the first Jesuit pope. 'Hello, it's Bergoglio…' became the prelude to a number of reports recounting how Pope Francis had made calls to old friends in Rome or Argentina and to tradespeople back in Buenos Aires. This was a Pope with an unprecedentedly common touch.

Later that morning he articulated both the intensity and optimism which characterised his faith, in an address to the College of Cardinals to mark the end of the conclave. In it he praised Pope Benedict, describing his decision to resign as a 'brave and humble gesture'. The cardinals, he said he had been told, were 'the Holy Father's priests'. The community, friendship and closeness that had developed among them in recent days would serve the Church well in the future. They should return to their dioceses – never giving in to the bitterness, pessimism and discouragement with which the Devil would try to entrap them every day but, rather, to continue their ministry 'enriched by the experience of these days that have been so full of faith and ecclesial communion'.

The next day, Saturday, he broke another precedent. He invited the world's media, who had been in Rome to cover the conclave, to a post-election papal press conference. As Archbishop of Buenos

Aires he had taken care to develop a good relationship with the media, which he saw as essential to the dissemination of the Church's message. Though he had hardly ever given interviews, he often gave off-the-record briefings and briefed to his press aide daily, sometimes twice a day. The head of the Vatican press office, Fr Federico Lombardi, another Jesuit, who had seen Benedict XVI rarely, was now getting direct access to the Pope. Francis had let the Vatican communications personnel know that he regarded what he intended to say at this first press conference as particularly important. It was to this assembly of around two thousand journalists that he revealed the story of how he had come to choose the name Francis. It was here that he announced what was to be the main theme of his pontificate: 'How I would like a poor church for the poor', Francis said.

He concluded with an additional signal. Francis, who has spoken in the past of his respect for atheists, ended by saying: 'Since many of you don't belong to the Catholic Church and others are non-believers, I offer this heartfelt blessing in silence, to each one of you, respecting the conscience of each person, but knowing that each one of you is a child of God.' His words were instead of the traditional blessing which Catholic journalists had expected. Many non-Catholics lauded the change as a welcome increased sensitivity towards them.

The next day he sent out a further important token of intent. Sunday was the new Pope's first Angelus from the balcony of St Peter's, two days before his official installation. Previous custom had it that the pontiff should speak in many languages. But although Francis has several languages – Spanish, Italian, French, German and a little English and even Ukrainian – he spoke at the noontime gathering only in Italian. The message this was intended to convey was underscored two weeks afterwards when he gave his first Easter blessing. The Vatican had prepared greetings in sixty-five languages, as was traditional. Francis chose not to read them. Again he spoke only in Italian, underlining his repeated presentation of himself not as 'pope', but as the 'Bishop of Rome', as if to reflect a less imperial conception of the papacy and a return to the role's historical roots.

That worldview was even more clearly reflected in the style of installation with which Francis chose to begin his papacy. For a start, the new Pope declined to select special readings for his inaugural Mass. Fortuitously a date was approaching which had great personal resonance for him: the following Tuesday, 19 March, was the Feast of St Joseph, the patron saint of both Bergoglio's boyhood church in which he had first heard the call to become a priest, and also patron of the *Colegio Máximo* in which he had spent much of his Jesuit formation. But the idea of sticking with the ordinary readings of the day fitted with Francis's love of the calendar of the saints and also with his sense that God is to be found in the everyday rather than in the special. Though political and religious leaders attended from all around the world – including six sovereign rulers, thirty-one heads of state, three princes and eleven heads of government from 132 states and international organisations – Francis did all he could to play down the pageantry. He chose a mitre and chasuble that he had had since he was a bishop. He selected a recycled papal ring based on one which had belonged to a former secretary of Pope Paul VI – and which was gold-plated silver in contrast to those of his predecessors', which were all solid gold. He wore a second-hand pallium, the woollen scarf which symbolises pontifical office. He pared down the liturgy and kept the music far more simple and plain than had been the norm under Benedict XVI, who had a predilection for lace and Latin. Instead of requiring every cardinal to profess their obedience to him at the ceremony he asked for a symbolic six, two of each rank: cardinal bishops, cardinal priests and cardinal deacons.

Far more important to him was the fact that this was the first papal installation ever attended by a Chief Rabbi of Rome; Francis had sent a invitation to the Jewish leader, Riccardo Di Segni, mentioning Vatican II, on his first full day in office. He had also invited Bartholomew, the Patriarch of Constantinople, who became the first head of the Greek Orthodox Church in nearly a thousand years to attend the installation of a pope – a bold step, on both sides, which augurs a major warming of ecumenical relations between the Orthodox and the Roman Catholic churches. To show his thanks Francis directed that the installation Gospel be sung in Greek rather than the usual Latin. 'Let us never forget', Francis said during his inaugural homily, 'that authentic power is service, and that the Pope too, when exercising power, must enter ever more fully into that service.'

As the days turned to weeks in the infancy of his papacy Francis showed, time after time, through signs and symbols, that change had come in a big way. Perhaps the most dramatic was his decision not to move into the Apostolic Palace, with its space for 300 people to live, but to remain in the Casa Santa Marta, the spartan modern guesthouse for priests and bishops visiting the Vatican for meetings and conferences. It was, like his decision to use the bus and subway had been in Buenos Aires, in part pragmatic. It allowed him to live in community with other priests and bishops and not risk being cut off from outside influences by Vatican officials. But it also sent a powerful signal to the world about Francis's hope for 'a poor church for the poor'. It said to the Church that here was a Pope for whom authenticity was a touchstone of the gospels. He reinforced that message with his decision to remain in Rome during the hot and sticky city summer, rather than decamping to Castel Gandolfo, the cooler papal summer residence in the hills to the south of the city. It was, Lombardi said, a sign of his solidarity with the poor who cannot afford to take holidays.

The gestures followed one on another. He invited the Vatican's cleaners and gardeners to attend his early morning Mass. On Sundays he led the worship at the little church of Santa Anna attended by Vatican staff, and stood outside to greet them like a normal parish priest. He was photographed by someone with a surreptitious mobile phone sitting humbly at the back of a congregation, rather than on the altar, during a meditation at Mass. He walked around the Vatican instead of taking cars. He would spend an hour after his Wednesday audience greeting people in wheelchairs, or order his

Popemobile to stop so he could leap out to embrace a disabled man. When the crowds chanted his name he told them to chant the name of Jesus instead. He chose a simple papal coat of arms and then conspicuously declined to have it emblazoned on any banners as his predecessors did. He briefly met members of the Grandmothers of Plaza de Mayo, a group that works to locate children and grand-children who disappeared during Argentina's military dictatorship – and which he had declined to meet when he was Archbishop of Buenos Aires. Inside the Vatican he signalled his unease at society's contemporary bonus culture by axing the €1,500 lump sum which Vatican staff were traditionally paid at the transition from one pope to the next. He ended the annual stipend of €25,000 awarded to each of the five cardinals who make up the supervisory board of the *Istituto per le Opere di Religione* – the Vatican Bank. He lifted the block the Vatican had placed on the murdered Salvadorian Archbishop Oscar Romero becoming a saint. He addressed the Vatican's trainee diplomats and warned them against ambition and careerism. Almost every week there was another story in the press about a 'Hello, it's Bergoglio...' phone call he had made.

Not everyone was impressed. His political opponents in Argentina dismissed it all as gimmickry. Estela De La Cuadra, whose family had appealed to Francis for help when he was Jesuit Provincial in 1977 and her pregnant sister, Elena, had been kidnapped by the Argentine military dictatorship, said: 'He's not really humble. All this paying the hotel bill is just a publicity stunt.' And the new Pope's rejection of Benedict's revivals of tradition outraged Catholicism's ultra-conservatives. The head of the SSPX, the Lefebvrist Society of Saint Pius X in South America, Christian Bouchacourt, denounced Francis's simple style as humiliating and undignified for the Church. A traditionalist blog, *Rorate Caeli*, catalogued the extremity of the ultras' indignation: Francis took off his stole in public; he removed the wall of candles Benedict had placed between celebrant and congregation; he said rather than sang certain prayers; he didn't make the deacon kneel before him for a blessing before the gospel; he preached without wearing his mitre; he folded his hands during the liturgy instead of pressing his palms piously together; he did not genuflect at the Consecration; and he gave the Kiss of Peace to deacons not just concelebrants. His solecisms were not just confined to liturgy, they bemoaned. He asked cardinals to wear black instead of red; he conversed with the Patriarch of Constantinople seated on an armchair rather than a throne; he used the phone, contrary to protocol; he drank *mate* tea in public when receiving the Argentinean president when popes should never be seen publicly consuming food or drink except the Eucharist; he insisted the Jesuit Superior General should use the informal Italian form 'tu' instead of Your Holiness; he signed himself plain Franciscus without the usual PP suffix, for *pontifex pontificum*; he didn't wear red shoes or white stockings – or cuff links! This catalogue of 'miserablist' errors was downright Protestant, the scandalised ultra-traditionalists complained.

Francis, however, had greater scandals in his sights. Each morning he established the custom of inviting different guests and Vatican staff to his 7 a.m. Mass in the fifty-seater Casa Santa Marta chapel. There he would deliver an extemporised homily based on the readings of the day. Each was characterised by his spontaneous thinking-aloud and his homely turn of phrase, a technique he carried over to sermons elsewhere. So he complained about the 'babysitter Church' which only 'takes care of children to put them to sleep' instead of acting as a mother with her children. Then he ridiculed 'God spray' – the New Age idea of an impersonal 'spiritual bath in the cosmos' God 'that is a bit everywhere but one does not know what it may be'. He issued warnings to those who did not share his belief that evil, like good, is embodied in a personal force: 'Whoever does not pray to God, prays to the Devil.' Next he criticised 'satellite Christians' whose conduct was governed by 'common sense' and 'worldly prudence' instead of the Gospel. Then there were priests who become 'collectors of antiques or novelties' instead of being shepherds who take on 'the smell of the sheep'. Priestly vestments at Mass are 'not so much about trappings and fine fabrics' as about 'the glory of our God'. The Second Vatican Council was 'a beautiful work of the Holy Spirit' on which there could be no 'turning back the clock' and those who resisted change should instead be asking themselves: 'Have we done everything the Holy Spirit was asking us to do during the Council?' In one sermon, with staff from the Vatican Bank in the congregation, he described their organisation as 'necessary up to a certain point' but told them to take care not to get its work out of proportion in the 'love story' the Church had to tell. In front of staff from the Congregation for the Doctrine of the Faith, the Vatican's enforcers of doctrinal orthodoxy, he made a joke about the CDF which did not amuse some of those present as much as it did those who heard the remark later reported on Vatican Radio. The Vatican's official newspaper *L'Osservatore Romano* edits out some papal asides which the radio station happily reports in the new spirit of openness which is abroad in Rome.

These off-the-cuff morning homilies were variously reported from the transcript Vatican Radio made available. Different media outlets reported them according to what suited their political agenda, ecclesiological or secular. Interpretations were sometimes partisan, ignorant or deliberately mischievous, as when Francis declared that Jesus had redeemed everyone, including atheists to whom he said: 'Just do good and we'll find a meeting point.' The media responded with all manner of jumbled nonsense about salvation, infallibility and heaven and hell. But the new Pope seemed determined not to let the risk of misinterpretation deter him from a style that St Augustine called the *sermo humilis* – which insists that even the most humble or homely phrases can be made holy when harnessed to the service of God. To Francis his risky on-the-hoof language embodied his preference for 'a church that gets out in the street and runs the risk of an accident' to a church that 'doesn't get out [and] sooner or later, gets sick from being locked up'.

All this altered the mood in Rome significantly. 'Today Rome is easy and smiling', one cardinal told me. 'The whole atmosphere is changed.' An archbishop in the Curia said something similar: 'Many members of the Church now feel able to say things they wouldn't dare say before.' A theologian said the same: 'We moral theologians were afraid of who would be the new Pope; now we are relieved.'

So striking were all these semiotics and signifiers that, after Pope Francis had been in office for a hundred days, many Vatican commentators, in preparing the usual pieces of journalism to mark the milestone, said that for all the signs and symbols there had been little at that point of shift in substance in the Franciscan pontificate. That was not entirely the case. One of his first policy pronouncements was on the case of the Vatican's previous attempt to clamp down on the activities of nuns in the United States. Conservatives in the Curia say the US religious women had been too concerned about social and economic injustice and not engaged enough on stopping abortion or gay marriage – and even dialoguing with radical feminists who questioned church doctrine. The media reported that Francis had reaffirmed the intention to rein in the female religious orders. But there was ambiguity in Francis's pronouncement and other signals from the Vatican suggested a 'wait and see' attitude was more in order. That seemed confirmed when reports after a meeting between Francis and nuns and priests from Latin America suggested that he had hinted to them that they should not be too bothered if they found themselves being investigated by the Congregation for the Doctrine of the Faith but just get on with their good work elsewhere.

There was nothing ambiguous, however, about the massive first step Pope Francis took towards reforming the governance of the Catholic Church. When a pope dies, or retires, all the heads of the various administrative departments in the Vatican automatically lose their jobs until a new pope is elected. One of the first acts of new popes, traditionally, is to reappoint the vast majority of these Curia bureaucrats and politicians to their old jobs for five-year terms. But Francis did nothing for several days. The Curia was held in abeyance. Then, when he did make an announcement, it was that the heads of the various congregations and pontifical councils should continue in office *donec aliter provideatur* – 'until other provisions are made'. The Pope's press secretary, Federico Lombardi issued a communiqué which said: 'The Holy Father, wants, in fact, to give himself a certain amount of time for reflection, prayer and dialogue before any appointments or definitive confirmations.' Dialogue was the key word in the statement. Significantly it made no mention of the Curia's most powerful department, the Secretariat of State, which is the office of what is effectively the Vatican's prime minister.

At first many commentators brought to mind the unwritten rule among Jesuits that a new superior should spend his first hundred days in office learning about the community before making any changes. One of the key techniques of discernment in Ignatius' Spiritual Exercises is called *Las Dos Bandera* – The Meditation on the Two Standards. It is used to clarify motives. It asks whether we are deluding ourselves that what we say we do in the service of God is in fact a disguised version of the values of this world with its illusions of security, reputation and power. Pope Francis spent a month meditating and then announced that he was 'taking up a suggestion that emerged in the course of the General Congregations preceding the Conclave'. He set up a groundbreaking kitchen cabinet of eight cardinals from all around the world to advise him on the running of the Church and the reform of the Vatican.

The official announcement spoke of a project 'of revision of the Apostolic Constitution *Pastor Bonus* on the Roman Curia'. This led the media to focus on the new group, which the *National Catholic Reporter* in the United States dubbed the G8, as a tool to remake the Curia in response to the recent Vatican scandals. One journalist joked: 'I'm reminded of Pope John XXIII's famed comment when asked how many people worked at the Vatican, he replied: "About half of them!"'. But Francis's decision was far more radical than talk of an overhaul of church bureaucracy suggested. Curial reform was only the second task. The first was 'to advise him in the government of the universal Church'. Close scrutiny of the eight men Francis had chosen suggested that their advice would be radical. They were not all of like mind, but they all shared a fierce independence of thinking. None had ever served in the Curia, seven had wide experience of running dioceses and only one was Italian. Some of them were among the most outspoken critics of the current Vatican system in the pre-conclave discussions.

The coordinator of the group was named as Cardinal Oscar Rodríguez Maradiaga, the Archbishop of Tegucigalpa in Honduras, a moderate figure with a passion for social justice and a longstanding critic of economic inequality. Significantly Rodríguez Maradiaga had a bruising encounter with the Vatican in 2001. He was president of the Church's aid agency network *Caritas Internationalis* when the Vatican's Secretary of State, Cardinal Tarcisio Bertone decided to refuse permission for the organisation's secretary general, Mrs Lesley-Anne Knight, to stand for a second term because she saw the aid agencies' primary task as assisting the poor rather than pushing Catholic doctrine. Rodríguez defended her, but lost the internal Vatican power struggle. Now that balance of power was to be reversed. Soon after his appointment was announced Rodríguez told journalists his group would 'certainly' be investigating the controversial Vatican Bank.

The new group was clearly intended to bring Pope Francis perspectives from around the globe. Many of the members are the head of the bishops' conference on their continent. Cardinal Reinhard Marx, the Archbishop of Munich, was president of the bishops' conferences of the European Community. Cardinal Laurent Monswengo Pasinya was Archbishop of Kinshasha and former head of the African bishops. Cardinal Oswald Gracias, Archbishop of Bombay, was president of the Asian bishops' federation. Cardinal Francisco Javier Errázuriz Ossa of Chile was a former president of the Latin America bishops. Cardinal Sean Patrick O'Malley, Archbishop of Boston, was a key member of the US bishops' conference. Cardinal George Pell, Archbishop of Sydney, though doctrinally solidly conservative was one of the most outspoken critics of Vatican management dysfunction. And Cardinal Giuseppe Bertello, a career diplomat, ran the Vatican City State. All were described as strong personalities. They were not Yes-men who would tell the Pope what they thought he wanted to hear. The first meeting of the group with the Pope in Rome was set for October 2013, but long before that bishops in their regions began to contact the G8 members with suggestions of what they should bring before Francis. They were perspectives, said Rodríguez Maradiaga, which normally do not get through to the Pope.

But the new Cabinet is more than a gesture to suggest that Rome should be accountable to the local churches rather than the other way round. It is more, even, than a sign of Francis's willingness to respond to what cardinals said they wanted during the speeches at the pre-conclave Congregations. It gives an embryonic structure to a more collegial system of government, shifting the balance of power inside the Church towards regional or national conferences of bishops. 'This move represents a highly significant rebalancing of forces within the government of the Catholic Church, and may pave the way for a form of representative Cabinet-type government instead of the model of an absolute monarchy that many believe has gone beyond the end of its useful life', said the international Catholic weekly *The Tablet*. 'The Pope's intention appears to be to translate into action the Second Vatican Council's desire for a realignment of forces within the Church that has remained largely theoretical over the last half-century.' Commentators from across the Church seemed agreed on the heft of the change. The Italian traditional liturgist Professor Mattia Rossi, editor of *Liturgia culmen et fons*, disapprovingly described the new group of advisors as a step toward the 'demolition of the papacy' which replaced the divinely instituted authority and stability of the apostolic hierarchy with a quicksand swamp of collegiality. At the other end of the spectrum Alberto Melloni, Professor of History of Christianity at the University of Modena and an expert on the Second Vatican Council, called it the 'most important step in the history of the church for the past 10 centuries'.

Nor was this the only indicator that change would be more that symbolic. Pope Francis has said he plans to make changes to the international Synod of Bishops to make it more collegial, as Vatican II intended. That intention had been undermined by the insistence of Benedict XVI, when he was head of the Congregation for the Doctrine of the Faith, that episcopal conferences 'had no theological significance', being mere collections of bishops whose collective weight was theologically no more than the sum of their parts. By contrast Francis told the fifteen-member coordinating council of the synod in June 2013: 'We trust that the Synod of Bishops will be further developed to better facilitate dialogue and collaboration of the bishops among themselves and with the Bishop of Rome.'

There were also hints at greater subsidiarity – the notion enshrined in Catholic Social Teaching that decisions and action should be taken at the lowest level possible. In May 2013 Francis addressed the Italian bishops' conference. Breaking with tradition yet again, he made no reference to Italian politics, as popes have usually done on this occasion. His speech was the shortest on record by a pope – just twelve minutes – prompting the Vatican-watcher Andrea Tornielli to dub the event the 'end of the era' in which the Church saw itself as a political power-broker. The focus was to return to pastoral essentials. 'Dialogue with the political institutions [of Italy] is up to you', not the Pope, Francis told the bishops. And the principle of subsidiarity was to cascade down. After the meeting one bishop said that henceforth it would be the job of the laity rather than the bishops to speak out when non-negotiable Catholic values were under threat. 'As far as political life [is concerned] it would be better for us bishops to keep out of it', said Archbishop Luigi Negri of Ferrara-Comacchio. 'The autonomy of the laity has to be respected.' The shift, according to the Italian sociologist Luca Diotallevi, talking to John Allen of the *National Catholic Reporter*, reopened 'an enormous space for the laity' to take the lead on the intersection of faith and politics. Other changes which were intimated at in the first weeks of the new papacy included sugges-tions of a revised role for the Congregation for the Doctrine of the Faith in expanding rather than restricting the interpretation of the Second Vatican Council as it had done under the previous two pontificates. The head of the CDF, Archbishop Gerhard Ludwig Müller, suggested in June 2013 that the war between the Liberation

Theology movement and Rome was over and that Liberation Theology should henceforth be recognised as "among the most important currents in 20th century Catholic theology". Francis also signalled his desire to reduce the number of Italian dioceses from their existing 225, a figure which is proportionately far higher than anywhere else in the world.

And the warmth and frankness of his discussions with the new Archbishop of Canterbury, Justin Welby, also led to speculation that Pope Francis intends to allow Benedict XVI's Anglican Ordinariate to wither on the vine. Diversity is something Francis has long embraced rather than fearing.

In his first weeks Francis, Bishop of Rome broke tradition after tradition in his attempt to strip away accretions to return to authenticity. Perhaps the most significant of the new Pope's breaches of precedent came with his decision in Holy Week not to celebrate his first Maundy Thursday in the church of St John Lateran, as popes customarily do. The Papal Archbasilica of St John Lateran is the oldest and highest ranking of Rome's cathedrals and the official seat of the Bishop of Rome. The Holy Thursday ritual commemorates the night before Christ's Crucifixion when Jesus washed the feet of his twelve disciples in a daring reversal of the usual relationship between leader and followers. Since the late twefth century at least, popes have marked the night by washing the feet of twelve priests or deacons. Most Catholic theologians suggest that canon law excludes women from the ritual.

But Pope Francis, for his first Holy Thursday, spurned the ancient basilica and went to *Casal del Marmo* juvenile prison. There he washed the feet of twelve prisoners. On his knees on the stone floor the 76-year-old Pope, vested like a deacon, washed feet which were black, white, male, female, tattooed and untattooed, and then kissed each one. The owners of the feet were Catholics, Orthodox Christians, Muslims and atheists. And two of them were women. No pope had ever washed the feet of a woman before, and the debate sparked by Francis's decision was like the debate surrounding his entire papacy in microcosm. Liberals welcomed the gesture as a sign of greater inclusiveness in the Church. Conservatives were aghast at the setting aside of tradition and the breach of the rubric church law involved. 'The rubric says *viri* – men', said the liturgist Mgr Andrew Burnham, who served on the Liturgical Commission of the Church of England before he converted to Catholicism. 'The Bishop of Rome setting aside the rubrics is a serious matter, with many consequences, some highly undesirable.' Conservatives lamented the Pope's 'questionable example'. But one senior Curia bureaucrat, who could see which way the papal wind was blowing, shrugged at the response. 'The Pope does not break the rules,' he told me, 'he just remakes them'.

Francis – who as Archbishop of Buenos Aires had washed and kissed the feet of drug addicts and hospital patients with AIDS – spoke to the young offenders before getting down on both knees at their feet. 'This is a symbol, it is a sign. Washing your feet means I am at your service', he said. 'Help one another. This is what Jesus teaches us. This is what I do. And I do it with my heart. I do this with my heart because it is my duty; as a priest and bishop I must be at your service.' After the ceremony he gave each of them a chocolate egg and an Easter cake in the shape of a dove. The detainees gave the Pope a wooden crucifix and prayer-kneeler they made in the prison workshop. As he left, Francis told the young people: 'Do not let yourselves be robbed of hope.'

That was his message not just to the young offenders of *Casal del Marmo*. It was his message to the wider world. 'He's totally aware that he must in some sense be a revolutionary Pope, not only for the Catholic Church but for the whole of humanity', I was told by Rabbi Abraham Skorka, who had known Jorge Mario Bergoglio for almost two decades. The first signs were that Pope Francis might just achieve that. 'Four years of Bergoglio would be enough to change things', said Cardinal Cormac Murphy O'Connor of Westminster, an old friend of the new Pope. 'But pray to God we have him for much longer than that.'

Afterword

For someone so celebrated for his simplicity Jorge Mario Bergoglio turns out to be a man of considerable complexity. The story of the Swiss Guard offers a revealing paradigm. One night, not long after his election as the Catholic Church's 266th pontiff, Pope Francis came out of his bedroom in the hostel of Casa Santa Marta. It was just before dawn and a young Swiss Guard was on duty by the door. Discovering he had been standing there all night the Pope went back into his rooms and brought out a chair. He told the young soldier to sit down. The guard said he could not. The rules did not allow it. Whose rules? asked the Pope. My captain's orders, the soldier replied. Well, he is just a captain and I am the Pope and my orders are that you sit down. The soldier sat down. The story has a coda. A few minutes later Francis reappeared with a slice of bread and jam – *panino con marmellata,* to add a little Italian verisimilitude – which the leader of the world's billion Catholics gave to the soldier with the words: '*Buon appetito,* brother'.

The tale went viral in the Catholic blogosphere, despite the fact that there appeared to be no serious news source from which it could be verified. To the re-tellers of the story that did not matter. It worked as parable or poetic truth to illustrate the authenticity of the humble Pope, a man whose greatness lay in his mastery of the smallest things. And yet, even as a myth, it contains some of the ambiguity which surrounds the real man, as was pointed out to me by one of his close aides, Guillermo Marcó, who was for eight years the public spokesman for Bergoglio as Archbishop of Buenos Aires. 'The story demonstrates a man with the common touch, true', said Marcó. 'But it also reveals him as a man with a strong sense of power. It shows him saying: "I am the Pope, I will decide. You do what I tell you".'

What verdict, then, are we finally to reach? Our journey from Argentina to Rome, from Bergoglio to Francis, has uncovered a pope of paradox – a man who is a radical but not a liberal, an enabler with an authoritarian streak, a self-confident man in constant need of forgiveness, and a churchman who combines religious humility and political wiles. It is also the story of a man who has undergone, if not a religious conversion, then at any rate a deep inner transformation which has wrought a profound and long-lasting change in both his personal and political vision.

Consider again the key points. The Pope who has shaken up the complacencies and self-certainties of the Vatican – deconstructing the monarchical model of papacy, stripping away its rococo affectations and accretions, and declaring his desire for 'a poor Church for poor people' – began as a religious and political conservative. In his 15 years in key leadership positions among the Jesuits of Argentina, from 1971 to 1986, he initially resisted the radical changes with which the revolutionary Second Vatican Council sought to revitalise an introspective Catholic Church. And, though he always had a deep love for the popular piety of the poor, until he was in his mid-forties he studiously avoided addressing the economic and social circumstances which made, and kept, people poor. Rather he was the hammer of Liberation Theology, that movement which sought to combine the spiritual and material improvement of the poorest. He was a charismatic leader, but one who was unyielding and domineering with the Jesuits in his charge. His clarity of purpose and autocratic demeanour – combined with his associations with the right-wing Peronist Iron Guard – divided Argentina's Jesuits into two camps – those who loved and those who loathed Bergoglio. So bitter was his legacy that when Bergoglio left, and was sent by his superiors into exile 400 miles away in Córdoba, eventually the Jesuit Curia in Rome had to send in an outsider, from Colombia, as Provincial. That came after three successive

Argentinean provincials failed to end the *Bergogliano* personality cult and heal the wounds.

The most livid of those wounds concerned the two Jesuit priests, Fr Orlando Yorio and Fr Franz Jalics, who were kidnapped and tortured – and held, hooded and shackled for five months – by one of the military death squads responsible for murdering as many as 30,000 people regarded as 'subversives' during Argentina's so-called Dirty War. Many unproven allegations have been made about Bergoglio's involvement in their disappearance. Most of them seem untrue. But Bergoglio was guilty in one key respect.

Jorge Mario Bergoglio was just 36 when he took over as Provincial in what amounted to a coup against his predecessor, Fr Ricardo O'Farrell, who was perceived as too liberal and too political by the conservatives within the Society of Jesus in Argentina. Bergoglio was determined to curtail, or expunge from the order, those Jesuits who had embraced Liberation Theology to the point of working actively in the slums in alliance with overtly political groups. The problem was that the two most prominent Jesuit practitioners of Liberation Theology, Yorio and Jalics, had once been his teachers and were both older than him.

The young new provincial locked antlers with the older men. They refused to obey his order to leave the slum and began writing documents, to Bergoglio and his superiors in Rome, explaining why. Bergoglio was outraged. One of the key vows a Jesuit swears is obedience. Yorio and Jalics were in flagrant violation of that, particularly so when he informed them that his command had been reiterated by Rome. Bergoglio declared that they had expelled themselves from the order and informed Archbishop Aramburu of Buenos Aires who withdrew the licences of the two men to say Mass.

There is unresolved controversy about whether Bergoglio also blocked their move to the jurisdiction of another bishop, Miguel Raspanti, who was prepared to allow them to continue their work in his diocese of Morón. But it seems indisputable that he allowed his anger with the men to cloud his judgement. The withdrawal of the two men's licences to say Mass was a sufficient signal to the military dictatorship that the Church had removed its protection from the priests. Bergoglio, who was both politically astute and well-informed about the tactics – and even the timing – of the military's repressive behaviour, should have seen the danger in which he was placing his two priests. Bergoglio behaved recklessly and has been trying to atone for his behaviour ever since.

All the other evidence suggests that Bergoglio behaved with considerable courage over the six years which followed as the Dirty War – which the military euphemistically called the *Proceso de Reorganización* – grew ever dirtier. As Jesuit provincial and then Rector of the order's *Colegio Máximo* he set up a clandestine network to smuggle out of the country fugitives from the military's reign of terror. He was, said one of those he helped to freedom, both 'personally and institutionally brave'. He did not speak out publicly against the military, but then most people did not, knowing that to do so was like signing your own death warrant.

But Bergoglio had done enough to trouble his conscience. When his term of office came to an end his Jesuit superiors in Rome decided he had to be removed from Argentina. He was sent to study in Germany, but came back sooner than expected. After an unhappy sojourn as an ordinary priest in various Jesuit communities in Buenos Aires he was exiled to Córdoba – a place for Bergoglio 'of humility and humiliation', said Marcó.

It was in that wilderness that Bergoglio, a prayerful man who spent at least two hours a day in the presence of God before the tabernacle, looked deep into his own heart and made a radical change. One of the standard techniques used in the fifteen-year Jesuit formation is a series of Spiritual Exercises devised by the order's founder, St Ignatius of Loyola. At their heart is a process of discernment which helps the practitioner to strip away his layers of self-justification and self-delusion, and penetrate through to the inner core of his behaviour and motivation. Bergoglio had long years to reflect on his divisive leadership of the Jesuits in Argentina – and on what he had done wrong or inadequately during the Dirty War. He had to confront the fact that, in his inexperience as a young leader, he had allowed the breakdown of the pastoral relationship between himself and priests in his care. Years later, after Yorio was dead, Bergoglio and Jalics met in Germany, where Jalics had fled to the safety of a Jesuit retreat house. In 2013, after Francis became Pope, Jalics issued a statement to say that the two men had been reconciled and had concelebrated Mass together ending with what Jalics called 'a solemn embrace'. What actually happened, an eye-witness said, was that the two men fell into each other's arms and wept.

Three years before he became Pope, when Bergoglio was still Archbishop of Buenos Aires, in a rare interview with two Argentinean journalists, Sergio Rubin and Francesca Ambrogetti, he looked back on those years and said:

> 'I don't want to mislead anyone – the truth is that I'm a sinner who God in His mercy has chosen to love in a privileged manner. From a young age, life pushed me into leadership roles – as soon as I was ordained as a priest, I was designated as the master of novices, and two and a half years later, leader of the province – and I had to learn from my errors along the way, because, to tell you the truth, I made hundreds of errors. Errors and sins. It would be wrong for me to say that these days I ask forgiveness for the sins and offences that I might have committed. Today I ask forgiveness for the sins and offences that I did indeed commit'.

Bergoglio's soul was touched profoundly in all this. To understand how deep the examination of his conscience went it is only necessary to look at his preaching. The need for forgiveness and for God's mercy have been his dominant theological refrains, both before and after he became Pope. 'Guilt, without atonement, does not allow us to grow', he has said. 'There's no clean slate. We have to bless the past with remorse, forgiveness, and atonement'. The final Lenten letter he left for the people of Buenos Aires before he left for Rome said: 'Morality is not 'never falling down' but 'always getting up again'. And that is a response to God's mercy'. In his first Sunday homily after his election as Pope he said: 'Mercy is the Lord's most powerful message'. From Jesus, he said, we will 'not hear words of contempt, we do not hear words of condemnation, but only words of love, of mercy, that invite us to conversion: 'Neither do I condemn you. Go and sin no more!' In his first Angelus message he told a packed St Peter's Square: 'Mercy, this word changes everything. It is the best word we can hear: it changes the world. A little mercy makes the world less cold and more just... The Lord never gets tired of forgiving, it is we that get tired of asking forgiveness'.

Inside the Sistine Chapel when a cardinal is elected Pope he is asked: *Acceptasne electionem de te canonice factam in Summum Pontificem* – do you accept your canonical election as Supreme Pontiff? The normal response is: *Accepto* – I accept. But Jorge Mario Bergoglio replied: 'I am a great sinner, trusting in the mercy and patience of God in suffering, I accept'. Even at that special moment – or perhaps because of it – contrition for his past filled his mind. As the world has learned, he never fails to miss an opportunity to ask those around him to pray for him.

Bergoglio's exile in Córdoba ended when he was made one of six assistant bishops in Buenos Aires. But he arrived in the city of his birth a different man. He returned to the capital with a new perspective. In his years of retrospection, in those long hours of prayer, he had discerned a new model of leadership, one which involved consultation, participation, collegiality and listening. There was, it turned out after all, a clean slate.

From the outset he focused his attention on the slums. There the process of change within him was deepened by his increasing contact with the poorest of the poor. As the years passed he began to create a new generation of priests dedicated to working in the slums. The numbers of these *curas villeros* – slum priests – quadrupled under his watch. He began to encourage the foundation of co-operatives and unions and other mechanisms by which the poor could empower themselves as well as challenging the dominance of the drug dealers who ran the slums. Working in shantytowns where large parts of the church congregations were single mothers or divorced altered his attitude to Church rules like forbidding the remarried to take Communion. He did not veer from orthodox Church teaching but did not allow it to overrule the priority of caring for individuals. 'He was never rigid about the small and stupid stuff', said Fr Juan Isasmendi, the parish priest in Villa 21 slum, 'because he was interested in something deeper'. But the poor reshaped his politics too. He repeatedly denounced the political and economic system, warning that oppressing the poor and defrauding workers of their wages were two sins 'that cry out to God for vengeance'. Extreme poverty and unjust economic structures were 'violations of human rights' which called for solutions of justice not just philanthropy.

The irony was that, 40 years on, he had arrived at a similar under-standing of social justice to that of Yorio and Jalics, the two Jesuits he had cut off because of their work in the slums. The Cold War was over and with it the need to see Liberation Theology as some kind of stalking horse for secularised anti-Church Communism supplanting Catholicism along with capitalism in Latin America. Liberation Theology had been more right than wrong, he began to conclude. Bergoglio started to honour the martyrs of Liberation Theology. As Pope he has unblocked the process to make a saint of Archbishop Oscar Romero of El Salvador. And, under Francis, the head of the Vatican's doctrinal watchdog, the Congregation for the Doctrine of the Faith, Archbishop Gerhard Ludwig Müller, declared that the war between the Liberation Theology movement and Rome was over. Liberation Theology should henceforth be recognised, he pronounced, as 'among the most important currents in 20th century Catholic theology'.

How deep is the change? The most striking fruit of Bergoglio's conversion was his humility. Humility, as a religious virtue, is not some kind of personality trait. It is a mode of behaviour which Bergoglio chose to adopt, after prayerful reflection that this was what God required of him. It was calculated. That is not to suggest that it was fake but it was thought-through – as has been his arrival in the papacy. 'Make no mistake about it Francis came to the job with a plan', as the Vatican watcher Alessandro Speciale put it. Bergoglio knew that calling himself Francis was a gesture of some audacity. What he wanted, he proclaimed, was a Church which practices what it preaches. It is the philosophy encapsulated in the words attributed to St Francis of Assisi – the inspiration for Bergoglio's papal name: You must preach the gospel at all times, and if necessary use words. 'That's what he's doing', said Speciale. 'His simplicity is a way of looking at reality from the point of view of the poor'.

But audacious humility is a high-risk strategy. When Bergoglio refused to appear as a witness before a Argentinean 'crimes against humanity' trial in 2010 – claiming that bishops were exempt under Argentine law – the families of those who had been murdered by the junta were scathing. The court was forced to decamp to Bergoglio's own office to take evidence from him. 'What kind of humility is that?' asked Estela de la Cuadra whose pregnant sister was one of the disappeared. Bergoglio told the court he had no knowledge of the stealing of babies from women like Estela's sister who gave birth in detention. But many in Argentina did not believe him. Being humble on his own terms was clearly not the same as being humbled in a court room. Yet all that underscored was that Bergoglio's humility was not some natural modesty, bashfulness or self-effacement. It was certainly far from the same thing as meekness. In Pope Francis humility is an intellectual stance and a religious decision. It is a virtue which his will must seek to impose on a personality which has its share of pride and a propensity to dogmatic and domineering behaviour. Humility is a consciousness which wrestles against the unconsciousness of the human ego.

That battle was on show in the 2010 court hearing where Bergoglio – who, on sex abuse by priests, insisted strongly that the Church must not put its institutional reputation before a search for the truth and the care of victims – was decidedly unco-operative in doing the same on the Dirty War. Perhaps that was because he knew that collusion between the Church and the military in that era was so widespread that he feared uncovering the whole sordid enter-prise could do more harm than good to the fabric of Argentinean society. There has been one sign that he may yet change his view on this. As Archbishop of Buenos Aires he repeatedly refused to meet with the Grandmothers of the Plaza de Mayo, a group dedicated to tracing the babies stolen from mothers killed during the Dirty War. Within his first few weeks of becoming Pope he had a brief meeting with representatives of the group who want him to order the opening of Church archives. They hoped to be able to trace the children if they could identify those priests and nuns involved in the scandal by finding 'good Catholic families', sympathetic to the military junta, to adopt the babies.

But if there is a paradox in the way that humility and power come together in Pope Francis it is far from the only one. Or, as one cardinal put it, rather more colourfully: 'The new Pope plays for the same team but kicks the ball in an entirely different direction'. So while Francis does not demur from the Church's official teaching against abortion he is, on his track record, far more likely to focus on child trafficking and sex slavery. Though he opposed the government's distribution of free contraceptives in Argentina he is just as likely to talk publicly about the fact that condoms can be morally acceptable where they are used primarily to prevent the spread of disease; and on family issues he is more likely to ask parents whether they make the time to play with their children properly. He has opposed same-sex marriage and gay adoption but spoken out strongly in favour of civil unions and equal rights for homosexuals. On euthanasia his public pronouncements have chiefly been about how contemporary society's neglect of the elderly, and poor care in hospital, constitutes a form of 'covert euthanasia' – with frequent references to the shame of a society where old people are hidden away in care homes, like discarded like old overcoats shoved into closets with a couple of mothballs in their pockets. On the place of women in the Church, though he has long insisted that women cannot become priests because Jesus was a man, he scandalised conservatives by washing women's feet in his first papal Maundy Thursday service – and emphasised that women, not men, were chosen by God to be the first witnesses of the Resurrection.

Doing something to raise the profile and the status of women is one of the touchstones by which the papacy of Jorge Mario Bergoglio will be judged. Early indications were that this was a priority for Pope Francis. After Cardinal Oscar Rodriguez Maradiaga was appointed co-ordinator of the Pope's ground-breaking new group of cardinal advisers, one of his first public statements was about women and the Church. He said that getting more women into key posts would be a central part of the reform of the Vatican with which his group was charged by Francis. Other benchmarks for Francis will include his openness to co-operating with the Grandmothers of the Plaza de Mayo – and allowing them to access Church records in their search for their missing relatives. And Bergoglio's old friend Rabbi Abraham Skorka is hoping Pope Francis will act upon his previous conviction that the Vatican should open its secret archives to lay bare the truth about whether Pope Pius XII did more to help or to hinder the Jews of Europe during the Nazi persecutions in the run up to the Holocaust.

In choosing to be called Francis the new Pope also issued an invitation to be judged by an additional criterion. 'Francis is more than a name – it's a plan', said Leonardo Boff, a founding father of Liberation Theology, who is Professor Emeritus of Ethics, Philosophy of Religion and Ecology at Rio de Janeiro State University. 'It's a plan for a poor Church, one that is close to the people, gospel-centred, loving and protective towards nature which is being devastated today. Saint Francis is the archetype of that type of Church'. A key moment in the conversion of the great saint from Assisi came when he heard a voice from the crucifix at San Damiano calling: 'Francis, rebuild my house, which is falling into ruins'. The saint's name became a byword for poverty, simplicity, and kindness but, according to Boff, it is a metaphor for much more. What is in ruins is not just the Church but the whole of Creation, for the modern world has eased to see it as sacred. The planet has instead become a place that we master and abuse rather than 'our Sister, Mother Earth', as St Francis called it, which instead ought to be cherished, preserved and healed. Understanding that is the most radical form of humility, grounded in the very *humus* of the earth, said Boff. In his first weeks in office the new Pope made several public references to the environment – most notably a condemnation of the developed world's 'culture of waste'. But he has also privately been in touch with Boff and asked the Brazilian theologian to send him what he has written on eco-theology. Francis told Boff that wants to issue an encyclical on environmental matters.

Perhaps the foremost issue on the agenda for Pope Francis is, however, the question of how completely his papacy can answer the call for greater collegiality in the governance of the Catholic Church. The cardinals made it very clear in their discussions in the General Congregations before the conclave that this was vital. The Second Vatican Council almost half a century earlier had concluded that the way that the Church was run must be reoriented. It needed to move away from the paradigm of the papacy as monarch, which had developed in the Middle Ages. In its place should be restored the principle that the Pope and the bishops together should share the responsibility for the governance and pastoral care of the Catholic Church. But the changes which Vatican II set out on the role of bishops' conferences had been undermined during the pontificates of popes John Paul II and Benedict XVI. Speech after speech, by cardinal after cardinal, in the pre-conclave meetings, had insisted this trend needed reversing to restore the intentions of the Second Vatican Council.

Within the first month of his papacy Pope Francis took a major step towards addressing this by announcing the formation of an official group of cardinal advisers to the Pope. Drawn from every continent it was intended to provide a conduit which would enable the views of the local church across the world to reach the ears of the Pope. By appointing to the group individuals who had previously been sometimes trenchant critics of the Vatican bureaucracy Francis sought to ensure that the advice he received would be genuinely independent. Then Rome would serve the Church, rather than the other way round.

Part of the agenda for this council of advisers was the reform of the Curia. The Vatileaks scandal led the media to focus on this aspect of its brief. That focus was reinforced by a meeting that

Pope Francis had in June 2013 with a group of nuns and priests from Latin America. In it he appeared to acknowledge that there was truth in earlier reports by the Italian media that a gay cabal within the Vatican was responsible for part of the infighting and intrigue which had bedevilled the workings of the Curia bureaucracy. Francis indicated that this was something on which he needed to take action. He reportedly told representatives from the Confederation of Latin American and Caribbean Religious (CLAR): 'In the Curia there are also holy people, really, there are holy people. But there is also a stream of corruption, there is that as well, it is true the 'gay lobby' is mentioned, and it is true, it is there. We need to see what we can do'.

There was considerable controversy about these remarks, which were contained in notes on the meeting taken by the Latin American religious. They were posted on a Chilean Catholic website *Reflexión y Liberación*. The nuns and priests later apologised for the leak, and the notes were taken down from the website. But it was generally assumed that the Pope had been reported accurately – especially when the note-takers conceded that their report did not necessarily reflect his choice of words (*las expresiones singulars*) but did convey the 'general sense' (*su sentido general*) of his comments. The Vatican pointedly did not deny them.

The media, in carrying reports of this encounter, followed the original translation and used the term 'gay lobby' though 'gay network' may be a more accurate term for what the Pope intended. But his words appeared to confirm Italian newspaper reports from before the resignation of Benedict XVI. These had said that the confidential investigation into the Vatileaks scandal, conducted by three cardinals at Benedict's behest, found actively gay networks, and a culture of blackmail and corruption, at work within the Vatican. Pope Francis, who had a hardline 'zero-tolerance' and 'no cover-up' attitude to clerical sex abuse as Archbishop of Buenos Aires, indicated that the issue would be directly addressed by his new council of advisers, in particular three of its members, Cardinal Rodríguez Maradiaga, Cardinal Errázuriz and Cardinal Marx.

But what many in the media missed was that there was much more to this council of advisors than the reform of the Curia. Francis clearly intended it to be part of a revolution to restore a more collegial vision to the Catholic Church in which the bishops of the local churches would influence decision-making in Rome as much, if not more than, vice versa. The new Pope gave an indication of the diminution of the central power of the Vatican in other remarks he made to the nuns and priests from Latin America, urging them not to take too much notice of the intrusive Vatican bureaucracy. He reportedly said: 'Perhaps even a letter of the Congregation for the Doctrine (of the Faith) will arrive for you, telling you that you said such or such thing. But do not worry. Explain whatever you have to explain, but move forward. Open the doors, do something there where life calls for it. I would rather have a church that makes mistakes for doing something than one that gets sick for being closed up'.

Not long afterwards he announced he had established another five-person commission specifically to address the troubles of the secretive and scandal-hit Vatican Bank. Its members were Italian cardinal Raffaele Farina, French cardinal Jean-Louis Tauran, a Harvard law professor Mary Ann Glendon, a Spanish bishop Juan Ignacio Arrieta Ochoa de Chinchetru and a US cleric Mgr Peter Bryan Wells. They were given powers in a chirograph document hand-written by Francis, to summon any documents and data they deemed necessary and told to report directly to Pope Francis, bypassing the Vatican bureaucracy.

But such issues, serious though they were, were peripheral to the core problem. Reform of the Curia was a secondary task. The first task of the new group of cardinal counsellors was 'to advise him in the government of the universal Church.' That went to the heart of the main problem besetting the church – that a monarchical from of papacy had replaced the earlier model of collegial government in which the Pope was not an autocrat but only 'first among equals' in the company of bishops.

A truly collegial Church would better reflect the reality that the global make-up of the Church has changed dramatically since the Council. More than two-thirds of Catholics now live in the southern hemisphere, yet Italy had more cardinals in the last conclave than the whole of Latin America. All this had been a source of irritation to Bergoglio as Archbishop of Buenos Aires, according to his then aide Guillermo Marcó who said: 'He didn't see why a lot of Italians with emptying churches should be telling bishops in countries with growing congregations what they should and should not be doing'. Catholics in Africa, Asia and the Americas, said Boff, were 'no longer mirror-churches of Europe but source-churches, with their own face and ways of organising themselves, generally in networks of communities'. Collegiality, by definition, has to come from the bottom not the top for the spirit blows where it wills. But Pope Francis had begun the business of finding a new structure to express that. What he had done, said Alberto Melloni, Professor of History of Christianity at the University of Modena, constituted the 'most important step in the history of the Church for the past ten centuries'. With Pope Francis a Church of the third millennium is being inaugurated, said Leonardo Boff, 'far from the palaces and in the midst of the peoples and their cultures'. A sense was abroad that, after the thin sunlight of a long dry Catholic winter, spring may at last be arriving.

Is Jorge Mario Bergoglio the man to usher it in? One of Spain's most distinguished Jesuits, Fr José Ignacio González Faus, has said that fears may come from Bergoglio's time as a Jesuit but that hopes should come from his time as an archbishop. What our exploration of the story of Bergoglio's life shows is that a man who has made mistakes has, though a difficult time of personal trans-formation, become aware of his own frailties and devised, through prolonged prayer, a strategy to handle them. Acutely conscious of the forgiveness and mercy of God he has determined that his future should atone for the mistakes of his past. It has made him both tender and strong. He is humble but steeled for the task.

Those who know him best said that as Pope he was, both psychologically and spiritually, in a good place. He is 'easily tough enough', said to his 64-year-old sister María Elena Bergoglio, who has reverted to her maiden name since she divorced. 'I get the impression he's very happy, and it made me think that the Holy Spirit must be right there with him'. Rabbi Abraham Skorka, who has known the new Pope for two decades said: 'From his recent phone calls he is feeling very at peace with myself. He's in a very good established spiritual moment. He's listening and analysing and meditating deeply. When he's arrived at a conclusion, he's unlikely to change his mind'. The human rights lawyer Alicia Oliveira, who has been a close friend for 40 years, said: 'He tells me he's having a great time. Every time I speak to him I tell him 'Be careful Jorge, because the Borgias are still there in the Vatican'. He laughs and says he knows. But he's very, very, very happy. He's having fun with all the people in the Vatican telling him he can't do things – and then doing them'.

Those in Argentina who find it hard to forget the past might well be counselled by Leonardo Boff who concluded: 'What matters isn't Bergoglio and his past, but Francis and his future'.

Timeline

Year	Life of Jorge Mario Bergoglio	Jesuit Provincials In Argentina
1936	Born 17 December in Flores, Buenos Aires	
1939		
	Attended primary school at *Wilfrid Barón de los Santos Ángeles*	
1946		
1950	Starts six-year vocational course at the *Escuela Nacional de Educación Técnica* leading to a diploma as a chemical technician	
1953	Recognises vocation during Confession on 21 September	
1957	Nearly dies from lung infection	
1958	Enters Society of Jesus 11 March Last time Bergoglio votes in an election	
1958		
1960	Takes first vows as a Jesuit Studies humanities in Chile	
1961	Begins two years philosophy in *Colegio Máximo*	
1962		

Argentina politics	Jesuit Superior Generals	Popes
		Pius XI, since 1922
		Pius XII elected 1939–58
Juan Perón, President 1946–55, 1st term	Fr Jean-Baptiste Janssens 1946–64	
Arturo Frondizi, President 1958–62 – overthrown by the military on 29 March 1962		
		John XXIII elected 1958–63
		Second Vatican Council 1962–65

Year	Life of Jorge Mario Bergoglio	Jesuit Provincials In Argentina
1963		
1964	Teaches in *Colegio de la Inmaculada Concepción* high school in Santa Fé for two years	
1965		
1966	Teaches in *Colegio del Salvador* in Buenos Aires	
1966		
1967	Studies theology for three years at *Colegio Máximo*	
1978		
1969	Ordained a priest, 13 December	
1969		Fr Ricardo 'Dick' O'Farrell 1969–73
1970	Tertainship at University of Alcalá de Henares in Spain until 71	
1971	becomes Novice Master 1971–3	
1973	Takes final Jesuit vows, 22 April Becomes Provincial, 31 July	Fr Jorge Mario Bergoglio 1973–79
1974		
1975		

Argentina politics	Jesuit Superior Generals	Popes
		Paul VI elected 1963–78
	Fr Pedro Arrupe 1965–83	
Juan Carlos Onganía, Dictatorial President 1966–70		
		John Paul I elected In office 33 days 26/8/78 to 28/9/78
Juan Perón, President 1973–4, 2nd term Isabel Martínez de Perón, President 1974–6		
	Jesuits' watershed 32nd General Congregation in Rome votes to embrace the option for the poor	

Year	Life of Jorge Mario Bergoglio	Jesuit Provincials In Argentina
1976	Two of Bergoglio's Jesuits, Orlando Yorio and Franz Jalics, are seized by the military, tortured and illegally detained for five months	
1977	Father of kidnapped pregnant woman, Elena De La Cuadra, appeals to Bergoglio for help	
1978		
1979	Becomes Rector of *Colegio Máximo* 1979–85	Fr Andrès Swinnen 1979–85
1980	Visits Ireland for two months	
1981		
1982		
1983		
1985	Organises international conference with Fr Juan Carlos Scannone on Faith & Culture	Fr Victor Zorzín 1985–91
1986	Finishes as Rector and visits Germany for sixth months PhD study. Returns to Argentina to teach in Buenos Aires and then joins Jesuit community in Córdoba as an ordinary priest	

Argentina politics	Jesuit Superior Generals	Popes
Military Junta seizes power. Thousands of political opponents are rounded up and killed in the *Proceso de Reorganización* which becomes known as the Dirty War 1973–83 Gen Jorge Videla, Dictatorial President 1976–81		
		John Paul II elected 1978–2005
Leopoldo Galtieri, Dictatorial President 1981–82 Falklands War (2 April–14 June) Galtieri orders invasion of British-held Falkland islands. More than 700 Argentinean soldiers killed. Argentinean junta falls		
Civilian rule returns to Argentina, and investigations into human rights abuses begin Raúl Alfonsín, President 1983–89	Fr Peter-Hans Kolvenbach 1983–2008	
		Regensburg lecture

Year	Life of Jorge Mario Bergoglio	Jesuit Provincials In Argentina
1989		
1990	Visits Córdoba for two years	
1991		Fr Ignacio Garcia-Mata 1991–97
1992	Becomes Auxiliary Bishop of Buenos Aires	
1994	Attends Synod of Bishops in Rome	
1997	Becomes Coadjutor Archbishop of Buenos Aires	Fr Alvaro Restrepo, a Columbian and former assistant to Superior General in Rome 1997–2003
1998	Becomes Archbishop of Buenos Aires, 28 February	
1999		
2000	Argentine bishops make weak Millennium Jubilee apology for Dirty War	
2001	Made a Cardinal, 21 February Appointed realtor at the Synod of Bishops in Rome	
2003		
2004		
2005	Attends conclave for Pope, April. Bergoglio is runner-up. Elected president of the Argentine Bishops' Conference until 2008, November	
2006		

Argentina politics	Jesuit Superior Generals	Popes
Carlos Menem, President 1989–99		
Amnesty laws passed to prevent prosecution of military junta		
Fernando de la Rúa, President 1999–2001		
Massive economic crisis in Argentina. Poverty soars		
Néstor Kirchner, President 2003–7		
Amnesty laws repealed and prosecutions recommence		
		Benedict XVI 2005–13
Abortion legalised in some cases		

Year	Life of Jorge Mario Bergoglio	Jesuit Provincials In Argentina
2007	At Aparecida, conference of all bishops of Latin America, Bergoglio is elected to write key document. It gives a central place to 'poor people's culture'.	
2008	Re-elected president of the Argentine Bishops' Conference until 2011	
2010	Appears as a witness at ESMA trial into crimes committed during Dirty War	
2012	Argentine bishops make another apology for Dirty War but take no institutional blame	
2013	Becomes Pope	

Argentina politics	Jesuit Superior Generals	Popes
Cristina Fernández de Kirchner President 2007-present		Attends Aparecida
	Fr Adolfo Nikolaus 2008-present	
Same-sex marriages legalised. 30th anniversary of Falklands War		
Videla is sentenced to 50 years for overseeing systematic theft of the babies of political prisoners		
		Francis 2013–

Timeline by Thomas Vallely

Acknowledgements

When a man comes to the attention of the world only at the age of seventy six he has an immensely long and complex back story. And when the public virtues he has cultivated are of simplicity, humility and authenticity that only enriches and complicates the search for the man beneath.

The intellectual and spiritual journey of Jorge Mario Bergoglio has been a story of twists and turns. Assembling enough detail to try to unravel them in the short time since his election has been a formidable challenge. Even more so has been the business of sifting and evaluating the facts from the fictions – and the partialities of the perspectives of those whom his life has touched. The task has been clouded by hagiography on one side and on the other by the bitterness that is perhaps inevitable in a country like Argentina which still has not come to terms with the legacy of what was a particularly nasty civil war. There is an additional problem; when a man becomes Pope there are also those who think it prudent or desirable to rewrite past encounters, for both good and ill motives.

I could not have managed to pick a path through all this without the assistance of a huge number of people. In Argentina, I was lucky to find as a *vade mecum* Cecilia Macon, a lecturer in the Philosophy of History at the University of Buenos Aires with a special interest in the politics of memory from the particular perspective of trials of crimes against humanity. She guided me through the maze of Argentinean politics, and the peculiar puzzle of Peronism, and was also both an unflagging 'can do' fixer and translator. In Rome, the Vatican correspondent of *The Tablet*, Robert

Mickens was unstintingly magnanimous with his time, knowledge, insights and contacts – and also happy to share his considerable acquaintance with Rome's little-known *ristoranti*. Others whose knowledge and perceptions helped me included: Rabbi Abraham Skorka, Alessandro Speciale, Alicia Oliveira, Fr Augusto Zampini, Austen Ivereigh, Catherine Pepinster, Clelia Luro, Clifford Longley, Cardinal Cormac Murphy O'Connor, Professor Eamon Duffy, Dr Emilce Cuda, Federico Wals, Dr Fernando Cervantes, Professor Fortunato Malimacci, Francis McDonagh, Gerard O'Connell, Gregory Burke, Fr Guillermo Marcó, Fr Gustavo Antico, Fr Gustavo Carrara, Hugh O'Shaugnessey, Ian Linden, James Alison, Rt Rev James Jones, John Cornwell, John Wilkins, Fr Jose-Maria de Paola (Padre Pepe), Fr Juan Carlos Scannone SJ, Julian Filochowski, Lisandro Orlov, Margaret Hebblethwaite, María Elena Bergoglio, Martin Pendergast, Fr Michael Campbell-Johnston SJ, Michael Walsh, Miguel Mom Debussy, Fr Miguel Yanez SJ, Fr Norman Tanner SJ, Mgr Paul Tighe, Philip Pullella of Reuters, Fr Rafael Velasco, Fr Ricardo Aloe, Tim Livesey, Fr Timothy Radcliffe OP. I'd also like to thank the considerable number of cardinals, bishops, theologians and Jesuits who spoke but asked for their names not to be listed here.

Thanks for the help in translating from Spanish and German to Isabel de Bertodano, Catherine Ramos and Barbara Fox – and to Ilenia Cuvello who deciphered the cursive 19th century Italian handwriting on the wedding certificate of Bergoglio's Grandma Rosa. Brother Mario Rausch SJ took considerable time to show me around the *Colegio Máximo* including the section of the seminary in which Bergoglio hid fugitives from the Argentine military death squads during the Dirty War and the old garage where Bergoglio as Provincial kept his car. Roger Williamson made available his copious research into the future Pope's conduct in the years of military dictatorship. And Mark Dowd, who presented BBC Radio 4's *The Report* into the Pope's past, and his producer Charlotte Pritchard were most generous in allowing me to hear all their unedited research tapes of extensive interviews with Horacio

Verbitsky, Luis Zamara, Fr Ernesto Giobando, Rodolfo Yorio, Fr Tony Panaro, Fr Andres Agare and Estela de la Cuadra before I set out for Argentina.

I would also like to acknowledge my debt to the interviews of Sergio Rubin and Francesca Ambrogetti in their book *El Jesuita* (2010) which must be the starting point for any research on Jorge Mario Bergoglio. His conversations the same year with Rabbi Abhraham Skorka in *Sobre el cielo y la tierra* (On Heaven and Earth) are shot through with revealing moments. And I have been grateful for the writings of Fr James Hanvey SJ on the confluences of Ignatian and Franciscan spirituality, to Carl Bernstein's research on the links between the CIA and the Vatican and to the perceptive reporting of the veteran *Vaticanisti* Gianni Valente, Andrea Tornielli and John Allen.

Jeffery L Klaiber's *The Jesuits in Latin America 1549-2000: 450 Years of Inculturation, Defense of Human Rights and Prophetic Witness* was very useful, as was Norman Tanner's *New Short History of the Catholic Church*. For background on the Dirty War I drew on Emilio F. Mignone's *Witness to the Truth: The Complicity of Church and Dictatorship in Argentina (Iglesia y Dictadura)* and Iain Guest's *Behind the Disappearances*. On Liberation Theology, Ian Linden's *Global Catholicism: Diversity and Change since Vatican II* was invaluable. Monika K. Hellwig's *What are the Theologians Saying Now?* was illuminating, as were the two key Vatican texts: *Instruction on Certain Aspects of 'Liberation Theology'*, 1984, which bears all the hallmarks of the style of Joseph Ratzinger, and the more positive 1987 *Christian Freedom and Liberation* from the Pontifical Justice and Peace Commission.

My editors Robin Baird-Smith and Joel Simons were unfailingly understanding, unperturbed by my shifting deadlines and ready with sage suggestions when needed. My son Thomas, an historian in the making, produced a Timeline to guide me through various parallel chronologies while I was working; it proved so useful that I have included it in the book, for which I give him many thanks.

But my most heartfelt gratitude goes to my wife Christine Morgan whose judgements about institutional politics and human psychology are infinitely subtle and intuitively correct. She brought them to bear on the range of delicate issues which arose during the research and the writing. She is also the best and most affirming editor with whom I have ever worked; her discerning insights are couched so gently that I would find myself happily rewriting a section after she had begun by telling me how good it was. And she uncomplainingly took up all the domestic slack during the months of research and travel. My thanks are boundless.

Despite all this help from so many quarters, any errors, omissions or things of darkness I acknowledge mine. But I have had such sterling assistance from so many quarters that I dare to hope that this book will go some way to unravelling the knots in the ribbon of Jorge Mario Bergoglio's life and offer some glimmer of what we might expect from the man who has become the first Pope Francis.

Index